the new lively rhetoric

READINGS
ANALYSES
ARGUMENTS

ALEXANDER SCHARBACH
RALPH H. SINGLETON

Portland State University

HOLT, RINEHART AND WINSTON, INC.
New York/Chicago/San Francisco/Atlanta/Dallas/Montreal/Toronto

*To the students in colleges and universities today,
our pledges for the bright new world of tomorrow.*

Library of Congress Catalog Card Number: 75-102792
SBN: 03-081217-8
Printed in the United States of America
1 2 3 4 5 6 7 8 9

Preface

Now, when not even the most secluded "ivory tower" is likely to escape noxious police gases or the bullhorn-magnified voices of the leaders of this or that demonstration, no one can doubt that ours is an age of violence and harsh rhetoric. Today the decibles of sound are often deafening. And what atmosphere is free of pollution?

Our mass media-nurtured generation, who are truly the children of the electronic tube, may well exemplify Marshall McLuhan's warning: "The medium is the message." Perhaps without even being able to speak of the "art of rhetoric," most of them already realize they are the constant targets of persuasion. Some have shown themselves quite adept in finding targets of their own.

As the selections and commentaries in this book evidence, the rhetoric of the 1970s has long since broken free of Aristotelian and neo-Aristotelian restraints. The revolt against what can only be termed "neoclassic rules" governing approaches to composition and literature began with I. A. Richards and Kenneth Burke in the 1930s and their influence upon the "new criticism." Since then, discoveries in linguistics and psychology have opened up the whole creative process of written communication. Taken together, they constitute what is generally called the "new rhetoric."

The authors of this book have found the "new rhetoric" as *lively* as the very recently published articles they have selected to serve as models of current professional writing. They have sought to apply many of these new insights and approaches to the problems that face college freshmen in composition courses. They have tried to combine the best of the rein-terpreted "old" rhetoric with the most helpful and stimulating of the "new" rhetoric.

The thirty-six articles and accompanying commentaries are grouped under the following headings: The Student Generation, Campus Issues, Personal Values, The National Conscience, The Media, Science and the Future, and Literature and Art. Some of the authors, like John Ciardi, Marshall McLuhan, Anthony Burgess, and Goodman Ace are well known. Others, like Brian McGuire, who graduated from the University of California at Berkeley in 1968 with the highest grade-point average of any senior in the College of Letters and Sciences, are intelligent spokesmen for the new generation of students.

As was the design and method in the earlier book, *The Lively Rhetoric,* each of these divisions presents, in turn, one of the principles of rhetoric and composition facing every writer, professional or beginner, when he sits down to express his thoughts. We are committed to the view that the student writer can learn only one thing at a time, and that he can best learn from examples and analyses illustrating the fundamentals he needs to know and to master.

Thus, the first section poses the problem, As Author: Who and What Are You? And once this primary question has been answered, it takes up the conventional structuring of one's thoughts into an introduction, a body, and a conclusion. Succeeding sections take up the following:

Choice of Topic: What Do You Have to Say? How do you limit your topic?
The Reader-Audience: Who and What Are They? How do you identify with them?
Arrangement: How Are You Going to Say It? How do you handle source material?
Suasive Strategies: How Are You Going to Persuade Them? What are the changes you might strive for?
Logic and Composition: Straight Thinking, Valid Judgments. How do you verify the truth of an assumption?
What is Style?: Sentences, Paragraphs, and Diction. How does one manage effective expression?

The first article in each section is provided with marginal comments and then an outline showing its structure and organization. Every selection is followed by an approach to the semantics of its language, as well as a wide variety of suggestions for writing assignments. Since a number of the articles are arranged to present a pro-con view of highly controversial subjects, engrossing to students of the 70s, they should furnish topics for lively and interesting essays, well within the range of student experience and observation.

The commentaries will immediately reveal our acknowledged indebtedness to those rhetoricians of the past and the present, such as I. A. Richards, Kenneth Burke, Wayne C. Booth, W. Ross Winterowd, and Francis Christensen. In addition, of course, we owe immeasurably much to others like Albert R. Kitzhaber, Marshall McLuhan, Josephine Miles, Richard Ohman, Kenneth Pike, and to the many contributors to *College English* and *College Composition and Communication*. We wish to give special thanks to Professor Richard Beal of Boston University, for his invaluable suggestions and comments, and to Jane Ross and Lois Wernick of Holt, Rinehart and Winston, Inc., for their assistance throughout the preparation of this text. Our grateful thanks go out, as well, to the many teachers and students whose comments on our earlier book have helped us in this alternate version.

And finally, we are most grateful to United Press International, for their permission to reprint the excellent photographs we have used in the text, to David J. Barrios, a student at Portland State University, for his outstanding cartoons created especially for some of the articles, and to the publishers and authors who have granted us permission to include their works in our book.

Portland, Oregon
January 1970

A. S.
R. H. S.

Contents

Rhetorical Contents

Persuasive Polemic

Ironic Humor

Personal Essay

Narrative

part I
THE STUDENT GENERATION

AS AUTHOR:
WHO AND WHAT ARE YOU?

Whenever we write we are moved to do so by some *motive*. Whether it be essay or short story, letter or diary, we write with some purpose, some end in mind. It is certain that each of the authors whose essays appear in this text had a compelling motive for writing what he did. From this purpose or need came the energy and the drive to say what he did.

It is not difficult to see what motivated Brian McGuire, "Berkeley's best student," to write the dramatic article "It Wasn't Worth It" that opens this section. Nor is it difficult to see what complex of desires and pressures aroused young Cecelia Holland to proclaim: "I Don't Trust Anyone Under Thirty." In both articles we find a clear-cut motivation which led to the author's putting words on paper and which gave the article a *tone* of conviction and self-confidence. Obviously, both authors know what they believe, and this assurance means that they know, rather well, who and what they are as persons.

The double question, "Who and What Are You?" may not seem pertinent, at this point, as you consider the motive behind the article. Yet this is the inquiry every person must face before he can begin to write. To be specific, let us consider the plight of a typical first-term college freshman, whom we will call "Mac." He has just been

1

asked to write an essay on his personal reaction to Brian McGuire's article.

As he sits there in front of a blank sheet of paper, with a welter of half-formed thoughts racing through his head, it is little wonder that Mac is in a sweat. He senses that he must arrive at some definite idea or view. If only he could get started! If only he could seize upon some "idea" that would get him going. Then, perhaps, he would be all right.

What he is really looking for is a *thesis*—some central, controlling concept. He is involved in a *drama* of choice, and since honest conviction almost always carries with it a creative strength, he searches for a stand, an attitude in harmony with his sincere beliefs.

At this point Mac would do well to take stock of himself and realize that he cannot write a worthwhile essay until he comes to some decision regarding his own personal values so far as he can decide upon them. Failure to do so means crippling himself as a person, and therefore as a writer.

Self respect, courage, hunger for truth—these are some of the traits we admire in every effective writer or speaker. They ring out in the *tone* of whatever he says, give it a consistency of character and, therefore, *style*. As critical readers we will be looking for that tone in every selection in this text, and from it we will determine the author's attitudes and values.

Let us get back to Mac. Mac cannot write effectively until he comes to terms with himself, asking himself the double question, "Who and What Am I?" So must everyone who wishes to write with the strength of conviction. Mac must strive to be honest and frank in examining what he believes, and, if he has no clear-cut beliefs, admit to being uncertain or undecided.

Here are some stimulating questions that can serve as a guide in such self-examination:

1. What do I know from experience about the subject?
2. How much am I influenced by what I have just read?
3. What solid reason do I have for feeling as I do?
4. Have I really thought through the subject?
5. What is right, wrong, or questionable about the views others have expressed?
6. What, honestly, are my motives for taking the stand I do?

After we have come to terms with ourselves, we can begin to adapt what we have to say to the conventional structure of an essay:

introduction, body, and *conclusion.* As the term suggests, the *intro-duction* is the opening section, wherein the writer begins "talking" to his reader-audience. "Talking," in this context, means pretending that writing is like speaking to someone. This awareness of the constant presence of a reader who is "listening" to every word helps one to be clear, direct, and concise. Both politeness and good sense require a writer to establish some rapport with his readers as he leads them into the subject of his essay and his particular views upon it.

Once he has secured their attention and prepared them for the main thrust of his discourse, he moves them from the *introduction* on to the *body* of his essay, where he presents his supporting facts and ideas. You can see how skilled professional authors handle the body or main part of their essay by studying the running comments in the margins of many of the essays in this book as well as in the analyses found in the commentaries.

The closing paragraph, or paragraphs, should try to leave the reader with some memorable impression. This *conclusion* should at least make the reader feel that what he has just read has been well worth his time.

In all of the essays in this textbook, look for two things that will help you shape up as a writer: Test each author with the double question, "Who and What Are You?"; then try to see how well he brings across his thoughts and impressions in his *introduction, body,* and *conclusion.* In addition, in any writing assignment your instructor may give you, ask yourself that same double question, "Who and What Am I?" so as to make clear your motive for writing what you do. Then organize your own thoughts clearly so that your essay will have a suitable beginning, middle, and end.

Berkeley's Best Student: "It Wasn't Worth It"

by BRIAN McGUIRE

Introduction

Dramatic opening statement on his record grade-point average and honors as student.

His surprising thesis—"It was not worth it"—and announcement of intention to go to Oxford.

By present standards of American education, I am a complete and utter success. In 1964 I was class valedictorian at Saint Mary's College High School in Berkeley. During my years at the University of California, Berkeley, I have attained the highest grade-point average of any graduating senior in the College of Letters and Science in the class of 1968.

After 16 years of success, playing the grade-point game, I have come to one overwhelming conclusion: It was not worth it. Now Harvard, Princeton and Berkeley have all offered me fellowships for graduate study in history. I have turned down their offers and will be doing research at Balliol College, Oxford, this fall. There I shall be evaluated for my work on a personal basis and not by a grading system.

My efforts to win high grades were not worth it for two reasons: Grades got in the way

Reprinted from *The Saturday Evening Post,* September 21, 1968, by permission of author.

of learning, and the 12 hours a day I spent studying in order to be a success made it almost impossible for me to develop any significant human contacts. My four years of university education, instead of helping me to become a man, have nearly turned me into an unfeeling, unthinking zombie, totally removed from the world outside my own specialized field.

A great deal of the fault was my own, for I made the choice to pursue high grades. But the tragic thing is that many educators and most parents uphold the value of high grades as an indication of genuine learning. And American professions and businesses frequently assume that the student who has made high grades is their best potential recruit. Such assumptions exist, I suppose, because it is more convenient to judge a person's ability by numbers than any other way.

It was foolish of me not to realize that by playing the grade-point game I was compromising my ideals about education and copping out to a dehumanizing system. But the university helped me to fool myself. Its homage to the grade-point standard made it easy for me to assume that, because of my grades, I was really learning about the world around me.

In May I gave a speech at a Berkeley Phi Beta Kappa banquet and received a standing ovation for my position against grades. Some people at the university answered my plea for reform by saying that since life is made up of games anyway, one has to learn how to play, and one might as well start at the university. If such is the case, then I think American politicians and educators should stop their platitudes about the greatness of college education, the broadening of the mind and the development of the individual. The truth, unfortunately, is that most middle-class students attend colleges today because they are under parental or internal pressure to prepare themselves for a well-defined career. Their parents are obsessed with making their way up the

Body
Two reasons why the efforts for high grades were unrewarding.

His mistake in accepting the wide-spread assumption that equates grades with genuine learning.

His university equally at fault in overstressing the importance of grades.
The grade game as another part of the general obsession with the idea that higher education is a way to financial success.

socio-economic ladder to the promised land of the "good life," the affluent society with a steak on every grill and three cars in every garage. These parents, and sometimes their children, have equated happiness with the earning power that a college education promises to bring.

But last summer parents all over America found out that their children had stopped believing in this equation. The brightest, most sensitive adolescents from the most well-heeled families began to drop out of society. Thousands of parents began to wonder about the way they had brought up their children. The cute little kids of the early 1950's were suddenly challenging the very homes, education, and society that had so coddled them.

As in our families, so too in our colleges. Abundance is accompanied by despair. The student is surrounded by material things, but he cannot enjoy them because of the void he finds in himself and in the people around him. When I first came to the university at Berkeley in the fall of 1964, I was amazed at the beauty of the place. The buildings, the trees, the huge library, the vast laboratories were all a source of amazement to me.

A few months later, in December, this beautiful image was shattered for me. One morning as I was riding my bicycle up Telegraph Avenue I found the way blocked by paddy wagons taking students to jail. I was upset and confused. I didn't understand what was happening. It was as if for months I had been looking at a beautiful wedding cake and then finally touched it, only to discover that it was made out of cardboard. The arrests were the result of a demonstration by members of the Free Speech Movement. It was the first revolt of the students of the 1960's against the impersonality and alienation that underlie so much of American mass education today. The particular, specific issues were not nearly so important as the feeling on the part of thousands of

Revolt against parents last summer (1968) a reaction to such pressures.

His early experience with the disparity between campus beauty and abundance and student needs.

His discovery that the university ignored student need for treatment as individuals.

Berkeley students that the university had lost touch with them as individuals.

I myself did not participate in the Free Speech Movement. I had not yet fully comprehended the game that the university had set up for me to play. Earlier that fall I had told myself that at Berkeley I was not going to worry about grades, that even if I got C's, it would be fine, as long as I was working hard, doing my best and learning. The important thing, I decided, was to develop myself as a person—physically, mentally and spiritually. But I soon discarded these high-school ideals. I found that with a great deal of work in the first semester, I was able to earn four A's and one B. After that, the 4.0 symbol (indicating all A's) was far too tempting.

His discarding of high-school ideals to enter the race for grades.

Getting all A's was the best way for me to distinguish myself as a person in the university and to prove to myself that I was really doing what the university expected of me, and I expected of myself. The grade-point symbol became for me the affirmation of my existence, the proof that I was worth something. Subconsciously I knew I was letting the system dominate me and demolish me as an individual. But I could always excuse myself on the grounds that I would need these high grades to get into graduate school.

His self-deception in thinking he was not injuring himself in joining the system.

In America we have become a society of anticipation and anxiety. We are losing meaning, values and purposes. For many young Americans education means nothing but preparation for a specialized career. Many teachers and students have despaired of asking the great questions and reading the great books. Instead, we have tried to replace belief in values with belief in the so-called scientific method. We still think that those with vast knowledge in a given field, especially one of the sciences, somehow hold the solutions to our personal and social crises. Scientists as scientists cannot be moralists or philosophers or theologians. Nevertheless, many people assume that those who are the

His final realization that intense specialization results in a loss of fundamental values—a real loss to American society.

most successful specialists in our society can somehow make the most valid generalizations about the ills of America.

Irony of the fact that being such a respected "specialist" himself, he is being given a respectful hearing now.

I am a case in point. No one would be listening to me now if I were not a specialist in playing the college game of high grades. There are thousands of students all over the country who are tired of struggling for high grades rather than a liberal education. Yet few people have listened seriously to such students because they did not make it to the top of the system. So we tend to dismiss them as lazy or weak. We only listen to the successful in America.

Why the materialism found in their parents and home turns young people against their elders.

Many Americans, young and old, are lost in their own bags. Those who want to pursue excellence are forced to spend all their time on their work in order to succeed. In the process they neglect their families and their own personal lives. Those who refuse to acquiesce to the pressure and anxiety of such an existence are often frustrated at their own failure. They feel guilty about their inability to provide their families with as much material affluence as others can. Children in turn see the materialism of their parents and, because of youth's wonderful naïveté, are shocked, disappointed and angered at the gap between what their parents say about the meaning of life and the way their parents and teachers actually live that life.

The same materialism in the university hurts the quality of college education and the teaching.

School and family reinforce one another. The materialism found at home turns up again in the universities. The preaching is about the higher values of education, but the performance turns out to be training for careers. The teachers themselves, usually fine people, are caught in the bind of taking care of a family, doing research, and teaching. In the great multiversity, teaching usually comes last on the list, for tenure is generally not given for being a good teacher, but for being a successful researcher with a prestigious list of publication credits.

I am not advocating an end to research.

Nor am I saying that the technical training college for the engineer or the chemist or the dentist should be dissolved. I am saying that our great multiversities, responsible for educating such a great number of American college students, are going to have to find ways to provide smallness within their bigness. Many worthwhile reforms are possible. All lecture courses could be supplemented with small seminars, run by graduate students who are not overburdened with their own research and study. Professors could be given frequent leaves of absence from their research and paid to concentrate exclusively on teaching. The individual departments within the multiversities, from Anthropology to Zoology, could arrange seminars on educational reform and hold informal meetings at which students and teachers could meet each other on a more personal basis.

All these reforms would be inadequate without a secure structure within the university to provide a basis for intellectual ferment and maturation. I propose the creation of interdisciplinary liberal arts colleges inside the multiversities. These colleges would be open to freshmen and sophomores who wanted to spend the first half of their university education in reading the great books of western civilization. The faculty would be drawn from the various departments of the university and would be expected to abandon or limit their research during their stay in the college. The college faculty and distinguished visitors would give frequent lectures. Every hour of lecture would be matched by an hour of seminar in which students would give their own critiques of the material with which they were dealing. Most seminars would be based on weekly reading assignments, which would cover the primary sources of civilization. Secondary sources, explaining and interpreting the core books, would be optional.

Students would not be expected to become

Need for reforms in the "multiversities," particularly the stress laid on professional research.

Proposal for establishing liberal arts colleges inside the "multiversities," with concentration on primary sources.

Further details of this suggested discipline, with its aim to humanize the undergraduate.

scholars or textual critics. They would be exposing themselves to great literature and history, learning how men think, write, live and die, so that they might themselves become more aware of their universal situation as human beings. The college would aim at expanding students' minds beyond their immediate cultural milieu. Students would have a chance to see, feel and appreciate other men, other periods, other life styles, and to relate these experiences and value systems to their own lives. In order to organize their observations and provide some sense of continuity, students would write frequent papers on topics discussed by the teacher and students beforehand. At the end of each semester they would write a few major essays and receive a personal evaluation by their teachers. By the time they reached their junior year and started specializing in majors, students from the interdisciplinary college would be able to think creatively and to deal with relationships between human thought and human experience. Because of their personal contacts within the liberal arts college, they would also feel themselves to be worthwhile, integral parts of a great university instead of cogs in an indifferent machine.

Proposed grading in this new system—personal evaluation.

In both the interdisciplinary college and in the traditional university, all grading should be based on personal evaluation. The letter- and the number-grading systems should be replaced by a pass-fail system in all courses except those taken in the student's major field. In that area the student, instead of receiving grades from his professors, would be given individual evaluations by his professors in consultation with his academic supervisor, whom the student himself would choose. The evaluation would not consist of word substitutes for a grade, like "excellent" or "fair," but a comprehensive statement summarizing the student's work and progress and the professor's or graduate student's reaction to that student. Such a personal evaluation would concede a fact that everyone knows already: Any system of evaluation cannot be completely objective— it is inevitably subject to the bias of the person who is evaluating. Grades should be abolished not because they evaluate, but because they pretend to be objective. It is the lie, the dishonesty, the hypocrisy of the grade-point system that alienates so many students today. It is time we admitted that even professors reading exams are human beings and respond humanly to the people in their courses. Evaluation is ultimately a human act. People cannot fairly evaluate other people by means of numbers or letters.

This mechanical system of evaluation throws light on a much more serious problem. Our universities are not turning out people. They are producing technicians whose feelings and thoughts are forced into mechanical patterns. The big universities are alienating the best of our young people. Administrators, teachers and, most of all, parents and taxpayers do not realize that young people desperately want to understand themselves and the world around them, want to develop ideals and values. Students are as responsible for the alienation as older people, for they often use their idealism as a weapon against their parents and friends instead of accepting these people as they find them. We still approach one another as symbols or ideals. We are still afraid to admit we all are separate individuals who share the same fundamental drives for love and unity.

The big university could transform the rat race by lessening the impersonality of the educational experience. It could well afford to pay more attention to students as people rather than numbers. Our large state universities are favored places where people can come together, learn together, live together, and find out in the microcosm of university life how to be beautiful and dynamic individuals in the macrocosm of the world. They must do this, or they do not deserve to survive.

The basic reason why personal evaluation is superior to the present grading system.

Conclusion
Some of the most harmful effects the present "mechanical system" is having on students.

Possibilities for the future if desired changes are, or are not, made.

OUTLINE

Introduction

Thesis: "After 16 years of success, playing the grade-point game, I have come to one overwhelming conclusion: It was not worth it," and our universities need major reforms to become liberal arts colleges instead of impersonal training schools for specialists.

Body

I. Not until graduation did Brian McGuire realize the serious shortcomings of his education and his university.
  A. He now sees his all-out efforts to obtain high grades did not help him to become a well-rounded human being.
  B. His fault lay in accepting the general assumption that grades are a measure of one's education.
    1. He blames the universities for fostering this view.
    2. He sees other students and almost all parents as being guilty of identifying "the good life" with the high income supposed to come with graduation and high grades.
    3. He now understands that events of 1968 showed the falsity of prevailing parental and university assumptions.
  C. His decision to give up his high-school ideals and take up the grade-point game has had grave consequences.
    1. He was injured as a person by letting "the system" dominate him.
    2. His typical acceptance of "specialization" as his goal prevented a search for values.
    3. He finds himself in the ironic position of being listened to because he had become such a "specialist."
  D. Many other young people are caught up in the struggle for financial success when they should be using their college years in searching for basic human values.
    1. They encounter materialism both at home and on the campus.
    2. Instructors are also infected by it.
II. McGuire believes certain reforms in the "multiversities" must be made.
  A. These vast universities should reorganize themselves into liberal arts colleges.
    1. Their faculty should be excused from doing research.
    2. They should match lectures with seminars.

   3. They should not expect their students to become "textual
      critics."
 B. These liberal arts colleges should educate students to become
    enriched human beings.
   1. As freshmen and sophomores they should read widely.
   2. They should write papers that receive personal evaluation.
   3. As upperclassmen they should feel they belong to the uni-
      versity and to the world of learning.
 C. All grading should be only on the basis of personal evaluation.
   1. McGuire defines this kind of evaluation.
   2. He regards it as superior to the old grade-point system.

Conclusion

He sums up the most harmful effects of the present "mechanical"
system and suggests the kind of personal values the university must
foster in the future.

COMMENTARY: SOME PREWRITING DECISIONS

It appears that the author of "It Wasn't Worth It" went through some
painful self-examination before he began writing this essay. He must
have asked himself questions such as, "Who and what am I as a college
graduate?" and "What did I get out of all this working for high grades?"
We have his candid answers showing he tried to think through the
many conflicting facts and ideas those basic questions must raise.

Apparently, the situation he cites in his introduction led to this
self-searching and then occasioned first a speech at Berkeley and
then this confessional article. He found himself offered a choice of
graduate study scholarships from Berkeley, Harvard, and Princeton.
Furthermore, he seems to have enjoyed a third alternative—study at
Oxford. Now most young men placed in such happy circumstances
would make their choices and go their way congratulating themselves.
But this is not so for Brian McGuire. As his opening frank statements
indicate, he was not happy with himself or with the present American
system of higher education.

After briefly stating his record as a student, he moves to the
thesis idea of admitting his successful attempts to win in the "grade
game" "have nearly turned me into an unfeeling, unthinking zombie."
Then he immediately attacks the widely held assumption, or belief,
that if you get high grades you must also have received a good
education.

McGuire follows with another very popular assumption enjoying almost unquestioned acceptance among many parents and students: the conviction that to attain financial success is the main goal in life, and the quickest way to reach it is to get a college degree. Now that he thinks back upon them, he realizes, however, that many of his fellow students who took part in the Free Speech Movement saw through such assumptions and could not accept them. He admits he did not take part in demonstrations aimed at a university system that "had lost touch with them as individuals." He confesses that instead he remained caught up in the grade-point game and sought his identity as a person in playing it.

His disillusionment leads him to criticize the "materialism" he finds affecting American life and values; he sees them as corruptive of family standards as well as of academic life. Deploring the emphasis placed upon specialization, he attributes the growth of what he terms "multiversities" and their impersonality to this pursuit of specialization. He proposes changes in the form of a system of liberal arts colleges, wherein faculty and students would come to know one another on a personal basis and where instructors would give students' work individual evaluations instead of meaningless grades. McGuire goes on to describe, at some length, the kind of humanistic education this liberal college system would provide for its students. On the whole, the goals he assigns those colleges are those usually associated with "liberal"—mind-freeing, humanizing—education.

Following the criticism and recommendations in the body of the essay he concludes with two paragraphs restating his views and making almost an appeal to his readers when he says, "We still approach one another as symbols or ideals. We are still afraid to admit we all are separate individuals who share the same fundamental drives for love and unity."

It must have been difficult for Brian McGuire to face the facts and admit to himself and to the world that the kind of university life he had chosen was only a "rat race." Obviously, before beginning to write he made some decisions regarding his role as student and person. How many other decisions regarding what he would include and what he would omit in the planning of this essay we do not know, but his *introduction* and *conclusion* testify to his having spent considerable prewriting time and perhaps much rewriting effort on various versions of this article.

Compared to the companion essay following, by Cecelia Holland, this one is somewhat loosely organized, but its sincerity and fervor carry the reader along to the final statement of warning about the future of our "multiversities."

WHAT DOES IT SAY?

Note: Since words are only symbols and not the things that the words themselves stand for ("the map is not the territory"), it is natural that any one word can have different meanings for different people. Our reaction to a word depends upon our previous experiences with that word and all that it suggests to us. This study of the emotional meaning, associative meaning, and impact of words is called *semantics.* The associated meanings of words are known as *connotations.* Skilled writers in their attempt to reach others rely heavily upon emotion-arousing, imagination-stirring qualities of language. Consequently, beginning with this first essay, every "What Does It Say?" will deal with the manner in which the author's choice of language is designed to affect the reader. The author, however, expects us to play fair. We are to supply only those meanings that are closely relevant and appropriate to the *context* in which the word appears. *Context is* the "verbal neighborhood" that clearly points out the kind of meaning the author desires the word to have.

1. In the context of the essay as a whole, what connotations do the words in the title—"It Wasn't Worth It"—have for you?

2. What does it mean for a student to be "evaluated on a personal basis"?

3. What are some of the chief features of the "grade-point game"?

4. What is the meaning of *games* in the expression ". . . since life is made up of games anyway, one has to learn how to play"?

5. From where do you think the author derived the expression "an unfeeling, unthinking zombie"?

6. Define *platitudes.* What are some "platitudes about the greatness of college education" that you are familiar with?

7. Is your college or university a part of a "multiversity"? What does the term mean? Why isn't the word found in most dictionaries?

8. How does a *seminar* class differ from a *lecture* class?

WHAT DO YOU THINK?

Note: Included under this heading are a wide variety of possible essay topics from which you can choose one for your own writing assignment. Always try to support any basic view you take on your subject with specific examples and instances taken from your own experience, as Brian McGuire did in his essay. Also, as McGuire did, give your essay a suitable *introduction* and *conclusion* to open and close the substance of what you have to say in the *body*.

Remember that you too, in thinking about your essay subject, will be answering the basic question: "Who and what are you?" Be honest with yourself and with your reader. It is worth it!

1. Write a one-paragraph "essay"—one having an introduction, a body, and a conclusion—on one of these topics:

   (a) Getting grades the hard way
   (b) Tests easy to pass
   (c) What grades meant to me in high school
   (d) Should parents reward their children for bringing home good grades?
   (e) Feeling lost and alienated on this campus
   (f) What high school did not prepare me for
   (g) A situation I can never adjust to
   (h) Ideals I once had about education
   (i) How relevant do I find my courses?
   (j) What Brian McGuire did not say but should have
   (k) Grades and draft boards

2. Brian McGuire makes some very controversial statements. Write a brief essay expressing your reactions to one of the following of his statements. Be sure to give specific facts in support of your views.

   (a) "But the university helped me to fool myself. Its homage to the grade-point standard made it easy for me to assume that because of my grades, I was really learning about the world around me."
   (b) "As in our families, so too in our colleges. Abundance is accompanied by despair."
   (c) "In America we have become a society of anticipation and anxiety."
   (d) "We only listen to the successful in America."
   (e) "Many Americans, young and old, are lost in their own bags."
   (f) "The letter- and the number-grading systems should be replaced by a pass-fail system in all courses except those taken in the student's major field."
   (g) "Grades should be abolished not because they evaluate, but because they pretend to be objective."
   (h) "Students are as responsible for the alienation as older people, for they often use their idealism as a weapon against their parents and friends instead of accepting these people as they find them."

3. In 1961, Max Rafferty, California Superintendent of Education, made a speech critical of grade- and high-school education that is said to have launched him into politics. The following is an excerpt from it:

> This sizable minority of spineless, luxury-loving, spiritless characters came right out of our classrooms. . . . The results are plain for all to see: the worst of our youngsters growing up to become booted, sideburned, duck-tailed, unwashed, leather-jacketed slobs, whose favorite sport is ravaging little girls and stomping polio victims to death; the best of our youth coming into maturity for all the world like young people fresh from a dizzying roller-coaster ride, with everything blurred, with nothing clear, with no positive standards, with everything in doubt. No wonder so many of them welsh out and squeal and turn traitor when confronted with the grim reality of Red military force and the crafty cunning of Red psychological warfare.[1]

How valid do you find Mr. Rafferty's judgments? Would Brian McGuire agree with him?

4. Does the following editorial statement appearing in *Time* have any bearing on what McGuire had to say? What are your reasons for agreeing or disagreeing with either or both?

> For all the U. S.'s faith in universal higher education, many of the nation's brightest youths have rebelled against mass schooling that seems to ignore their burning questions: What is the good life, the nature of justice, the remedy for society's evils?[2]

[1] *The New York Times Magazine,* September 1, 1968, pp. 30–31.
[2] *Time,* August 30, 1968, p. 21.

I Don't Trust Anyone Under Thirty
by CECELIA HOLLAND

Militant, committed, articulate and radical, the generation under 30 claims to be the hope of the world. Our parents believe it. They contrast the purity of our motives and the energy of our commitments with their own corrupted morality and corroded traditions and decide that everything we say *must* be right. "Don't let the kids down,"says an advertisement for Gene McCarthy. Not since the Children's Crusade in the early 13th century has an older generation entrusted so much of its salvation to the young. Not since the Renaissance have we wielded so much influence over our elders. (Did Cesare Borgia trust anybody over 30?).

Much of the work in the civil-rights crusade is done by people under 30 years of age. Almost all the protesters of the Vietnam war (and the great majority of those fighting in it) are under 30. There are very few hippies over 30, and the hippie movement stands out as the single most visible protest against the syndrome commonly called the American Way of Life. My generation is the most idealistic, the most dynamic and the most liberal in history; just ask us, we'll tell you. We're strong on freedom and long on love, and there are enough of us around to change the very definitions of the words to make these statements fact.

Are we strong on freedom? It would be hard to find a young person outside the South who isn't all for the Negro revolution. The freedom to protest the Vietnam war—to protest anything (except the protesters)—is as hallowed as the bones of a saint. Yet to hold a conservative viewpoint, however honestly, can only be a sign of cowardice. Anybody over 30 will ask first what your opinion is on the war. Anybody under 30 will automatically assume you're against it; if you aren't, you're a heretic.

Freedom and free speech should mean that anyone can hold any opinion he wants on the Negro or the war in Vietnam, as long as he doesn't try to enforce his views on anybody else. But our generation's conception of freedom goes more like this: "Do your own thing and all will be well, as long as your own thing is certified pure by the rest of us."

But what if your own thing doesn't happen to conform to that of the hip world, the militant students, the nonstudents or any other faction? There are, after all, people in this world who manage to live entirely within the existing social structure, and who do so by choice. There are people who find it possible to go through life neither rebelling nor conforming. Are they all hypocrites? To the under-30 group, nonalignment is as abhorrent as slavish devotion to the *status quo.*

Let's face it, my generation is *not* strong on freedom. Basically, we simply want to do what we like, without being bothered by anything silly like antique conventions and laws. But why the devil can't we just say so and let it go at that? Why do we dress our preferences in the vestments of a quasi-religion?

Part of the reason, I suspect, is that we're still bound by at least one antique convention: doing things for the right reasons, the socially acceptable motives. We have a party line, certain things and opinions that must be professed under certain conditions. Deviation labels one unfit. Anybody who's ever ventured into the wilderness of conversation with more than one hip or militant student or political fanatic or fellow-traveler knows that there is a striking similarity, not only in the lines of argument taken on almost all subjects but in the words and slogans used, not only within each faction but across partisan lines. Doctrine has hardened into dogma. (I am a fellow-traveler with the "straights," which means that sometimes I'm self-consciously hip; and making the transition from one vernacular to the other is difficult enough to suggest that the differences are not merely linguistic. Hip-think doesn't require logic or clarity, which makes it easier, of course, to sound profound.)

The drug issue is a good example of our dogmatism. If you don't smoke or pop pills, you're narrow-minded, tradition-bound and a chicken. Your reasons for denying the Nirvana of drugs make no difference. There are people for whom "grass," "acid," "speed" and their relatives hold no interest, just as there are people who dislike roast beef. Usually they manage to commune with the infinite quite well without an interpreter. Yet these people are as square to the drug-user as the housewife who won't wear short skirts because the neighbors might talk.

What does love mean to the Love Generation? It can mean purging oneself of hatred and prejudice and welcoming everyone else as a brother, and it can mean preaching the gospel while pushing Methedrine. It can mean the L.A. Diggers, a group of well-off, sympathetic people who give runaway kids a place to stop and catch their breath, and it can mean the "rank sweat of an enseaméd bed." There's something of calf-love in all our uses of the word, and something else that's just a little weird: The widely published off-campus living arrangements of college students like Barnard's Linda Leclair is another indication, with *Playboy* magazine and Ingmar Bergman, that sex is rapidly becoming a spectator sport. Why is it we can't love without announcing it to the world in infinite detail?

Love, as the song-makers know, is a private thing, and those who proclaim it in public tend to slip a little in the practice. Whatever the Columbia students were thinking about when they threw rocks, mailboxes and desks at the cops during their recent fit of self-expression, it wasn't love. If it was, it lost a lot in the translation.

Actually, when you cut out the preaching and look at the action, we're all sharpshooters—in the old sense—and our major target is that famous bogeyman, the world we never made. We think our parents made it—the hypocrisy, the prejudice, the materialism, the hatred, the uncertainty—and we know we have the answers for improving it. It takes the wisdom that comes with some age to realize that if the solution looks simple you probably don't understand the problem. And it takes the kind of minds we haven't got to realize that what you say means less than what you do.

The hip world isn't the whole of our generation, but it's a good microcosm. Its values and flaws characterize us all. The hippie drops out of society. But luckily for him, society sticks around, because the hippie is a parasite. The straight world supports him. Without this country's prosperity, there could be no hippies. They'd have nobody to bum from, nobody to give them easy jobs to tide them over the winter. There would be no leisure time in which to practice being hip, and no straight public to be titillated and fleeced. The hip world is neither self-supporting nor self-perpetuating, and it's hypocritical to claim that it is.

This kind of hypocrisy creeps into almost all our debunking of the Bad World. The institutions that create the atmosphere conducive to protest are inextricably bound up with the institutions we protest against. If it weren't for the Establishment, what would we fight against? And if we couldn't fight, who knows but—horrors—we might become Establishment ourselves? History is full of rebellious crusades that demolished the *status quo* and wound up becoming the *status quo* themselves.

To protect ourselves, we try to cover the deck with protests—prove our unimpeachable nobility by knocking everything in sight as ignoble. How well do we listen to what we say?

Materialism in this country has taken the odd turn of becoming a form of idealism: things put aside for tomorrow. Our parents live for tomorrow, in a thingy kind of way. They dream of the bright world ahead, a utopia which we find rather pathetic because we quit believing in utopias a long time ago. We live for today. We grab what we can get, now. Tomorrow never comes anyway. And when it does, it's just like today. Actually we aren't even particularly cynical about it, just sad.

The deadly corollary to this kind of thinking is that what you have to work for isn't worth having. (A woman's magazine recently declared that the emphasis is on "roles, not goals," a decent square translation of "do your own thing.") We think knowledge that must be learned isn't valuable; only intuitive, revealed knowledge is worth while. The college "grind" is a pitiable figure. It's so much easier to fake your way through. College isn't a place where you learn; it's an object to be revolutionized. You don't find knowledge, it comes to you, complete with bright colors and dogs barking flowers.

If we work, we do just enough to survive. A job exists to keep one fed—we accept employment as a token reason for accepting a living. We're a generation of grasshoppers.

We love Marshall McLuhan because he makes it impossible, and therefore unnecessary, to think logically. Our passion for J. R. R. Tolkien is, I think, due not to the clear-cut moral position he espouses but to the blatantly mythological character of his books; they aren't about the real world, which makes them safe to handle. ("We can dig the morality, but we don't have to do anything about it, because we aren't mythological people," says my sister, who is 17.) The fads borrowed from Oriental and Indian cultures are deliberate archaisms. We long for the safe, still, dead worlds in which all values are only reflections of eternity. We don't like change, and we doubt we can cope with it, so we pretend it doesn't exist. Reality has become elusive, painful, a blind god that isn't dead but probably isn't human either, so we prefer ambiguity. Nevertheless, we feel ourselves entitled to hold an opinion on everything, whether we know anything about it or not. And we've discovered that the less we know about something, the easier it is to hold a strong opinion about it.

Heaven preserve us from our own children.

COMMENTARY: PURPOSE AND CHOICE OF TONE

Cecelia Holland, at 24, belongs to the generation she criticizes. Already the author of three novels, she might well be regarded as a "complete and utter success," which is what Brian McGuire indicated he could be termed by "present standards of American education." Her essay demonstrates that she is an outspoken young woman who obviously knows what she stands for and has no hesitation in stating it. She is quite willing to attack current attitudes and practices that she considers false and hypocritical and to defend causes that are unpopular but, in her eyes, worthy of support.

In the opening paragraph of her *introduction,* we detect at once a note of disapproval: ". . . the generation under 30 claims to be the hope of the world." The word *claims* tips us off to her attitude. She herself is not ready to accept that assertion.

In the second paragraph she launches into the irony that is the characteristic tone of her attack: "My generation is the most idealistic, the most dynamic and the most liberal in history; just ask us, we'll tell you." We know now, for sure, that she is not on the side of the young people she has been describing. Her *thesis* sentence, the last one in Paragraph 2, is also clearly ironic. It *says* that these young people are "strong on freedom and long on love," but it *means* the reverse. These are the boasts that she intends to attack.

She begins her attack at once in the third paragraph, the initial one of the *body:* "Are we strong on freedom?" It takes her just six short paragraphs to explain why she must answer that question with a resounding "No!" Two more paragraphs make little of the claims that the militant young are "long on love."

In the remainder of her criticism, Miss Holland singles out typical attitudes and acts of the young that she considers hypocritical. In doing so, she dares to defend the Establishment and show sympathy for parents. Toward the end she runs through a list of the specific things she disapproves of in the young, a list running from "doing your own thing" to adopting Oriental and Indian-influenced fads. Her *conclusion* consists of a dramatic and ironic one-sentence paragraph: "Heaven preserve us from our own children."

Although Cecelia Holland and Brian McGuire obviously differ in many of their views, they both have one great trait in common: Both write with sincerity and perfect candor. The reader has no difficulty in determining just where each stands on the important *issues* (debatable points) in such questions as the idealism of youth, the materialism found in the home, and the status of the college "grind." Each shows strong feelings and much evidence of having thought through matters that had puzzled them.

The titles of their essays—"It Wasn't Worth It" and "I Don't Trust Anyone Under Thirty"—suggest that two writers may defend conflicting points of view without either being guilty of any loss of integrity. In both essays we find a strong tone of conviction which earns our respect. Both young persons have found strength in daring to follow through to the end of the lines of thought and feeling they considered right. Encouraged by that confidence, they have discovered facts and ideas to support their respective theses.

That Cecelia Holland is ironic in tone does not detract from her effectiveness. She does not always speak out in her own straightforward voice as does Brian McGuire. Instead she chooses the mocking, ironic voice we have pointed out in her opening. Evidently she finds this approach natural to her personality and talents, just as McGuire probably does his. Each in his own way convinces us that he has at some time answered our question: "Who and what are you?" From their answers came their topics, their content, and their way (style) of writing.

WHAT DOES IT SAY?

1. The opening sentence contains four words describing "the generation under 30": *militant, committed, articulate, radical.* Consult your dictionary and show what meaning these words have in common and what special, distinctive meaning each has.

2. Can you quote any slogans or give examples of any public acts that Cecelia Holland might be referring to when she speaks of "the purity of our motives and the energy of our commitments"?

3. The author makes use of *allusions* to historic events and persons to make her point about the present great influence of young people. Look up the following in a dictionary or encyclopedia and show their relevance to what she says: the *Children's Crusade,* the *Renaissance, Cesare Borgia.*

4. Look up the word *syndrome.* What national attitudes and practices

are suggested by the expression, "the American Way of Life"? How can this style of living be called a "syndrome"?

5. Miss Holland seems to favor attitudes which might be termed "conservative viewpoints" by those who disagree with her. What does *conservative* mean here?

6. What does she mean when she says, "I am a fellow-traveler with the 'straights,' which means that sometimes I am self-consciously hip . . ."?

7. What do the following expressions mean?

do your own thing	hip-think
to pop pills	grass
the *status quo*	acid
deviation	speed
the straights	sharpshooters—in the old sense
hip	dig

8. Who is J. R. R. Tolkien? What is meant by "the blatant mythological character of his books"?

WHAT DO YOU THINK?

1. Write a one-paragraph "essay"—one having introduction, body, and conclusion—on one of these topics:

   (a) Campus clubs—whom are they for?
   (b) Football and books—do they mix?
   (c) What I didn't come to college for
   (d) What I wish a friend had told me
   (e) They call it "orientation"
   (f) So that's the "generation gap"!
   (g) Must we have political interests?
   (h) Trying to be honest with yourself

2. Select *one* of the following controversial statements made by Cecelia Holland and, by using specific examples drawn from your own experience and observations, explain why you agree or disagree with her statement as it appears in the context of her essay.

   (a) "Freedom and free speech should mean that anyone can hold any opinion he wants on the Negro or the war in Vietnam, as long as he doesn't try to enforce his views on anybody else."

(b) "Hip-think doesn't require logic or clarity, which makes it easier, of course, to sound profound."

(c) "We're a generation of grasshoppers."

(d) "The fads borrowed from Oriental and Indian cultures are deliberate archaisms."

(e) "To protect ourselves, we try to cover the deck with protests—prove our unimpeachable nobility by knocking everything in sight as ignoble."

3. The practice on many campuses of permitting recruitment by representatives of the Armed Forces has aroused considerable controversy. Here are two arguments in the form of typical statements. Explain in some detail your agreement or disagreement with the opinions expressed in them.

> The Marine Corps was recruiting in the Job Placement Office. The nature of the Marine Corps is not to place job-hunting students in a fulfilling life-work. Rather, it is the instrument of our government's immoral and illegal military activities. In fact, compulsory service is synonymous with involuntary servitude, which is given by Webster as a synonym for slavery. In short, military service is a system of slavery for the murder of human beings.

> Freedom of choice is one of the major reasons for education; to provide as many choices as possible is the job of the placement office. The offer of employment by the Marine Corps is just as valid as employment by IBM, Xerox, or any other firm or organization that offers an exchange or payment for services performed.

4. In a brilliant article, "The War Against the Young,"[1] Richard Poirier made some incisive statements, two of which are listed below. Select one of these as a possible basis for a 500-word essay of your own, developed out of your thinking and experience.

> The intellectual weapons used in the war against youth are from the same arsenal—and the young know this—from which war is being waged against other revolutionary movements, against Vietnam, against any effective justice, as distinguished from legislative melodrama, in matters of race and poverty.

> What is happening to the youth of the world deserves the freest imagination, the freest attention that older people are capable of giving.

[1] *Atlantic,* October, 1968.

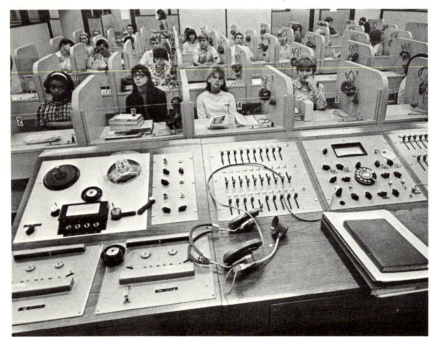

part II
CAMPUS ISSUES

CHOICE OF TOPIC:
WHAT DO YOU HAVE TO SAY?

Who gets through any day without having an argument of some kind? We constantly find ourselves in positions involving some conflict. In driving a car, for example, what silent or vocal remarks do we make regarding the competence of the driver who turns or brakes his car while we were momentarily looking elsewhere? Whose fault is it when we pick up a parking ticket? Most people easily convince themselves they are never wrong about anything. Listen to their accounts of the stupidity, blindness, or stubbornness of anyone who happens to cross them or disagree with them. Whose fault is it if a battery runs down, a meal is poorly cooked, an assignment left undone, someone's feelings hurt, money recklessly spent, or a room left untidy?

What do we always want in any argument?—To win, of course! Since "to win" is always the main purpose in engaging in arguments, let us consider some definitions of that verb. Common dictionary entries include these meanings: "to gain the victory in any contest; to triumph, prevail; succeed; to gain in competition or contest; to influence so as to gain the favor of." Psychologically, we always try to win in order to assure ourselves that we are in the right. As Brian McGuire must know, it is hard on the ego to acknowledge we may have been in the wrong.

27

Given this fact, we can understand how wars begin, racial conflicts erupt into violence, and family quarrels break out. For the same reason we even buy one "brand name" product rather than another and defend it against its rivals.

As citizens of a highly organized social structure, we are compelled to enjoy, as well as observe, the rights and duties of that status. As a result, we often find ourselves in conflict with elements of society. The essays by Brian McGuire and Cecelia Holland point out some of these dramatic conflicts, as will the authors of the upcoming selections: a young activist, a famous poet-critic, and a *Newsweek* reporter. In our times, we cannot escape such clashes of opinion; nor can we easily avoid expressing our own views on their issues.

The three authors in this part chose topics that they know are controversial; they are aware that the subjects they are dealing with have many sides and affect many interests and many people. But like all other authors, they plan and write their articles hoping that readers like us will be won over to their side of the argument. This fundamental purpose, or goal, of gaining the approval and support of others governs not only writers but also businessmen in conferences, experts in symposiums, and politicians in conventions and elections. Only a crafty propagandist, paid for his work, will select a topic he knows from the outset is worthless and hopeless.

As the first great philosopher to treat rhetoric as persuasion, Aristotle dealt at length with the judicious process of selecting a "winning" topic. Like his predecessor, Plato, he based his rhetoric on his understanding of how the human personality works. Their views on this differed, and, of course, so did those of their historic successors during the succeeding centuries. Today, rhetoricians such as Kenneth Burke and Wayne C. Booth enrich the old rhetoric and transform it by approaching it in the light of modern knowledge. They no longer think in terms of Aristotle's 37 sources of topics and their mechanical application. They no longer regard the study of rhetoric as the "art" of finding the means, in ready-made formulas, for winning cases or defending causes.

Instead, they regard the *whole* of a literary work as comprising its rhetoric. They see the essayist, the poet, the writer of fiction as one seeking *identification* with those readers who respond to him, and this recognition and sharing occur when the readers discover they share identical interests, needs, and aspirations with the author. Read the Commentaries to see how the author prepares for this identification.

It is through *analysis* of how the authors define their topics and present them effectively that the "new" rhetoric can best be demonstrated; yet there is one thing on which all rhetoricians, past and present, agree—the topic must be "limited."

LIMITING THE TOPIC

To turn again to our friend Mac, once he finds a topic that really grips him he may feel that he could "write a whole book on the subject." But he knows that his instructor will settle for two or three pages. The problem, then, is "How does he *limit* his topic?" or "How does he narrow down a wide, general subject to one that can be adequately discussed in the time and space available?"

There are various ways in which Mac, and you, can go about limiting a topic, thereby reducing it to one that can be *developed adequately* within the space (number of words) you intend to devote to it. (*Remember:* To give a topic *adequate development* means to make certain that you have provided the reader with enough details so that he can clearly see the point you have been trying to make and the support you have given it.)

1. Consider as "too wide" any social institution, organization, or pattern of behavior such as the following: religion, politics, crime, war, poverty, education, music, art, morality, freedom, science, or labor.
2. Narrow the scope of such a general topic to one particular problem or aspect. One way to do this is to come down what semanticists call "the abstraction ladder," as in the following example:

Freedom

Constitutional rights

Demonstrators at _____ University who "occupied" the president's office

Their leader _____ who was arrested and jailed

Why he should, or should not, be suspended or expelled

3. Make sure that you know enough details about the topic you have finally decided on and that the material is specific and concrete enough for you to handle in a short paper.
4. State your final limited topic in the form of a complete sentence—a thesis.

Coming down the abstraction ladder provides opportunities for discovering what your *thesis,* your main purpose, should be. You will find the "ladder" most helpful. By using it you can bring almost any subject down to your own level to see how it affects you, personally. If, for example, you have first-hand knowledge of the confrontation the militant student staged against the president, you will find him a most suitable subject for a brief essay. An obvious thesis that practically suggests itself might thus be: "I think this student should (not) be suspended or expelled for his actions."

The side you take in such a controversy will appear in a forthright statement in your essay and will be your *thesis.* The reader, encountering this statement in the *introduction,* will know what to expect in the *body* of the essay, and possibly the general direction of the *conclusion.* This thesis serves as a foundation for the discourse you will build upon it.

On Whose Side Are the Universities?
by MICHAEL NOVAK

Ten years ago college kids resented being called
kids. Today they call one another kids with
pride and solidarity. Today students have power;
they do not need to play pretend.

Introduction
Opening with a startling
fact: "Today students have
power."

What happens in the colleges in 1968 may
be decisive for the next 30 years. Small but
articulate groups of students have attained an
astute political consciousness and are promising disruption and rebellion. The Congress—
that band of old men two generations removed
from reality—is threatening reprisal. A nation
founded by an armed revolution and still pledg-
ing allegiance to unfulfilled revolutionary principles—like liberty and justice for all—does not
wish to educate rebellious students.

Thesis states an irony:
Our country was founded
on revolution but "does
not wish to educate rebellious students."

What, then, is an education for? In the
minds of many, a kid who "turns out right"
moves into the social network of American industry with an affable smile, an easygoing man-

Reprinted from *Christianity and Crisis,* October 14, 1968; copyright by Christianity
and Crisis, Inc., 1968. Reprinted with permission.

Body

Rhetorical question asked and answered: The kind of students now graduated are made to order for a technological society.

ner and the reliable, efficient, pragmatic style on which our technological society depends. Hardheaded, realistic and committed to the demands of the present order of things, such a promising young man is encouraged to indulge in sentimentalities about defending freedom.

One sees his friends in Viet Nam: crew-cut, clear-eyed, soft-spoken, determined. One sees them everywhere in the universities: clean-shaven, hard-working, bright, smooth. These are the "silent students," not represented by the radicals who dominate the news; for there is nothing new about them. The American educational system has been geared to turning out millions of them.

They are the "silent students" who support the *status quo* and Viet Nam.

Again the key rhetorical question followed by other questions suggesting what education should not be.

What is an education for? To keep the clocks ticking, the factories humming and the planes flying? To keep American democracy strong? To keep the young loyal? To teach them to be happy with bread and circuses?

The liberal answer that higher education should produce progressives is no longer a serviceable compromise.

The liberal answer to that question during the past 30 years has been to use the schools as agencies of progressive political and social enlightenment. And, indeed, public opinion polls regularly show a marked correlation between length of education and progressive views. But the liberal solution was a compromise with the ongoing system. Against utopianism and apocalypse, liberalism under Franklin D. Roosevelt chose pragmatic adjustment from within the system. The fruits have been many. But the compromise appears, now, to have broken down. The evidence is the malaise felt almost everywhere.

Can schools supported by the wealth and power of a social system be expected to produce students who will rebel against that society?

The public schools are supported by public money and the private schools are supported by industry and government. How can such schools prepare students to be revolutionaries? How can any system prepare young people to transcend itself? The problem is even more vexing than the problem the institutional church must face: how to catechize prophets. For in the society at large, all the wealth, power and force of arms of the social system are preserving the system on its present course.

Where revolutionary criticism is neither promoted nor heeded, moreover, those who strike the revolutionary pose for its own sake— desiring neither power nor its responsibilities but inner exaltation—are difficult to distinguish from genuine men of power. Without the hot-blooded, the romantic and the profoundly confused, on the other hand, no revolution can proceed. A revolution is not an act of reflection but of passion. Tom Paine's instability is not an argument against the validity of 1776, and it is unfair to discredit the present revolution merely by denouncing its tactics or the personalities of some of its leaders.

The "present revolution" should not be judged by the tactics or personalities of its spokesmen.

Do we want a political revolution in the United States, a serious rearrangement of the bases of power, wealth and prestige? That is the fundamental educational question. If we do not want a serious revolution, then we should allow our various educational systems to function as they are. The logic of such a political choice would lead us to: (a) squash the student revolutionaries forcibly, or (b) co-opt their energies in pseudo-revolutionary programs (place them on committees). Generally, it is the liberal administrator who is the slowest to grasp the force and the origin of such logic. That is why he is the most hateful in the students' eyes.

The fundamental question: Is a political revolution in the United States wanted? If not, let the education system continue unchanged.

There has not been much serious revolutionary passion in the U.S. since the days of Reinhold Niebuhr's *The End of an Era.* But the doors of the Pandora's box closed by World War II have again flown open. Can a capitalistic democracy possibly serve the ideals of "freedom and justice for all"? Or is the whole system inherently contradictory?

Two more critical questions expressing doubt of possible reforms in the system.

When young radicals close down one or another university during this school year or next, it would be a mistake to imagine that merely procedural issues are at stake. A stream-

The revolution taking place in universities is a real one.

lining of the administrative process or functional adjustments that relieve the pressure at concrete points of protest will not meet the issue. (In liberal pragmatic theory, issues are swiftly reduced to functional, operational terms.) The revolution that has begun on the campuses is not raising a procedural issue; it is substantive.

That revolutionary issue has two parts. In the first place, the crew-cut, affable American is not an attractive human type. He is repressed, empty, quietly and blindly savage, without an interior life, boring and bored. The first substantive issue has to do with inhibitions, repressions and diminished imaginative and affective capacities.

In the second place, the revolutionary issue is concerned with economics, technology, the mass media and political machinery. What is good for Texas money does not, clearly, promote "freedom and justice for all." The "law and order" that police forces now defend does cruel and arrogant violence to too huge a number of human beings; it is not tolerable. The interests that dominate social and political decision-making in the U.S. are unfaithful to the revolutionary ideals on which this country is founded.

Faced with such a revolution, on whose side are the universities? And do they dare to say so? There is no other basic educational issue.

First, this revolution affects the repressed, average students.

Second, this revolution is in the spirit of the American revolution but contrary to the present controlling forces.

Conclusion
The dilemma the universities must face up to: The universities must decide where they stand.

COMMENTARY: CONFRONTING THE READER WITH CHOICES

In fewer than one thousand words, Michael Novak presents us with a carefully thought out analysis of what lies behind some of the unrest found in American universities today. If we accept his interpretation of these disturbances, we will also have to accept the dilemma put to us in the conclusion of his essay. Whether we agree with his analysis or not, we must admit that he is convinced he has something important to say. Even those readers who may be appalled by what he has written must respect him for having taken a firm position on a controversial issue.

His many questions and positive statements suggest his intense feeling, just as the scope of his inquiries reveals the aspects of life and education in America that he has brooded over and struggled to understand. This intensity probably accounts for the briefness of some of his fourteen paragraphs, wherein questions and statements have the sting of whiplashes.

Look at the confident, bold statements in the opening paragraph of the *introduction:* "Today students have power; they do not need to play pretend." Is it true?

One after the other, he hits us with accusations such as the one in the fourth paragraph, wherein he labels the "clean-shaven, hard-working, bright, smooth" students as "the silent ones." What is his attitude toward them? Does it anger you?

Michael Novak knows what he wants to say and how to say it so as to get the reactions he wants.

All of the explanations and assertions he makes in the *body* are aimed at reinforcing the dilemma confronting the reader in the *conclusion.* By definition, a dilemma is a statement, or argument, forcing one to choose between two alternatives, both of which are painful and unpleasant, and so are called "the horns of the dilemma."

If you will examine the whole essay again in the light of the marginal comments, you will find that Novak has taken care to steer the reader directly onto "the horns" of the dilemma. Skillfully, he has tried to block off any third or fourth alternatives his readers may want to choose when the final choice must be made. He maneuvers his readers into an almost inescapable predicament. They face a *confrontation.*

WHAT DOES IT SAY?

1. Novak describes the campus rebels as "articulate groups of students who have attained an astute political consciousness." What does he mean?

2. What typical scenes and situations do you associate with "the reliable, efficient, pragmatic style on which our technological society depends"?

3. Who are the "silent students"? What are they silent about? Why?

4. What is the difference between *progressive, liberal views* and the kind Novak favors?

5. Who was Thomas Paine and what "instability" was he criticized for?

6. How can placing of student revolutionaries on committees enable the administrators to "co-opt their energies in pseudo-revolutionary programs"?

7. Who was Reinhold Niebuhr and what is "Pandora's box"?

8. List four of the "revolutionary ideals on which this country is founded."

WHAT DO YOU THINK?

Write a 500-word essay, having an introduction, body, and conclusion on some aspect of one of the following topics most familiar to you. Remember to come down the "abstraction ladder."

1. Is there anything wrong in wanting to become one of the following?

teacher	accountant
engineer	scientist
welfare worker	forester
nurse	pilot
salesman	professional athlete

2. Militant Black students are also confronting our institutions of higher learning with dilemmas. Write your considered reaction to the kind of statements made by Eldridge Cleaver, Black Panther leader and author of *Soul on Ice:*

   > We want to break ground for a revolutionary movement, including blacks and whites, that can really deal with the situation. There are certain hostile elements in the white community that control the black community—businessmen, politicians and the gestapo—and they work in conjunction with the parasitical class in the black community. We need to have revolutionary blacks and whites working on both fronts. Everything we're doing aims at pulling these elements into functional coalition machinery.[1]

3. A recent *New York Times* article reported the following cases as evidence of "Teen-Age Revolt." Write your opinion on *one* of these patterns of behavior.

[1] As quoted by William Hedgepeth, *Look*, January 7, 1969, p. 35.

Howie S. is organizing a revolution against American society in the high schools with the skill of a little Lenin.

Jamie G. started at Radcliffe College this fall with no clear idea of what kind of life she wants to prepare for, but sure that it must be different from the affluence in which she was raised in Great Neck, L. I.

Joe S. is a weekend marijuana smoker ("I got turned on in summer camp," he said) and now is selling pot to his friends in Westchester to make enough money to go to India on a Diogenes-like quest for "God, a guru or just a really good man."

Joan McW. is having what she calls "marriage tryouts" with boys, protecting herself against pregnancy with a bootlegged supply of birth-control pills that she bought with her piggy-bank savings last June.

All these young New Yorkers, members of the current generation in their middle-teens, share a common background of comfortable homes, loving parents, good schools, high intelligence, excellent health, and almost unlimited opportunities for self development. In short, they have all the advantages that many of their mothers and fathers, growing up in the Depression and World War II years, were denied.[2]

---

[2] Michael Stern, "Teenage Revolt; Is it Deeper Today?" *The New York Times,* October 7, 1968.

Unsolicited Opening Day Address by Prexy

by JOHN CIARDI

Ladies and gentlemen, welcome—and welcome back—to Diehard University. I shall start the academic year by describing the contract you have entered into by the act of enrolling in this university. That contract is clearly set forth in the university catalogue, but since literacy is no longer prerequisite to admission, let me lip-read the essential points of our agreement. As you emerge from this convocation you will be handed a digest of these remarks in attractively prepared comic-book form with all dialogue limited to basic English and with the drawings carefully designed to help you over any grammatical difficulties. Those of you, moreover, for whom the requirements of Sub-Literacy One have been waived, may dial AV for Audio Visual, followed by 0016, and a dramatized explication will appear on your TV sets.

Diehard, as you know, is no longer dedicated to excellence. The trustees, the administration, the faculty, and the federal government—not necessarily in that order—have concurred that excellence has been outnumbered. The restated policy of Diehard University is simply to salvage what it can from what little it gets from the too much being thrust upon it.

We recognize that the achievement of any given intellectual standard is no longer prerequisite to a bachelor's degree. The insistence of any educational institution is defined by its minimum standards, and Diehard no longer has any. As a contractual agreement, the faculty undertake to confer a bachelor's degree upon you in acknowledgment of four years of attendance.

If you are willing to settle for that degree, I suggest you do not waste money on textbooks. The presence of a textbook may tempt you to open it. The psychological consequences are obvious: if you must actually open a textbook in order to meet nonexistent minimum standards, how will you ever be sure you are not a moron? Your whole future career could be warped, in such a case, by guilt and uncertainty. Our educational activities, let me say, are so organized that any member of the in- or out-group of the affluent society can stroll through them in the intervals between political rallies, draft-card burnings, love-ins, water fights, sit-ins, sit-outs, sympathy marches, student elections, anti-raids and generalized adolescent glandular upheavals. These programs have been carefully constructed to assist your social development as students. I urge them upon you as the social duty of every minimalist. Diehard would serve no purpose were it to allow an intemperate emphasis on learning to deflect its minimalists from the fullness of their undergraduate social development and thus, indirectly, from future computerization.

To further that social development, Diehard imposes no rules of extra-curricular behavior. We shall not act *in loco parentis*. With a mild shudder of revulsion, we return that function to your legal parents. We have problems enough with our own failures and cannot accept as ours the genetic failures of others.

This university has eliminated dormitories. Where you live, with whom you live, and what you do off campus are matters between you and your parents, or between you and the police, as the case may be.

You are free to demonstrate on all matters of conviction, or, simply, on all matters. For your convenience we have set aside a fireproof, waterproof, open-occupancy convention center called Hyde Park Hall. You are free to occupy it and to harangue in or from it at your pleasure. You have full license for all non-criminal acts that occur in Hyde Park Hall. Any criminal actions you may engage in there will be, of course, between you and the police.

Should you choose to act unlawfully in any of the otherwise assigned buildings of the university, you will be warned once that your actions are unlawful, and the police will then be summoned to take normal action against a breach of the peace.

The university will seek your advice on all matters of student organization, social development of the university, and community relations. We shall seek that advice temperately and with as much open-mindedness as we can achieve in our senility. In seeking it, however, we do not pledge ourselves to be bound by it. Where your views seem to be reasoned, they will be honored in reason; where they seem intemperate or shortsighted, they will be rejected in reason. A faculty-student board will be elected to study all grievances.

In no case, however, will that board, or any body of this university, consider a general amnesty as a condition for ending a demonstration that violates lawful procedure.

Diehard will not consider any request made by a minimalist for changes in the curriculum, faculty, or academic qualification. On these matters we ask nothing from you and we will hear nothing.

We do confess to a vestigial nostalgia for the long-honored and now outmoded idea of the university as a bookish community of learning. While most of you are pursuing your social development, therefore, the faculty will direct such students as are inclined to volunteer for it, in a course of study leading to the degree of Laureate in Arts or in Science. We shall continue to grant the Bachelor's degree in Arts or in Science without requirement, though to assist your social development we do invite you to attend various discussion groups to be held at carefully spaced intervals.

With those who elect the Laureate program, the university insists on a different contract. It insists that in the act of electing such a program, the student will have submitted himself to the faculty as candidate for a degree to be conferred at the discretion of the faculty. The faculty, having already thrown away minimums, must insist on reserving to itself the right to formulate maximums for those who are willing to reach for them. It is the student's business to qualify, or to revert (without prejudice), to the social development program leading to the degree of Bachelor.

I ask all those who are interested in a course of study to return tomorrow to start our further discussions. The rest of you may now return to your pads to drop out, turn on, and tune in. If you are arrested between now and your graduation, the university will credit the time up to your conviction toward your attendance and will do its best to readmit you upon completion of your sentence. By decision of the board of trustees, days of attendance completed while out on bail pending an appeal will be counted toward a degree.

If the police, that is, are willing to let you out of jail, and if you are willing to check in on the roster, we are willing to keep the attendance records and to grant appropriate degrees upon satisfaction of the requirement.

We are not willing to have our reading and discussion time interrupted by protest, no matter how passionate, that breaks the law. Nor are we willing to police the law. Criminality is the proper concern of the police; ours, we believe, is reasoned discussion. When the discussion goes beyond reason and to the point of interfering with the curriculum of those who have chosen one, we reserve the right to suspend or to expel you from the hazy premises of our failing venture into education for those few who are interested in the unlikely.

Hello. Goodbye. And may your standardization be your fulfillment.

COMMENTARY: THE USES OF BITTER IRONY

Is poet-critic John Ciardi unhappy about what is happening in and to our universities? As soon as we encounter the name of the university, "Diehard," we know, of course, that this "Opening Day Address" is going to be a satirical one, full of ironic comments and ridiculous overstatements made to make the *Saturday Review* readers smile and weep at the same time. Instead of honest, forthright protest and plain indignation, Ciardi has chosen to express his displeasure with certain aspects of our universities under the guise of satire and mock seriousness.

Like Jonathan Swift, pretending to be serious about selling the babies of starving Irish as delectable table fare for the rich, in that great masterpiece of deadly irony, "A Modest Proposal," John Ciardi plays at being serious in his president's plan for granting a Bachelor's degree merely for attending a university for four years. After the first three paragraphs, which make up the *introduction,* he begins taking up, one after the other, the main points of the proposed new program. It has five distinct features: (1) Diehard will require no textbooks, (2) it will not act *in loco parentis,* (3) it will grant full freedom to demonstrate lawfully, (4) it will seek student advice and have a faculty-student board of grievances, and (5) it will have a special Laureate program for students who really want to learn.

Throughout the essay, we can detect a *tone,* a mood of despair. He seems to regard the majority of those who come to college as young people who come for reasons of social "improvement" and not at all for learning; he calls this majority "minimalists" and apparently sees no hope whatsoever in them. He lumps them together as "the in- or out-group of the affluent society" who take part in "political rallies, draft-card burnings, love-ins, water fights, sit-ins," and so on. He states in the opening paragraphs that they are illiterate, and that they rely on television and comic books for their minimal instruction. In the last sentences of his *conclusion* he again speaks most pessimistically about the possibility of attracting many students to enter and complete a real program of learning. He calls this program "our failing venture into education for those few who are interested in the unlikely."

Yet the speech does contain some positive, illuminative comments that in places seem to flash through the satire as deadly serious standards for any university. His repeated statements such as the following indicate the policy he really favors: "Any criminal actions you may engage in there [Hyde Park Hall] will be, of course, between you and the police. . . . Nor are we willing to police the law. Criminality is the proper concern of the police; ours, we believe, is reasoned discussion." It would appear that he advocates all universities adopting such policies, even though they are not willing to give Bachelor degrees to their own "minimalists."

In the closing paragraph his basic objection to present university education and practices stands in the most prominent and dramatic position any speech or essay can offer—the final words. They are: "And may your standardization be your fulfillment."

David J. Barrios

WHAT DOES IT SAY?

1. What is a "diehard"? Why is this an appropriate name for Ciardi's fictitious university?

2. He calls the relationship between his institution and the entering student "a contract." Is it really such?

3. How would you recognize his "minimalist" student if you saw one?

4. How possibly can he describe such activist moves as draft-card burnings, sit-ins, and student elections as being "generalized adolescent glandular upheavals"?

5. Does your university or college act on the policy of *in loco parentis?* If so, in what ways?

6. He says his faculty have "a vestigial nostalgia for the long-honored and now outmoded idea of the university as a bookish community of learning." What is the meaning of *vestigial nostalgia?*

7. Why the final "Hello. Goodbye"? What is he suggesting?

8. How is his term "the Laureate program" an apt one for the students it is designed to attract?

WHAT DO YOU THINK?

1. Think about what you can say that makes good sense to you on *one* of the following topics; then write an orderly essay of 500 words on it.

   Why I came to college

   Are most of us "minimalists"?

   What's wrong with looking for "social development"?

   What my high school did not prepare me for

   What does our university expect of us?

   Is student government important here?

   How much say should students have on college committees?

   Part-time jobs versus time in the library

2. Select one of the following statements as a basis for your essay:
   (a) Howie Swerdloff, 17-year-old organizer of the New York High School Union:

The main thing that's taught us in school is how to obey the rules, dress in our uniforms, play the game and NO, DON'T BE UPPITY! Oh, we're trained for participating in the democratic process—we have our student governments—they can legislate about basketball games and other such meaningful topics. Don't mention the curriculum. THEY'LL tell us what to learn.

Asked what he hoped to accomplish by radicalizing his fellow students, Howie replied: "We don't want to take over the government. We want to destroy it. I believe people should have power over their own lives, but not over other peoples' lives."[1]

(b) Abraham H. Lass, principal of Abraham Lincoln High School in Brooklyn, New York City:

Abraham H. Lass, principal of Abraham Lincoln High School in Brooklyn, also finds himself troubled by the intransigence of young rebels. But, he said, "I have more compassion than anger with these kids because the trouble begins basically with adult delinquency."

High school radicals do not have to look to the universities for models, Mr. Lass said.

"There are manifestations of violence all around them," he said. "It is almost a form of approved social behavior. Look at teachers, policemen, firemen, sanitationmen, nurses, doctors, social workers. These once were people who were thought to be so dedicated to the public welfare that they never would do anything to imperil it. They were the embodiment of the idea of settling differences peacefully.

"But now they strike and withhold their labor for their own ends in defiance of law. Is there any wonder that students see nothing wrong in using lawless methods for what they want?"[2]

(c) Professor Raymond Aron on the French university revolt of May 1968:

It was not the student revolt in itself which may have dealt a deathblow to the liberal universities, but the support given by a minority of teachers and lecturers to a movement initiated by the students, and the methods used to "intimidate" those who refused to turn the place upside-down and rush through reforms at a time of intellectual turmoil and open or concealed violence. For the first time in university history, members of university staffs tried to be both teachers and professional revolutionaries, both within and outside the university. The leaders of SNESUP openly proclaimed themselves *syndicalistes universitaires* and, from 27 May on, made no secret of their revolutionary activities. What is without precedent, they refused for several days to recognize the legally constituted government of the country as a valid party to the debate. Although, as functionaries of the bourgeois State they were as concerned as ever for their grade and salary, they sought to overthrow

---

[1] *The New York Times*, October 7, 1968.
[2] *The New York Times*, October 7, 1968.

the power which has granted them all the freedoms denied to their colleagues in the East—freedoms of which they were cheerfully prepared to deprive their French colleagues. And then they clamoured for university solidarity!

This revolutionary, or pseudo-revolutionary, posture on the part of a teachers' union was a breach of the unwritten law of the university community, which was even more gravely violated by their action within the university. That many students and teachers have wanted, and still want, "structural reform" is undeniable. But who is going to believe that for years past the sole aim of these teachers has been to entrust an unspecified degree of power, its precise nature and limits still undetermined, to student-teacher parity committees? And who will believe that votes by a show of hands in plenary or general assemblies can express the genuine intention of teachers and students?[3]

(d) From "Free Speech in 1968," a pamphlet distributed by the American Civil Liberties Union:

As long as protest is orderly, however annoying, it is protected, and interference by private citizens is at once unlawful and unwise.

When a protest seems most annoying it may be well to remember the Supreme Court's wise admonition:

A function of free speech under our system is to invite dispute. It may indeed best serve its high purpose when it induces a condition of unrest, creates dissatisfaction with conditions as they are, or even stirs people to anger.

[3] *Encounter*, September, 1968, pp. 61–62. Reprinted with permission.

An Outcry:
Thoughts on Being Tear Gassed
by PETER BARNES

Last Tuesday, I was gassed twice in Berkeley. It hurt. The police and National Guard no longer bother with simple tear gas. They are using a chemical called CS—the kids call it pepper gas—that the Army uses in Vietnam. It not only stings the eyes but sets fire to the nose, mouth and throat, and made me, at least, feel groggy and mildly nauseated.

Many other people, of course, got hurt far worse than I did. They were clubbed and shot as well as gassed. One 25-year-old onlooker was killed by buckshot pellets the size of a marble. So this is not in the nature of a personal complaint; it is rather an outcry against what is happening in California, and by extension, what is happening to America.

In many ways, the violence of the past few days in Berkeley is more frightening than the violence that exploded in Chicago last August. In Chicago, as the Walker report concluded, the police erupted into a riot. But at least no one was killed, the national media told the story to the world and, among his critics and defenders alike, Mayor Daley was held responsible for the cops' behavior.

Brutality: In Berkeley, under cover of Governor Reagan's three-month-old "state of extreme emergency," police have also gone on a riot, displaying a lawless brutality equal to that of Chicago, along with weapons and techniques that even the authorities in Chicago did not dare employ: the firing of buckshot at fleeing crowds and unarmed bystanders, and the gassing—at times for no reason at all—of entire streets and portions of a college campus.

The Berkeley rioting could perhaps most accurately be described as an outbreak of class warfare between cops and students. To the cops, the young and shaggy-haired denizens of Berkeley have become "niggers," subject to clubbing and gassing for what they are, rather than for anything they might have done. To the students, most policemen have become "pigs," brutish representatives of a power structure so up tight it could not even cope with the spontaneous creation of a "People's Park." Few students actually threw anything more dangerous than epithets, but a sizable number, goaded by gas and gunshot, were increasingly willing to be led into cat-and-mouse tactics of guerrilla provocation.

Unlike Chicago, the lines of political authority in Berkeley have been so confused that it has been almost impossible to affix direct responsibility for the violence—or, more important, to discover avenues for bringing it to an end. The mayor of Berkeley and the Berkeley police chief have had little control over the situation: the forces present have included Alameda County Sheriff deputies, the California Highway Patrol, the San Francisco Tactical Squad, the National Guard, and police from Oakland and other neighboring communities—none of whom is responsible to Berkeley authorities. Berkeley chancellor Roger Heyns, whose initial misjudgment turned the People's Park into a battleground, has lost control over the forces of "law and order" on his campus.

War Games: For seven days in May, the effective rulers of this occupied city and university were 3,000 unknown men in uniform, headed by two generals and a sheriff playing war games with real people's lives.

In the end, however, one man—Gov. Ronald Reagan—is responsible for what is happening. He is the only man who can stop it now and—in terms of the popularity he has gained from it for the moment—he is its only beneficiary. Far from the scene of his officers' violence, he has projected himself as the virtuous foe of an insidious clique of unruly revolutionaries. Reagan's approach is far more sophisticated than Joe McCarthy's and, in my view, far more ominous: Joe McCarthy never controlled the National Guard, nor did he contribute to the polarization of our society with bloodshed.

The real danger in California is not the students, nor the tree-planting street people, nor even that handful of genuine revolutionaries that Reagan so piously condemns. It is the uncontrollable use of paramilitary force without responsibility; it is the helplessness of such representative institutions as the Berkeley City Council (whose meeting during the violence was a charade); it is the fearful reluctance of moderate public officials to speak out.

Tactics: No one denies that there is a group of revolutionaries in Berkeley and throughout the country who are determined to provoke confrontations. No one questions the fact that tens of thousands of American students feel alienated from society as they see it. But you do not diminish alienation or defeat a hard core of revolutionaries by gassing and clubbing and shooting indiscriminately.

Quite to the contrary, such a primitive response only plays into the revolutionaries' hands and takes attention away from specific issues that are negotiable and should be negotiated. The olive-drab National Guard helicopter that sprayed pepper gas over the campus may have cleared Sproul Plaza for twenty minutes, but it radicalized hundreds of nonrevolutionary, nonviolent students for far longer than that, and did little toward settling the controversy over the People's Park.

While the escalation of armed force undoubtedly benefited Reagan politically and gave some policemen and militant students a chance to prove their virility, it did no one else any good at all. What was called for in Berkeley—whatever the provocation—was not pepper gas, buckshot and bayonets, but reason, restraint, and as much good faith as possible.

Beyond the smoke and confusion of last week's tragic events in Berkeley are some broader questions. When youthful citizens can be wantonly gassed and beaten, all because of a small, unauthorized park, what has happened to America? What has happened to our sense of perspective, our tradition of tolerance, our view of armed force as a last—never a first—resort?

COMMENTARY: RESTRAINT AND PASSION

How, without raving and growing incoherent, do you manage to describe your anger and outrage in having suffered and witnessed an event of unjustifiable brutality? That was Peter Barnes's problem in preparing his first-hand report for *Newsweek*.

His training as a reporter helped him to keep his feelings in restraint while relating the painful events of the campus violence. At the same time, his concern for the "Why?" of this violence enabled him to treat the experience from the viewpoint of an observer who is only too well acquainted with other such episodes of violence and the pattern they are creating. We find one basic question unifying both the introduction and the conclusion: "When youthful citizens can be wantonly gassed and beaten, all because of a small, unauthorized park, what has happened to America?" Peter Barnes thus sees the events at Berkeley as part of a highly disturbing pattern of police and military reaction spreading across the country.

His restraint appears in the barebone facts of his opening: "Last Tuesday, I was gassed twice in Berkeley. It hurt. The police and National Guard no longer bother with simple tear gas." Beneath that simple phrasing we sense his passion; it almost surfaces in that phrase— "no longer bother with simple tear gas." His description of the effects of the "CS" gas as he experienced them are likewise almost clinically objective: "It not only stings the eyes but sets fire to the nose, mouth and throat and made me, at least, feel groggy and mildly nauseated." The honesty of that qualifying adverb *mildly* testifies to his professional effort to be an honest reporter. He is no more hesitant to say that the police regard "denizens of Berkeley" as "niggers" than he is to record the students' epithet of "pigs" for the police.

In considering the causes of the tragic events he witnessed, Peter Barnes—rightly or wrongly—places the responsibility for all the grim happenings of this "class war" upon "one man—Gov. Ronald Reagan." But he also admits that there are "revolutionaries" at Berkeley and elsewhere who are seeking to bring about such confrontations. And he acknowledges the fact that "tens of thousands of American students feel alienated from society as they see it." Still he holds "gassing and clubbing and shooting indiscriminately" to be far from the means of meeting such opposition. In place of violence, he urges government adoption of "reason, restraint, and as much good faith as possible."

By viewing this Berkeley park episode as the latest one of a disturbing series of such violent police and military reaction, he elevates the event he is reporting to a level of national importance. He ends by virtually asking his readers to identify with him in his moral protest against what is happening to the American "tradition of tolerance."

WHAT DOES IT SAY?

1. How can the author term his article "an outcry" when its language and protests are what they are?

2. When do police actions deserve to be called a "police riot"?

3. What is the original meaning of *class war?* What is the author's basis for terming the behavior of police and students in Berkeley as "a class war"?

4. Rephrase in standard English the expression "a power structure so up tight . . . ."

5. In saying "a sizable number" of students "were willing to be led into cat-and-mouse tactics of guerrilla provocation," what manner of "tactics" did the author have in mind?

6. Why is the term "law and order" placed in quotation marks in the statement saying that the chancellor lost control over those forces?

7. Is there any evidence for the author's claim that Governor Reagan profited politically from his "state of extreme emergency" policy and practices?

8. How would you define Peter Barnes's meaning of the word *tolerance?*

WHAT DO YOU THINK?

1. Here are some possible essay topics related to Peter Barnes's "outcry." Select one.

   (a) A potentially explosive problem on our campus

   (b) A "recipe" for "student unrest"

   (c) Can't anything be done about _____?

   (d) What I learned about "confrontation"

   (e) How our local police regard us

   (f) What really has happened to America?

   (g) Who was Joe McCarthy?

2. Compare or contrast Peter Barnes's treatment of the Berkeley "Peoples' Park" violence with one by Barbara Schreiber:

   > James Rector is dead.
   > An Alameda pig cleans his gun and washes his hands.
   > The steel fence around People's Park gleams in the sunlight.
   > The Establishment begins its analysis of "what actually took place in Berkeley during the latest 'rioting' and who was responsible."
   > The Establishment will put out 500 copies of their analysis on expensive paper and schedule another meeting.
   > The Establishment will "tell it like it is."
   > Ronnie, Wally, Roger, forget it. Don't bother.
   > If you were in the streets you know what happened.
   > If you weren't in the streets all the rhetoric and verbiage you command is worthless.
   > We don't need another report, another mass of lies and propaganda.
   > We don't need a City Council meeting to debate whether or not we

should share our food with a starving brother or share our love with a starving community.

We don't need your guns and clubs and tear gas, your murderers who take our lives, your thieves who steal our joy and leave behind a waste of mud and dying flowers.

We don't need you.

But you need us.

You need someone to talk to. You cannot be silent. You cannot afford to be silent and think of what you have done. Or what you are. You are not pigs. You are the servants of pigs. You are at the mercy of their guns. If we die, you are next in line.

We hold in our hands all that is beautiful. We hold life in our hands.

You have only death on your side.

While you sit in the dark, insane with the fear of living, we will fight.

We will fight with strange new weapons. With dirt and water. With flowers and trees. With singing and dancing. With our naked bodies. We will bury you under truckloads of dark, rich earth. We will plant a park that will encompass the world. We will love each other and laugh in the face of your guns and bayonets.

Each day we will grow in number. Each year we will grow in power. We will be an amoeba, a vine, a silent army of seeds carried by the wind. Can you legislate against the earth? We will be the earth.

We will grow ten thousand more street people, ten million more James Rectors, a nation of human beings. We will take back the land that is ours. We will feed our brothers and sisters from the earth. We will be free. We will live.[1]

[1] Reprinted from *The Berkeley Barb,* May 30–June 5, 1969. Copyright © 1969 by Barbara Schreiber. Reprinted with permission of the author.

Courtesy of United Press International

part III
PERSONAL VALUES

THE READER-AUDIENCE:
WHO AND WHAT ARE THEY?

Besides his skill in expression, perhaps the main reason that the professional writer is successful where the beginner-amateur is not, is that the professional knows the tastes and interests of his readers. He is constantly aware that he is writing for a specific body of readers with well-defined tastes, united by similar backgrounds and interests. In appealing to those interests, or in making allowances for them, he is following the practice urged by every rhetorician from Aristotle down to your present writing instructor.

Before anyone can expect his readers to *identify* with him and his message, he must first be able to identify with them himself. To do so he will ask a variant of the basic question he posed about himself: "Who and what am I?" This time he will ask about his readers: "Who and what are *they?*" Before he addresses them he will want to know what makes them tick: what they hold sacred, what they tend to condemn, and what are their passions and their prejudices. When he has this knowledge, he can judge accurately how they are likely to react to what he wants to tell them, and also the manner he should adopt in saying it. He decides, in other words, on what rhetoricians call his *stance;* that is, his attitude and approach to his readers.

Let us take again our student-friend Mac. Like the rest of his class he has read William Zinsser's witty piece "Ladies: Why Not Creative Cussing?" which heads the group of essays in this section. He has also read, under the heading of "What Do You Think?," the quotations from *Life* and the *Chicago Sun Times* about the mounting use of "four-letter words" in print, and the provocative comments and statements in the other items. Perhaps he has noted the appearance of some of these four-letter words in his own campus newspaper or literary magazine and has been surprised or shocked or delighted or just amused by their appearance. Whatever his reaction to Zinsser's article, the quotations, and his own observations, he feels stimulated to say something on his own. His emotions are aroused, and he knows exactly what he wants to say. Therefore, he pulls out a sheet of paper and sits down to write a letter to the editor; a letter that is, in reality, a short essay.

Here, one notes the difference between Mac and the professional writer. The professional picks up where Mac leaves off. As one who makes his living by selling what he writes, the professional makes sure that he knows almost everything to be learned about his reader-audience. Mac, perhaps, has a general idea about the people who might read his letter if he is writing it for his college newspaper. He knows the Teds and Bills, and Sharons and Sandras who might applaud, or condemn, or sneer at what he has to say. And he may have a fair idea of what certain faculty members might think from remarks made in class or overheard by him in the halls. What's more, since this newspaper is addressed to a college audience, Mac will have a pretty fair idea of what that audience is like.

But for the professional even this knowledge is not enough. If he intends to publish an article he makes an intense study of the publication he may be writing for in order to learn all he can about its readers who will be his audience. He examines the typical articles of the magazine, its fiction and special features, its letters to the editor, its cartoons, photographs, illustrations; even its advertisements. The editors may have announced unabashedly their editorial policy, but whether they have done so or not, that policy can be discovered in the kind of material they publish—all of which reveals the tastes and age of their subscribers. Whether it be *The New Yorker* or *Seventeen,* *The Saturday Review* or *Ramparts, The Washington Post* or *The Chicago Tribune,* each publication knows pretty well what group it is appealing to and what its readers expect to find in its pages. The professional, therefore, directs his message in the form and in the language that he feels will appeal to those readers.

You can be sure that William Zinsser realized he was writing for the readers of *Life,* just as Anthony Burgess aimed at those who read—or page through—*Vogue* when he wrote his frank essay "The Private Dialect of Husbands and Wives." The other two authors represented in this section found their immediate audience in the often surprising *Christian Century.* As psychologists and sociologists point out, every body of readers usually shares a common background of values and experience, giving them a strong sense of "belonging." They may be united on the basis of age or sex, ethnic origin, social status, occupation, religion, or politics. Effective writers, such as those included in this text, consequently frame their message in the language, tone, and form most likely to gain a favorable response from the special body of readers whom they are addressing.

As student writers, you properly assume your reader-audience will generally consist of your instructor and your classmates. Because you are one of the group, you may make the mistake of assuming you already know enough about their backgrounds, tastes, beliefs, and prejudices. (By the way, is every statement you do not agree with a "prejudiced" one?) But unless you have observed how your instructor and the rest of your immediate reader-audience react to what is read and discussed in class, you may not really know them at all and, therefore, as a result, blunder into arousing hostility when such was not your purpose. If you are challenging views expressed in your class—especially those of the instructor—you should know enough about them to make a tactful approach so as to gain a favorable hearing.

And if, like Mac, you want to communicate with a wider audience and persuade them to agree with your opinions on a controversial matter such as the propriety of the use of four-letter words in campus publications, you will need to know more about your possible readers. Here are some preliminary questions you may want to ask yourself regarding your reader-audience:

1. Who are they and what are they like?

2. What exactly do I want of them?

3. How friendly or hostile are they likely to be?

4. How much do they know about my topic?

5. How can I get their good will, or at least their tolerance?

6. What "feedback" (information from similar persuasive attempts by others) is available?

Inquiries such as these will also make more clear your own *motives* and *message* in writing anything intended for publication. (If your instructor selects your essay to be read in class, that is one form of "being published.")

Once you have thus sized up your readers and reappraised yourself, you may find yourself either in agreement with, or in opposition to the majority. At this stage, as an "author" of integrity, you need to consider once more the merits and importance of your views. But, as we shall see later, no matter how unpopular those views may be, the writer who has mastered rhetorical techniques and strategies can make a considerable impression upon even hostile readers. You may not, for example, have liked what John Ciardi said in his pretended role as a college president addressing his new students, but his rhetorical skill probably won your grudging respect if not your full approval. As an editor of the *Saturday Review*, John Ciardi knew that his regular readers would very likely applaud his criticism of institutions of higher education.

In brief, then, follow this advice: (1) know yourself; (2) know your subject; and (3) know your reader-audience. In the four essays that follow, look for the writer's awareness of his audience, and then try to emulate those writers in your own work.

Ladies: Why Not Creative Cussing?
Bad Language by Women
by WILLIAM ZINSSER

It was just a simple accident—the pretty girl sitting next to me at dinner spilled something on her dress—and I wouldn't have noticed it at all except for her unusual reaction.

"D--- it!" she yelled.

"Mercy me!" I said. "What's the matter?"

"How the h--- do they expect us to eat this cr-p?"

"Land sakes, who are you talking about?" I asked.

"Those sons of b-----s out in the kitchen," she snapped.

"Gracious, a thing like that could happen to any of us," I told her, and that seemed to calm her down. Still, the incident left me shaken and I didn't know what to make of it. Then I saw a headline in the New York *Times:*

Introduction
Opening with a dramatic scene experienced by the author and illustrating the topic: "Bad Language by Women."

A newspaper article showing the timeliness of the topic and the author's reactions.

WOMEN INFRINGING ON
ANOTHER MEN'S PREROGATIVE:
THE FREEDOM TO CURSE

"Tarnation!" I said to myself (for the headline really made me mad). "Will they never stop this blasted infringing!"

The article said that "the use of obscene language among women, from coeds of the New Left to proper matrons at swank Manhattan cocktail parties, has risen sharply. Police have been amazed by the obscenity issuing from the lips of apparently demure girls at political demonstrations."

Body

Behavior of "the beautiful people" as a possible cause of this lamentable usage.

But why would an apparently demure girl want to do a thing like that? One theory suggested that the inhibitions came down when "the beautiful people and female movie stars started doing it." The theory is all right as far as it goes (which isn't very far), but it has one major flaw. For when the beautiful people started using foul language, didn't they become less beautiful people, or even somewhat ugly people? That's the trouble with having the beautiful people around as a new American class. Just when they're so beautiful it almost makes you want to cry, they turn around and do something gross, and then all our values go p--f.

Sense of power derived from such language another possible cause.

So if it isn't a question of beauty, what is it a question of? Raw power, says a psychologist who taught at Columbia last spring and found that Barnard girls were much more likely than Columbia men to "curse a cop" during the campus riots. "They were aware that cursing was a weapon, one of the few they had," and they used it for two revolutionary ends—to exploit class differences and thereby enrage the police, whose own women don't curse in public, and to establish equality with Columbia men.

What if cursing is the ultimate weapon of feminism?

Thus feminism finds its ultimate tool—the four-letter word—and drives for total victory. And who shall hurl it back, this Anglo-Saxon tide? I don't mind women having the vote, or holding male jobs, or going to men's colleges, or any of that stuff. But how can the toughest cop withstand the obscenity of an apparently demure girl? Let him spray her with Mace; she will spray him back with expletives and he will crumple. So much for law and order.

And how can a husband come home at night to a family where he is not only outvoted but outsworn? This was one of his few areas of domestic competence—a rude skill, but at least his very own, the vestigial reward of his army years when he fought for his country, that immemorial proof of manhood, while the little woman stayed home and made apple pie. Now the little woman stays home to read dirty novels and practice her vocabulary, and a husband who opens the door to announce that he had a heck of a hard day, or that he got a darn good raise, will find himself blown back out on the sidewalk, a victim of the new equality. So much for the American home.

Sad results if the American male finds himself outsworn.

Well, swear away, girls, if that will make you feel manly. But at least break some new ground. Surely it's no victory just to use the same few tired words in which men have tried so long to wrap their virility or to bury their frustrations. Invent! Be creative! Bring feminine grace and feminist intellect to profanity's arid shores.

Conclusion
Thesis: "Invent! Be creative! Bring feminine grace . . . to profanity's arid shores."

If a cop gets too nosy, call him scrutator. If you see him stealing an apple, tell him he's full of usufruct. Accuse him of manumission at least once a day. Taunt your husband for being intestate. Complain that he drinks too much to labialize. Say you caught his pullulating in the garden animadverting on your best friend. Coeds, demand formication in the zoology lab and rectorial rights on Sunday. Shout the new words with gusto at riots and rallies: sphagnum, flocculate, surd, ropery, ort, fuscous, lingulate, faciend, nard. They're all there in Webster's, ladies—hundreds of them. If you really want a weapon, *that's* how to knock the futtock out from under the ship of state.

Humorous suggestion of some new and effective words to be found in Webster's and recommended as substitutes for male cursewords.

OUTLINE

Thesis: Girls—"Be creative! Bring feminine grace and feminist intellect to profanity's arid shores."

I. The author pretends to be dismayed at discovering that well-bred women use "bad language" once heard only from men.
   A. He is startled to hear a pretty girl use profanity.
   B. He pretends he does not use such language himself.
   C. He expresses mock concern over a *Times* news story, reporting that women are taking over "men's prerogative."
II. He plays at being serious in presenting the causes for this shocking change.
   A. He cites the behavior of "the beautiful people" as a cause.
      1. He ridicules them.
      2. He is in mock despair over them.
   B. He cites the feministic desire for "raw power" as another cause.
      1. Barnard girls said to have used cursing as weapon in the Columbia demonstrations.
      2. They attacked mace-squirting police with it.
III. He humorously deplores the effects of this kind of feminism upon the American male.
   A. They have lost their masculine prerogative.
   B. They are browbeaten at home by cursing wives.
IV. He mockingly recommends a new list of words that sound obscene but are not.

COMMENTARY: THE HUMOROUS STANCE

Usually people who object to the way other people behave will complain, scold, or protest. They are in such a hurry to unburden themselves that they are likely to blurt out almost anything. That is how bitter quarrels and fights begin, and how one finds himself more involved than he ever wanted to be. An unskilled speaker or writer may make the same blunder in giving vent to his unhappiness over some situation. But the professional will not, because he has learned that there is a cause and effect relationship between himself and his audience: he knows that what he says will definitely arouse emotions, because nobody likes to be criticized. But the skilled writer who wants to chide his readers also wants to avoid a barrage of verbal brickbats and wants to win over those he criticizes by persuading them to like him and to agree with him.

William Zinsser shows us how it can be done by means of the humorous stance. Like Mark Twain, Art Buchwald, and other humorists who have coaxed laughter out of victims still smarting from the wounds dealt them, Mr. Zinsser has adopted the stance of gentle ridicule. With it he attacks the growing practice of women in polite society to resort to the coarse language formerly used only by males in their off moments. (By *stance,* you will recall, we mean the attitude and approach a writer chooses as the one most likely to win him a favorable reception from his readers.) Mr. Zinsser does his best to make his victims chuckle even though they may resent what they are reading. If you have ever succeeded in making an angry person laugh, you may have used the same techniques he has used in this essay.

How does his stance as humorist-critic work? First of all, note the role he immediately assumes as the first-person author, "I," in the opening incident with "the pretty girl":

> "D . . . it!" she yelled.
> "Mercy me!" I said. "What's the matter?"

As his "Mercy me!" shows, the author is pretending to be a man who would never use vulgar language in the presence of ladies. In fact, as shown by his mild "Tarnation!" on reading the newspaper article, he is not given to the use of four-letter words even when alone.

In this same, apparently naive, manner, he goes on trying to restate theories on why "demure" girls have come to adopt coarse obscenities. He becomes comically sentimental in lamenting the crudity of those once considered "the beautiful people," but in complaining how as a result "all our values go p . . f," the author reveals his conscious irony. Likewise, when he recognizes women's cursing as their "ultimate" weapon in the battle for equality, he is only pretending that he no longer objects to this usage.

His final plea to women not to rob men of their virility by taking over the usual male obscene expressions is also in character with his role as the timid male. His list of suggested substitute words, startling as they may first appear, again ends up revealing the ironic humor of the author who is playing at being the gentle, slightly ridiculous protester.

Obviously Mr. Zinsser found his humorous stance enjoyable. Do you find it persuasive as well as amusing?

WHAT DOES IT SAY?

1. How can "the freedom to curse" be considered "a prerogative" of men? What is a "prerogative"?

2. Whose names would you include in a list of "the beautiful people" of our time?

3. What is the four-letter word in this expression: ". . . and then all our values go p . . . f"? It is no obscene word, and so why is it not spelled out? And what about the closing expression: "to knock the futtock out from under the ship of state"?

4. Briefly describe three scenes or images you associate with the word *feminism* as found in the context of this essay.

5. How accurate do you think Zinsser's picture of "the American home" is in this description: "This [cursing] was one of his few areas of domestic competence—a rude skill, but at least his very own, the vestigial reward of his army years when he fought for his country, that immemorial proof of manhood, while the little woman stayed home and made apple pie"?

6. What do the words *scrutator, usufruct,* and *manumission* really mean? Why, despite their sound, are they really polite terms as applied to the policeman mentioned in the closing paragraph?

7. What actually would a husband have been doing if his wife accused him of "being intestate," unable to "labialize," and was caught "pullulating in the garden animadverting on your best friend"?

8. How appropriate and "correct" are the "new words" Zinsser recommends for use by coeds?

WHAT DO YOU THINK?

1. Choose and limit one of these topics so as to make your essay specific and interesting in details and examples. If your instructor approves, you might try to adopt a humorous stance.

   How a certain group on campus act and talk

   How women in television commercials act and talk

   The politer vocabulary of military life

   Children's use of "bad" language

   The kind of language I hear daily

   Our campus and four-letter words

2. What inferences or conclusions do you draw from the following quotation? Write a short essay pointing out your agreement or disagreement with its thesis.

Irreverent obscenity and outrageous vulgarity are ancient and splendid weapons for social protest. Aristophanes had people flinging clods of manure around the stage, and there is much to ponder in the yippie with the four-letter word painted on his forehead who said, 'After the napalming of children, nothing is obscene.' Yippies, in truth, brim with moral outrage and are capable of greater indignation than the most choleric congressman.[1]

3. What are your views on any or all of the following statements that appeared in a Chicago *Sun Times* news story by William Braden? Consider you *stance* and write an essay developing your views.

Writing that used to be seen only on washroom walls has now become commonplace in college newspapers across the nation.

At the University of Wisconsin, the regents objected when the *Daily Cardinal* printed a syndicated story supplied by the College Press Service. The story was sprinkled with obscenities. *Michigan State News* reprinted the classical obscenities contained in the *Cardinal* editorial— and the paper's adviser threatened to cut editorial salaries. The student-faculty judiciary will conduct a hearing.

The four-letter syndrome appears to have infected college journalism in all regions of the country. Except for the four Midwestern cases, however, most college papers at the moment seem to have no serious problem with official censorship.

The University of Chicago's paper, the *Chicago Maroon,* has earned something of a national reputation for the scatological content of its classified advertising. . . . The ads include dirty jingles, lewd comments on the passing scene, lascivious personal messages and other amusements.

One college journalist who has absolutely no use for obscenities is Michael Walters, associate editor of the *Depaulia* at Depaul University, a Chicago Catholic school.

"We won't use a dirty word even if it is relevant, whatever that means. Any idiot can get up and swear, after all. What brain power does that take? I always thought a college was a place where literacy stands for something. So why not be literate?

"Some of these college papers. I wish their editors were a little less worried about substance and more about form. I mean, it would be nice if they knew how to spell and use punctuation . . . Dirt and filth aren't journalism. They're just dirt and filth. . . ."

"I'm afraid we may lose some of our important four-letter words," said Dr. Kostrubala, assistant professor of psychiatry at the Northwestern University Medical School.

According to one school of thought, excessively early toilet train-

[1] Shana Alexander, "The Loony Humor of the Yippies," *Life,* October 25, 1968.

ing produces resentment that may be expressed years later in the form of filthy language—dirty words being used as "aggressive ammunition" with which to bombard offending parents.[2]

4. Write a brief essay explaining and illustrating your agreement or disagreement with the view expressed in the following quotation.

> It [obscenity] is a substitute for real communication, a form of cliché, the effect of which is banality. The person who throws out a succession of four-letter words doesn't have to think. If everything he says is an obscenity, then his language becomes flat. Speaking in terms of style, not social action, the great defect of obscenity lies in its monotony.[3]

---

[2] William Braden, *Chicago Sun Times,* as quoted in *The Oregonian,* December 8, 1968.
[3] Ralph H. Singleton, *Style* (San Francisco: 1966), p. 29.

The Rhetoric of Conscience
by DONALD L. BERRY

Appeals to conscience are frequently heard these days as conflicting courses of action are confronted on the college campus and in the national arena. Conscience is described as that guide for action which overrides all other obligations and all other concerns. On grounds of conscience people have acted unexpectedly and beyond the limits of ordinary procedure in regard to such issues as the war in Vietnam, racial justice, the national election campaign. In each case—request for conscientious objector classification, participation in demonstrations and sit-ins, support of a particular candidate rather than a political party—the transcendent authority of conscience is invoked in terms similar to Martin Luther's famous refusal to recant at the Diet of Worms, saying: "Here I stand; I can do no other." Yet there are those who volunteer for military service in the Vietnam war, who refuse to abandon party affiliation despite the likelihood of an unsatisfactory candidate, who though fully opposed to every form of racial discrimination join in neither demonstration nor sit-in—and who likewise invoke the transcendent authority of conscience to justify their positions and actions.

The old adage "Let your conscience be your guide" appears in modern translation as "Do your own thing." Many people assume that citing some variation of the appeal to conscience settles the matter and closes off all possibility of and need for discussion. But what sounds like a defense of personal liberty can easily become a camouflage for tyrannical denial of such liberty, be it tyranny of religious idolatry or of political domination.

For the Christian—indeed, for anyone whose style of living is informed by biblical faith—the appeal to conscience is not enough. The devil himself could say, "I must do my own thing." The voice of conscience is never unambiguously the voice of God. It is incumbent on us all to reflect on how Christian faith illumines the problem of conscience. We need to be as clear as we possibly can about the degree to which the Christian may appropriately appeal to conscience as the authority for his decisions and actions. Indeed, one of the functions of the church today may be to provide the setting in which such reflection can take place, and one of its less popular tasks may very well be to insist on such reflection.

I

Surely the foundation for this reflection is recognition that freedom of choice can be neither completely surrendered by any individual nor completely taken from him by any other person or by any group. The language of conscience is personal language; it is a way of talking about the self as a concrete, inviolable center of willing and acting —a way of talking about the self in its capacity to commit and entrust. Our very language about conscience-decisions is evidence of their unassailable personal dimension. We speak of the pain, the anguish, the loneliness, the risk, the alienation of such moments of deciding and committing. Sometimes the rhetoric of conscience is extravagantly personal; witness the words of the late Martin Luther King, Jr., about the strategy of violence, to the effect that even if the whole world took up the way of violence he could never walk that way himself.

But no matter how personal a conscience-decision is to a person, the decision is never private—because the person is never totally solitary. The self comes into being only in dialogue, in encounter, in mutuality, in meeting, in community with others. Everything would seem to turn, then on the nature of the self's dialogue with others, on the way the individual is related to the community. Biblical faith makes our involvement with others essential and inescapable. But it sees as demonic an involvement with any community—a social club, a political party, a student organization, even the church—that entails the surrender of the conscience, the obliteration of personal responsibility, the total and ultimate commitment which the man of faith can give only to God. It is not surprising that many people are willing, sometimes even eager, to hand their consciences over, as it were, to a community, for to do so seems to lighten the burden of risk and anguish that always accompanies personal decision. But when any community functions in such a manner it becomes what Kierkegaard called "the crowd." The individual is submerged, and the crowd is "untruth" because it denies the truth about personal existence.

II

Each man has to "do his own thing," for no one can do another's believing, trusting, loving, or dying. But how do we decide what our "own thing" is? Or, in more traditional language, how is conscience able to be our guide? Our conscience is not a part of our self in the sense that a brain, an arm, or a vital organ is. Conscience is simply a way of viewing the totality of the self in its moment of committing and trusting. As such it does not function in any way that is divorced from the kind of person we are. Our conscience is informed at every moment by our personal history, our scheme of values, our personal hierarchy of preferences and concerns. Conscience is the voice of this intricate fabric of trusts and loyalties, not some private inner voice discontinuous with the rest of our life; when conscience guides us, we are guiding ourselves from the depths of our being, in the context of the constellation of decisions and loves that have made us what we are.

For this reason the man of biblical faith insists that the only way he can permit his conscience to be his guide is first to allow his conscience to become captive to God. That captivity liberates him to do what he thinks must be done, to struggle for whatever justice is possible in the human situation. He no longer needs to make a particular form of justice his god for the moment; he knows that God will forgive his sin, and trusts that God will be able to use whatever he can contribute toward that community of brothers who are free to do what love requires of them—a community of brothers who know themselves loved by God in spite of their unlovability. "My conscience is captive to the Word of God"; therefore, said Martin Luther, "Here I stand; I can do no other." *That* the devil could never say.

There are no guarantees for the man of faith that it is really God who rules in his life. After all, he walks by trust, not knowledge. But there are some marks, some clues to which the man of faith appeals in his concern that it be God and not the devil, not some relative good absolutized as God, that is controlling him, ruling his life, informing his conscience. They are not proofs, but guidelines. Though not infallible, they can be useful. *If my act is directed by a conscience captive to God:*

(1) It cannot involve an ultimate-final-unquestionable-unambiguous commitment to any finite good, no matter how great.

(2) It cannot insulate me from the possibility of suffering, nor give me special privilege over others.

(3) It will contribute to the building of a community of justice and openness.

(4) It cannot require the easy sacrifice of the human rights of any person—friend or foe, supporter or rebel.

(5) It cannot isolate me irrevocably from the world of others, with whose destiny I am bound up.

(6) It will make me available and responsive to all others who encounter me. I will regard them as persons sent to me, not as persons whom I have selected in order to secure my own well-being. The self that is captive to God does not need to search for security or status, to wall himself off from possible encounters. Accepting himself as a child of God, he finds he has the only status that matters.

COMMENTARY: THE MORAL STANCE

No one reading this essay can doubt the earnest sincerity of its author in attempting to lay down some guidelines for the development of a right conscience. Dr. Berry feels, thinks, and writes within the spirit of the Judaic-Christian ethical code of our common social inheritance. He assumes the role of a moral guide speaking to us very rationally, as we would expect a distinguished professor of philosophy and religion to address us. His tone and attitude thus create for him a stance as moralist that most readers sharing his traditions and backgrounds can respond to favorably. And it is this group that he is counseling.

But Dr. Berry is also a skilled rhetorician, a writer who knows how to reach his readers. Consider the first three paragraphs that make up his *introduction.* The opening paragraph immediately relates the topic of conscience to "conflicting courses of action" faced by all on "the college campus and in the national arena." He then quickly lists specific instances of such conflicts demanding painful choices.

In the second paragraph, he continues to speak the readers' language by daring to define a centuries-old definition of *conscience* in modern slang terms: "Do your own thing." He follows this with a brief warning that he will later enlarge upon. And in the third paragraph, he defines the basic concepts and attitudes on which he will finally build his six-point guideline.

Notice, however, that the words "God" and "Christian" do not appear in the opening two paragraphs. He avoids coming on strong with religious terms until he feels he has won the respect of his reader as being something of a realist, or even a social scientist. But when at last "God" and "Christianity" do enter in, even the most nonsectarian reader probably is prepared for them.

His subsequent warnings against surrendering one's conscience and one's private sense of right and wrong to "the crowd" are again both timely and reasonable. They touch home with their explanation of the personal loneliness and the risks everyone who wants to keep his conscience alive must face in making important decisions. Bringing in current psychological terms such as "alienation" helps bridge the gap a reader may encounter in trying to identify "doing your own thing" with God, the devil, Martin Luther, and Martin Luther King, Jr.

Finally, Dr. Berry comes to his six-point guideline and fits it into a kind of everyday reality framework of checkpoints, whereby anyone who shares his common beliefs can, he thinks, see whether "my act is directed by a conscience captive to God." How successful this author has been in persuading his readers to see the logic and good sense of his views will have to be decided, of course, by each reader. But whatever the verdict, it will surely be given with sincerity equal to Dr. Berry's, and we can be sure that he would ask for nothing better.

WHAT DOES IT SAY?

1. In a reference book look up "The Diet of Worms" and then explain the historic significance of Martin Luther's famous refusal to recant: "Here I stand; I can do no other."

2. Would you agree that "Do your own thing" is a "modern translation" of "Let your conscience be your guide"?

3. Who is "the devil" and would he say, "I must do my own thing"?

4. What to you does the term "freedom of choice" mean in the context of this essay?

5. How do you interpret the meaning of the word *rhetoric* in Dr. Berry's statement: "Sometimes the rhetoric of conscience is extravagantly personal; witness the words of the late Martin Luther King, Jr., about the strategy of violence, to the effect that even if the whole world took up the way of violence he would never walk that way himself"?

6. What does Dr. Berry mean when he says, "The self comes into being only in dialogue, in encounter, in mutuality, in meeting, in community with others"?

7. Who is Kierkegaard and how is his concept of "the crowd" interpreted in this essay?

8. How can one tell whether or not he is "a man of biblical faith"?

WHAT DO YOU THINK?

1. Write an essay wherein you restate in your own words and give examples for what you understand Dr. Berry is saying in each of the six points of his guideline for conscience.

2. From one of the following statements select either the *one* that you approve of most or disagree with most. Using examples and specific reasons, explain why you hold the views you do on this particular subject.

   (a) God gives everybody a conscience.
   (b) A person has to learn to forgive himself.
   (c) Conscience is wholly conditioned by public or family mores.
   (d) Everyone has to decide for himself what is right or wrong.
   (e) Whatever does not hurt you or anyone else is morally right to do.
   (f) There is no such thing as the devil.
   (g) The Bible is so full of myths that it is not a reliable guide for one's conscience.
   (h) Conscience is the still voice of God.
   (I) "Conscience doth make cowards of us all."

3. Decide upon your own "moral stance" and write on some one aspect of any of the following topics:

Sin and guilt

The conscientious athlete

A fair day's work

Shoplifting

The honor system

The conscientious objector

Conscience and racial in-
justice

God and space exploration

Happiness and forgiveness

The chiseler

The hypocrite

Drugs and conscience

How to train a conscience

Home training and conscience

The Private Dialect of Husbands and Wives
by ANTHONY BURGESS

I remember an old film about Alcatraz or Sing Sing or somewhere, in which Wallace Beery, having organized the killing of several wardens, broken up the prison hospital, and kicked the deputy governor in the guts, said in his defense: "I was only kiddin'." I've never gone so far, but I fear that my own kind of kidding may be the death of me. Like giving a college lecture on a purely fictitious Elizabethan dramatist called Grasmere Tadworth (1578–1621). Like writing a pseudonymous review of one of my own books. Like, when asked by the editors of *Who's Who* to give the names of my clubs, answering with Toby's Gym, the Nudorama Strip Club, the Naked City and so on. This is not really funny. When the same editors asked me for hobbies, I gave *wife* as one of them, and they let that go through. There it is now, perpetuated from edition to edition, waiting for *Who Was Who,* and sooner or later I was bound to be asked what the hell I meant, mean.

It's tempting to retreat into that high-school thicket of evasiveness, the dictionary. Thus, my wife is a small species of falcon, *falco subbuteo*. My wife is a horse of middle size, a pacing horse, a stick or figure of a horse on which boys ride. My wife is (Old French *hobin*) a stupid fellow. All right, all right, stop fooling about; try the defini-

Reprinted from *Vogue,* June 1968 by permission of Anthony Burgess, c/o Marvin Josephson Associates, Inc. Copyright © 1968 by The Conde Nast Publications, Inc.

tion "favourite pursuit" and don't, for God's sake, say: "Ha, ha, I stopped pursuing her a long time ago."

I recognize a number of horrible possibilities, most of them appropriate to the evenings and weekends after the honeymoon, but those are not really applicable. The other possibilities are sentimental, so I reject those too. Popular songs used to approach the woman-in-one's-life as something of either gold or silver—nubile nymph or fulfilled mother—but they never hymned her in middle age. In middle age she has none of the properties of a cult. Not being an icon, she is not a thing. She resists being used and she resists being worshipped; she is at her most human.

My wife and I have now been married over twenty-six years, and I recognize that by the standards of our milieu—an artistic one—we have not played quite fair. We should have changed partners at least once before now, and there was a time, just after World War Two, when we tried. That was a period of almost mandatory disruption, and there was no shortage of new marital opportunities. But things went wrong; she and I found it more interesting to discuss what we proposed doing than actually to do it. The prospect of learning somebody else's language, of building up new mythologies from scratch, seemed shamefully wasteful. So we just carried on as we were, carry on as we are.

The lure of a fresh young body seems to me quite irrelevant to questions of marriage; the desire to regenerate one's glands is only a valid excuse for divorce in communities where adultery is a civil crime. A marriage is really a civilization in miniature, and one breaks up a civilization at the peril of one's soul. The vital element in any civilized community is language, and without language there can be no marriage. By language I mean something more subtle, and much less useful, than the signals of commerce and the directives of the law: I mean sounds, noises, grunts, idioms, jokes, bits of silliness, inconsequential stupidities which affirm that a special *closed* community exists. They are a sort of shorthand way of summing up a whole complex of feelings; time (history, if you like) has given them a meaning; they totally resist translation.

They can be explained, but then their significance disappears. Explain a joke, and there is no laughter. Explain a poem, and the poem dissolves into nonsense. If, at a party, I am asked to play the piano, and if I play the piano for too long, my wife has only to call "Mary!" for me to stop playing. The reference is to the scene in *Pride and Prejudice* where Mr. Bennet says, to his piano-playing daughter, "Mary, you have delighted us long enough." This is a fairly public example of marital shorthand; the private ones tend to wither in the air of disclosure.

"Blue, honey?" doesn't mean what it says. It's a common memory from some old trashy woman's magazine story, invoked in mockery during a needless posture of depression. A reversion to dialect (the Lancashire *aye*, for instance, instead of the Southern English *yes*) denotes an instinctive testing of a metropolitan pretension (our own or someone else's) against the earthier standards of my, or her, regional background.

I needn't labour this point about the marital language, or about the marital mythology which contains characters from literature or films, real relatives, the fat Birmingham woman who said "I down't eat enough to keep a baird aloive," the man who comes into the pub belching, dead cats, living dogs, the Holy Ghost. Every married man or woman knows what I mean, but may not be willing to see the importance of it. It can only be built up over a long tract of time, and after a quarter of a century it can become rich, subtle and allusive as Shakespeare's English, though less long-winded. But, unlike literature, it is relaxed, and it promotes relaxation. It can even encompass long silences broken by noises, rude gestures, lines of filthy doggerel, rows of isolated vowel-sounds, bursts of *bel canto*, exaggerated tooth-picking.

I seem to derive as much spare-time fulfillment from this sort of unproductive communion as other men get from boats, golf, stamp collecting, and drilling holes in the kitchen wall. Working at home as I do, I'm prepared to waste a whole morning on it; it's a two-way communicative process, which is more than can be said for hammering at a typewriter. It can be helped along with games of Scrabble, gin, doing the crossword in the morning paper, kicking the dog's flank with one's bare foot, seeing how long one can hold one's breath. It ends with guilt and astonishment when the Angelus is tolled at midday from the nearby church; the shopping has not been done, lunch is unprepared (but does one deserve lunch?), not one word has been fired at the sheet in the typewriter. A hobby shouldn't get in the way of one's work.

Am I using this term *hobby* correctly? It probably denotes a sub-creative process, like constructing model cathedrals out of matches, and it goes more easily with plurals than with singulars. *Wives,* as with some notable serial polygamist, fits better than *wife,* and it connotes collection as well as sub-creation (very sub: a brief marriage is hardly worth the making). There's also a strong whiff of the impersonal, or depersonalized, about it. I see now that, hobbled by *hobby,* I've presented my wife as a very intricately programmed phatic communicatrix (or whatever the sociological jargon is). Let me straighten out my own usage.

We talk about our hobbies because we're shy of mentioning the word *vocation*—unless we earn money from a vocation, when it promptly turns into a profession. And yet a lot of hobbies are true vocations—the fugues composed by the nightclub pianist, the paintings of a customs officer called Rousseau, the house that the bank clerk builds on summer evenings. In this term *vocation,* creation and religion combine. If one has a vocation for writing lyric poetry when the shop is shut for the day, one may also have a vocation for the priesthood. I think I have a vocation for gaining the maximal social fulfillment, which means communicative fulfillment, which means even a kind of spiritual fulfillment, out of living with a particular woman. But, frightened of the big words, and also incurably facetious, I have to talk of my wife as a hobby—the culminating item in a list that contains piano-playing, musical composition, and language-learning. Yet the term *hobby* is not really inept, since it implies enjoyment and not just, like *vocation,* a sort of pretension to uplift. One of Kingsley Amis's characters talks about going to bed with his wife as being ennobling but also good fun—as though some stunning work of literature were also a good read. That will do pretty well for most levels of marital intercourse.

My *Who's Who* avowal has been taken by some people as a misprint. Once I had to give an after-dinner speech, and the chairman, introducing me, said that *wife* was undoubtedly meant to be *wine.* The right facetious response is to say that a wife transubstantiates life into wine. The right highbrow response would take in the new communication philosophers—Marshall McLuhan in America and Roland Barthes in France—and point out that the basis of living is semiological, which means concerned with all possible modes of human signalling—from vulgar lip-noises to sublime poetry. In a marriage, you have an opportunity to erect the most subtle and exact semiological system civilization is capable of. It takes a long time, but it's worth it. So, apart from what else she is, my wife continues to be my non-professional vocation. Or, not to leave the fun out, my hobby. I hope to God I continue to be hers.

COMMENTARY: THE "CONFESSION" STANCE

Anthony Burgess, the famous English novelist, is making what can perhaps best be described as a confession, the revealing of secret, intimate aspects of one's life. Like all such revelations this one rings with the kind of delightful candor and honesty to be found in a person who has discovered drama as well as pleasure and rewarding work in his daily life. He feels secure enough in self identity to grant us a glimpse of the things that give him this euphoric sense of well-being. You may even wonder whether this essay is not something of a boast rather than a laying bare of the soul. Yet the prayerful note with which the essay closes does add to the confessional tone of the whole.

From the beginning we become aware that the author is *speaking* to us. See how he opens: "I remember an old film about Alcatraz or Sing Sing or somewhere. . . ." The first person "I" is taking us immediately and directly into his confidence, and he is very much at ease with us. Even his syntax in the opening paragraph suggests this lack of formality and restraint; he gives us four examples of his own "kidding," each a prepositional phrase starting with *like* but capitalized and punctuated as though each were a sentence. He does not even allow his central idea or *thesis* statement to frighten him into becoming more formal: ". . . and sooner or later I was bound to be asked what the hell I meant, mean." We know then, of course, that the rest of his essay will tell us just what he does mean by calling his wife "my hobby."

Like all writers, Anthony Burgess delights in toying with words. He runs through dictionary derivations of the word *hobby* and puns on the synonym "favourite pursuit." As if realizing he has gone too far and almost lost himself in his gameplaying with words, he comes down to what can be called a direct confrontation with his image of who and what his wife really is in their relationship.

Now begins the frank telling of what makes the union of a man and a woman truly a *marriage,* as he knows it after his twenty-six years experience with it. Without any false shame or shyness he admits there was once some discussion of a divorce between them; yet he can not refrain from tossing in here an ironic statement: ". . . I recognize that by the standards of our milieu—an artistic one—we have not played quite fair." And now comes, too, the first allusion to the title of the essay, "The Private Dialect of Husbands and Wives." By *dialect* he means all the forms of language whereby a married couple learn to communicate with one another: a language—like a *dialect*—which only the initiated or "the natives" can understand and which makes a marriage what he properly terms "a special *closed* community."

Once more in his pleasant, intimate tone and manner he confides in us specific examples revealing direct insights into the nature of this "closed community" consisting of only himself and his wife. He gives us several examples and then shows us how this private language and mythology give him pleasurable distraction from his writing chores. Then becoming serious again, he returns to his attempt at a definition of *hobby* and considers his marriage in the light of a *vocation* and a *profession*.

His distinctions between these synonyms are witty and even moving as he works out his final meaning of *hobby* while thus speaking to us. All of these candid admissions lead us to agree with him that the private dialect between him and his wife certainly makes her his "non-professional vocation" or "hobby," and we can infer from this conclusion that any marriage developing such a private language will also be successful.

WHAT DOES IT SAY?

1. What is the difference between a "nubile nymph" and a "fulfilled mother"?

2. What does his statement mean to you: "A marriage is really a civilization in miniature, and one breaks up a civilization at the peril of one's soul"?

3. What is a "closed community" as Burgess uses the term, and is its language really untranslatable?

4. Why is "marital shorthand" an apt synonym for the "dialect" he finds present in good marriages?

5. Can you now distinguish between *hobby, vocation,* and *profession?*

6. What has Kingsley Amis written, and why is the allusion to one of his novels appropriate?

7. If you are not yet familiar with Marshall McLuhan, turn to p. 207 and explain why he thinks "the basis of living is semiological."

8. Can marriage be called "a semiological civilization"?

WHAT DO YOU THINK?

1. Adopt a "confessional stance" of your own, and tell your readers what you are learning about some common concern in life such as one of these:

Having a roommate	Coping with racism
Trying to be a brother (sister)	Keeping a car going
Writing letters home	Understanding neighbors
Being engaged	Using the library
Relating to space exploration	Attending family dinners
Trying to stop smoking	Going steady
Overcoming a hang-up	Dealing with the draft board

2. If you have a kind of "closed community" language, or dialect, which you share with one or two roommates whom you like or with a group of intimate friends whom you pal around with, tell us about it and its importance to you.

3. After studying several issues of *Vogue* Magazine, write an essay describing who and what *Vogue* readers are, and why, therefore, you think the editors chose the Burgess article.

4. A seventh grader, Jeffrey Dryer, wrote a classroom composition that parallels one of the main points that Anthony Burgess has made in his essay. Let your own imagination dream up a world order of your own, and describe it on paper. Read Jeffrey Dryer's article first.

> Every Thanksgiving we go and see all our friends, or stay home and do nothing. Sometimes someone comes up for a couple of hours for dinner or lunch.
> One year we had a fishing spree for trout in our creek. We caught 30 of them and they almost spoiled.
> I wish that Thanksgiving was 10 days long, and everyone all over Oregon came here for a picnic of five days straight.
> Then all the wars stopped for Thanksgiving, and everyone played games and talked and made friends with each other. The scientists and other people traded ideas with each other.
> Kids would hunt and play games with each other, and compare ideas of what they want to be later on. And at night a lot of people would tell stories.
> Everybody spoke the same language so you could understand them.
> Then when Thanksgiving was over, no one could start the war again because everyone loved each other too much to fight him.[1]

5. In your own way, define, by examples and details, one of the following terms as it is related to someone you know very well. In the beginning of your essay make clear what audience it is that you are trying to persuade to accept the meaning that you are giving the term.

Beatle music	Vietnam tour of duty
Soul music	Folk singing
Drag racing	Acid
Pop art	Marijane
Parachuting	Surfing
Bussing	Skiing

[1] Reprinted from *The Oregonian*, November 28, 1968.

Courtesy of United Press International

Sex Is for Play

by FREDERICK KIRSCHENMANN

Whatever is wrong with sex in our culture today, it certainly isn't because we don't get enough information about it. On the one hand we have the prophets of technique who tell us that sex is primarily a matter of pushing the right buttons at the right time. On the other hand we have the prophets of love who tell us that sex expresses a deep relationship and that sex without total immersion in love is illegitimate. Now certainly there is nothing wrong with knowing something about the physical techniques of sex. A bungler, in any field, is a bungler. And surely few would suggest that love in sex is undesirable. But overemphasis on technique and love devalues the whole sexual experience. When we use sex to demonstrate our physical competence or to produce a deep love relationship, we lose some of its natural joy and pleasure. When we make sex something we want to *accomplish,* it's hard to relax and enjoy it.

I

Back in 1937, in his book *The Spirit of the Liturgy,* Romano Guardini made some observations that we can apply to sex. Guardini argues that liturgy is misconceived when we saddle it with a deep or austere purpose. Liturgy, he suggests, is really childlike play:

> The child, when it plays, does not aim at anything. It has no purpose but to exercise its youthful powers, to pour forth its life in an aimless series of movements, words and actions . . . all of which is purposeless, but full of meaning nevertheless. . . . That is what play means; it is life, pouring itself forth without aim.

In other words, liturgy is not meant to curtail freedom by constraining the individual to perform certain chores—praising God, confessing his sins, and so on. Rather, liturgy is an occasion to let oneself go, to become freely involved, to be oneself and to lose oneself, to pour forth one's being. It is in such free participation that one experiences the rich and playful joy that praising God can be.

Sex, like liturgy, should be more like play than work. But we have saddled it with too many serious purposes, thereby transforming what should be exciting play into a solemn chore or a dreary bore. The 19th century preacher and theologian Horace Bushnell made some distinctions between work and play that throw light on what has happened to sex in our culture:

> . . . work is activity *for* an end; play, activity *as* an end. . . when a child goes to his play, it is no painstaking, no means to an end; it is itself rather both end and joy. . . work suffers a feeling of aversion, and play excludes aversion. For the moment any play becomes wearisome or distasteful, then it is work; an activity that is kept up, not as being its own joy, but for some ulterior end, or under some kind of constraint.

We have placed so much emphasis on the "how to" of sex that sex as a joy and an end in itself has become subordinate to sex as an act performed to arouse the greatest possible physical response. We have placed so much emphasis on deep love in sex that sex as a joy and an end in itself has become subordinate to sex as an act performed to produce an intimate relationship. In either case, we have to work at it. The whole sexual adventure has become work for us; we cannot help sensing the "feeling of aversion" that it produces.

Hugh Hefner's playboy philosophy of sex doesn't offer much help: with all its stress on free and playful lovemaking his philosophy of sex, ironically, has no room for real freedom. A playboy must apply the right techniques, must cultivate the art of being a great lover; he is not free just to relax and let sex happen. Sex as an end in itself is subordinated to the task of becoming good at it. So sex is really work, not play. Hefner is afraid to view sex simply as a joyful, purposeless opportunity to "pour forth one's life in an aimless series of words, movements, and actions."

The same thing can be said of sexologist Albert Ellis. Perhaps because we humans have turned all of life into work we need books like Ellis' *The Art and Science of Love*. But simply applying his techniques for lovemaking will hardly make sex a joyful experience. To suggest that the success of lovemaking hinges on knowing and using the right techniques is to reduce sex to a function to be performed, a chore, an "activity that is kept up, not as being its own joy, but for some ulterior end."

The prophets of love—those who would have us use sex as a means to deeper interpersonal relationships—have also reduced sex to work. You can't create a love relationship by the sex act; such relationships come as the by-products of a free and joyful sharing of life. Martin Buber's distinction between the deep, receptive I-Thou relationship and the more superficial I-It relationship is relevant here. The experience of I-Thou—of transcending the ordinary subject-object relationship —comes to us, says Buber, only as a gift; "it is not found by seeking." In the very act of attempting to contrive an I-Thou relation I put myself over against the Thou I wish to enter, and so necessarily into an I-It (subject-object) relation. The only way one can enter the deeper dimension of communion is by being in the place where communion is likely to happen and letting oneself go. Likewise, when one consciously sets out to play—that is, when one works at playing—play is impossible. But he who lets himself go, who pours himself forth, will share in a deeper relationship with others, a relation in which he loses his sense of standing against the other and the rest of life. We go to bed, and the opportunity to participate in a free pouring out of life is there. But when we go to bed for the express purpose of effecting such a relation, it won't happen. The very relationship we want becomes an object to be achieved, and sex turns into work. While those who say that sexual intimacy should be a deep expression of love are right in that sex is the kind of joyful play in which such love is possible, they are wrong in insisting that one must have this purpose before entering the sexual relationship.

II

The view of sex as play certainly does not sanction "free love." Rather, it suggests new ways of looking at the old problem of marital vs. nonmarital sex. If we saddle sex with ulterior purposes, we must look at this problem in terms of whether or not these purposes can be satisfied, or even more readily satisfied, in a nonmarital context. One danger in that approach is the assumption that if a certain purpose is not realized in premarital sex one has only to try again after the marriage license has been signed. Many couples have gone into marriage only to discover that the noble goals they sought to achieve through sex are still out of reach on the other side of the marriage bureau.

In any case, when we view sex as play the relevant question is not whether nonmarital sex can realize predetermined goals, but how the sex act can be an act of play, how we can free sex so that it can become a spontaneous outpouring of life. Promiscuity is not the answer; I think it would be difficult for two people to be that free with each other without mutual trust growing out of a prolonged period of continual contact with each other. Such a free and open letting-go-of-oneself probably requires some sort of responsible living together.

But even under the best conditions we shall never be able to experience sex as play until we stop taking it so seriously. The old Mae West movies had the right attitude toward sex; they demonstrated its precariousness and showed how absurd it is to expect too much from it. By diminishing the reverence and intensity which are so often associated with sex, those movies created the healthy, relaxed atmosphere in which play is possible. As long as we take sex seriously, saddle it with sacred purposes and expect it to produce profound effects, it can never be an aimless pouring forth of life. Our concern with its seriousness and importance will always stand in the way, transforming an essentially playful act into a task. As long as we think of sex as sacramental we shall be preoccupied with doing just the right thing at just the right time under precisely the right conditions, making it impossible to let ourselves go in joy.

Perhaps man is such an anxious animal that he will always take himself too seriously and transform everything into work. But after all, man already has enough tasks to perform which properly fall into the category of work. If he recognizes that he is converting a potentially joyful act into a solemn exertion, maybe he'll be able to stop, relax, and discover that sex is not work, but play.

COMMENTARY: THE PHILOSOPHICAL STANCE

What were your first reactions to the title of this essay, "Sex Is for Play," by Dr. Kirschenmann, a prominent religious leader? Did it please you or shock you? How you feel and think, now that you have read it, you alone can tell. But however you feel, we can learn much about effective persuasion by examining the philosophical stance the author chose in presenting a very controversial topic.

In the second sentence of the opening paragraph we find the first "horn" of the traditional dilemma being jabbed at us: "On the one hand we have the prophets of technique. . . ." Next comes the other "horn" threatening to impale us: "On the other hand we have the prophets of love. . . ." Then the author comes to our rescue by admitting the merits of those two views but at the same time leading us to escape what he considers to be harsh and wrong alternatives. His concluding two sentences in this paragraph clearly tell us the way out. In fact, we are presented with a third alternative, one making him a "prophet" of sex for sheer enjoyment—a view likely to be objected to by readers favoring one of the other two alternatives.

Dr. Kirschenmann knows how to use the kind of rational, philosophical approach that his thesis—considering his readers—requires. He begins the support of his thesis in the *body* of the essay by finding analogies (comparable situations) in the works of two theologians, and he skillfully ties them in with his thesis, which he repeats in slightly different terms.

He turns next to attack Hugh Hefner of *Playboy* fame and Albert Ellis, sex technique author, as representative prophets of the "hard-work" school. To show also the errors of the "love" school of thought, he refers to the teachings of Martin Buber, one of the most original philosophers of our time. In Buber's doctrine he again finds confirmation of his view.

He prudently anticipates possible objections occurring to his readers at this stage of his persuasive argument. Chief among these fears would be that of promiscuity growing out of such a philosophy of sex. But certainly even his admirers must be startled to find old Mae West movies being recommended as embodying the kind of playful spirit the author advocates. And some critics may consider the concluding paragraph to be "begging the question;" that is, assuming his thesis has already been established beyond all question. But, on the whole, we have in this essay an excellent example of how a most daring view can appealingly be offered in contrast to two other widely-accepted philosophies of life and sex.

Throughout the essay we should note also how its language supports the philosophical tone and mood. The author treats a serious subject in direct, yet dignified, terms, as for example in the concluding sentence: "If he recognizes that he is converting a potentially joyful act into a solemn exertion, maybe he'll be able to stop, relax, and discover that sex is not work, but play."

WHAT DOES IT SAY?

1. Why is the author's choice of the term *prophets* in "prophets of technique" and "prophets of love" the right term considering his purpose?

2. How do expressions like "sex is primarily a matter of pushing the right buttons at the right time" and "A bungler, in any field, is a bungler" establish a personal relationship between the author and the reader?

3. What in religion is the meaning of *liturgy*?

4. What are the connotations (the suggested images, associations) of his term "the whole sexual adventure"?

5. Can you restate Martin Buber's "I—Thou" philosophy in your own terms?

6. How does "free love" differ from "sex as play"?

7. What inference would you draw from the teaching that sex must be "sacramental"?

8. Why does the author consider man "an anxious animal"?

WHAT DO YOU THINK?

1. Try to adopt a philosophical stance in discussing your views, observations, and experience in relation to one of the following topics:

Petting

Pre-marital sex

Chastity and self-control

High school "crushes"

Teenage marriages

College-age marriages

Friendship and "love"

2. Study and analyze a current issue of *Playboy* and organize a written report on the "philosophy of sex" that you find characterizes its editorial policy.

3. Write an essay explaining what significance you find for yourself and your future life as an adult in the following brief book review. (You may want to buy the paperback edition of the book and base your comments on it.)

> More than 40 per cent of American college and university educated women now experience premarital sexual intercourse, compared with less than 30 per cent in the 1940s.

From 1940 to 1963, the rate of illegitimate births in the United States tripled, rising from 7.1 per 1000 unmarried females of child-bearing age to 22.5.

These are among the findings reported in *The Sexual Wilderness,* by Vance Packard (McKay, $6.95), a study of "the contemporary upheaval in male-female relationships."

As an epigraph for his book, illustrating his view of the modern trend in sexual practices, Packard borrowed the following quotation from "de Laud" in Marc Connelly's "The Green Pastures": "Everything dat's fastened down is comin' loose. . . ."[1]

4. Do you agree that "play becomes work" when the attention is shifted from the game activities to the end or goal set for such play? Consider some of the "games" you have enjoyed in the past as mere play or sports taken up just for the immediate pleasure you found in them. Then write an essay telling what conclusions you have come to regarding "play" and "work."

5. Realizing that newspaper reports often produce muddled versions of what their interviewees actually said, assume that the following account is correct. What do you think of Pastor Siefkes' three-point program for creating "a better order"?

Not enough young people are "hooked" on love and they have to learn to be if they hope to change "the establishment," a Lutheran minister said here Saturday.

"Young people today—as well as adults—don't know how to make friends. I'm not talking about superficial friendships but those friend-ships that mean a willingness to go all the way with people," said Pastor James Siefkes, western regional director of Stewardship, American Lutheran Church, during an interview at the Hilton Hotel.

"In order to learn what people are like, you have to go out and learn what they smell like. Once you know that you're hooked—then you're starting to love, to feel," said Pastor Siefkes, 39-year-old resident of Palo Alto, California.

The strategy to love and friendship is as follows, Pastor Siefkes said:

1. "Tune in to God."
2. "Wait patiently—get your nerve endings raw, your eyeballs going."
3. "Penetrate—go where the action is, where the people are."

"Penetration is most important. Unless you've penetrated you won't have friends," said Pastor Siefkes. "If you have penetrated and you have developed friendships, then you can advocate—that is, speak for those friends who haven't learned how to speak, whether they be the poor, the blacks, or anybody for whom you wish to speak," he said.

If advocacy comes before understanding and friendship you have

---

[1] *The Sexual Wilderness* reviewed by Rollo Mays, *The New York Times,* October 13, 1968.

paternalism—"and it's not the job of the church, or youth working within the church, to be big daddy to the world."

Pastor Siefkes was guest speaker Saturday night at the ninth annual convention of the North Pacific District Luther League, being attended by 1,500 young people, at the Hilton Hotel.

In a talk entitled "The Impossible Dream," Pastor Siefkes challenged the young to create a better order out of what he said is "a changing system."

The young have to do it because the adults "have too many barnacles on their tails—too much property, too many possessions that tie them down."

As the new system emerges, it must be honest—"pass accurate information within the system"; it must be flexible—"be willing to accept others who aren't like you," and it must be responsible—"accept change, but more importantly initiate change."[2]

---

[2] Reprinted from *The Oregonian*, December 1, 1968, "Pastor Says Few People 'Hooked' on Love." Reprinted with permission of publication.

part IV
THE NATIONAL CONSCIENCE

ARRANGEMENT: HOW ARE YOU GOING TO SAY IT?

Sentences grow out of words, and paragraphs grow out of sentences, or, as the rhetoricians phrase it, "Discourse generates discourse." Here is what the noted linguist Noam Chomsky says about this generative process:

> The normal use of language is innovative, in the sense that much of what we say in the course of normal use of language is entirely new, not a repetition of anything we have heard before, and not even similar in pattern . . . to sentences or discourse that we have heard in the past.[1]

Sadly enough, however, this generative process does not necessarily organize one's ideas in the logical sequence that readers demand. Doing so requires concentrated thought—preconception, in fact.

We have noted in the analyses of the essays in this text some of the principles of arrangement, the patterns of thinking and feeling, that give *order* to all effective essays. So far, however, we have discussed only the general arrangement of an essay in an *introduction, body,* and *conclusion.*

One way to organize one's thoughts is to put them down in some

[1] Noam Chomsky, *Ethics,* October, 1968, p. 6.

89

form of outline. As we have seen in our analyses of the professional essays reprinted in this text, it is always possible to make an outline of a well-organized essay. The outline of the essay by Brian McGuire, "It Wasn't Worth It," revealed a careful organization of his arguments under two main headings. First, he dealt with what he believed to be serious faults that exist in present American university practices; next, he discussed the new policies he felt were needed in reforming the universities, to make them more effective as educational institutions.

We do not know whether or not McGuire began with a detailed outline comparable to ours on page 12, but it is safe to assume that his thoughts did not fall "naturally" into this pattern as he pounded away on his typewriter or scribbled away with his pen. He might possibly have dashed off a first draft, relying on a generative flow of language to carry him along, while channeling his ideas roughly into paragraphs. But somewhere along the way from first draft to finished essay there had to come a time when the process of organization set in, and he arranged his thoughts in some kind of coherent and pleasing design.

Analysis also revealed that the light and humorous essay by William Zinsser, "Ladies: Why Not Creative Cussing?" has just as logical and orderly an arrangement as the serious and formal discussion of birth control by Sir Arthur Bryant. It seems reasonable to conclude that, for professional writers like these, skill in organizing their thoughts comes from considerable practice and from quite deliberate adherence to standards of design and arrangement.

Finding a suitable arrangement for what we have to say remains a problem until we can identify the kind of thinking the essay topic is demanding of us. From the little that experts have learned so far about the creative process called "writing," we know that it involves various kinds of mental activity, including the following:

1. Deduction: the drawing of inferences of the application of general statements to particular situations.
2. Induction: the examination of particulars and individual instances and then drawing from them a generalization or conclusion.
3. Comparison and contrast (analogy): the discovery of similarities and differences between things that resemble one another.
4. Chronological tracing: the revelation of how an action or a process works by examining the procedure, step by step, in a time sequence.
5. Definition (or identification): the discovery of the distinct, recognizable character or nature of something by placing it within certain boundaries and then distinguishing it from everything else within those limits.

6. Classification: the sorting out and placing together like things in distinct categories or classes.
7. Causal analysis: the seeking out of a possible cause in order to understand the effect, or the prediction of an effect from a given cause or number of causes.

All of these forms of thinking involve memory, imagination, and the process of analysis. And, to some extent, we use all of these in deciding upon a design for an essay. We apply them when we ask ourselves such questions as these: Why do I believe what I am trying to persuade others to accept? How do others feel about it? What dangers do I see for myself and for others in a contrary view? What should I take up first, and then what next?

An analysis of Sir Arthur Bryant's essay on birth control shows how he answered such questions to obtain the main divisions for his criticism of the Papal Encyclical. We can observe how he carefully defined and classified the problems raised by that important episcopal message. He considered, realistically, the Roman Catholic and the Protestant views regarding the morality of using contraceptives. He was led, we might say, almost inevitably into the pattern of arrangement that he followed, one of comparison and contrast, which seemed clearly the most natural arrangement for his thinking on the subject.

The so-called "library" paper or "source" paper or "term" paper, as it is variously called, makes a special demand upon the writer in the way of careful preliminary planning. Once the writer has sufficient information in the form of notes that he has gleaned from his extensive reading, he is faced with considering how to arrange those notes in some kind of logical order. As the commentaries of the various essays in this section of the text will indicate, the "natural" order of development might well vary depending upon his subject, his concept of the subject, and his own special approach to it. As this "natural" order begins to emerge in his mind, he can then arrange the parts or divisions according to that order, always keeping in mind, as well, the need for introduction, body, and conclusion.

Although the introduction and the conclusion demand special attention, it is the body which most seriously worries the writer and takes up most of his planning since it must present his facts, evidence, and thinking. In planning the body, he immediately runs into the question as to which kind of order or sequence will be best suited to his topic and his readers. He has several arrangements to choose from, as the commentaries of the following selections will show: arrangement by comparison—contrast, by deduction, by causal analysis, by inductive arrangement, by definition, by chronological order, and by classification.

What each of these means of arrangement is and how you can adapt it to your writing needs, you will find explained and illustrated in the commentaries and the writing suggestions accompanying the articles. Along with all the "new" rhetoricians, we believe that such principles are best discovered and taught through analysis of works containing them.

Courtesy of United Press International

Birth Control: Dilemma of Conscience

by SIR ARTHUR BRYANT

The controversy over the Papal Encyclical on birth control is part of the eternal attempt —as old as time—to reconcile man's faith and ideals with the material circumstances in which his lot on earth is cast. Unless he hitches his wagon to a star he is less than the meanest brute, yet all the while the harsh realities of the human situation force him to pursue terrestrial courses which seem incompatible with his ideals. The Pope, who represents—though not solely—the greatest of all man's ideals, after long and painful cogitation has once more nailed to the mast of the Catholic Church, in the face of bitter and widespread opposition, the standard that affirms, in its most extreme and uncompromising form, the ideal of the universal sanctity of all human life. "Thou shalt do no murder," is the most emphatic and solemn of all the divine commandments that

Introduction
The historic importance of Papal pronouncements and how the Papal Encyclical on birth control forbidding use of contraception fits into Roman Catholic traditions.

Reprinted from *Illustrated London News,* August 17, 1968. Reprinted by permission of A. D. Peters & Company.

concern the purely terrestrial sphere. The interdiction applies, the Catholic Church teaches, not only to pre-natal human life, but even to human life before it is physically conceived.

At this point, so far as a reasoning individual can judge for himself, the Catholic Church goes beyond the actual teaching of Christ as enshrined in the recorded words—inevitably incomplete and, possibly, imperfectly transmitted—of the New Testament. Respect for all human life, even the humblest and least accounted, is a necessary corollary of Christ's philosophy of love to all men. But though, since life begins in the womb, abortion under any ordinary circumstances may seem abhorrent to a Christian, it is difficult to see, on purely rational grounds, why contraception should necessarily be so. As God made man not only the master of his terrestrial destiny but the sole means of initiating the process of human gestation and birth, it seems irrational to deny him and his sexual partner, woman, the right to judge and decide when that means should be employed. Neither Christ nor the Church ever put forward the doctrine that it is man's duty to create life whenever he has the opportunity to do so. And it is not easy in reason to see the moral distinction between one means of not exercising that power and another. So far as reason can pronounce on such a matter, Catholic and non-Catholic devices for refraining from initiating life seem in this respect on a par. So does a decision—against the prompting of nature—to refrain from sexual union.

Body

How the Catholic and Protestant attitudes differ on matters of faith; the author's support of his Protestant tradition despite his appreciation of the role of Papal authority in preserving Christianity.

This, however, is where the Catholic and Protestant attitudes on such matters diverge. In the last resort the Protestant applies to them the test of individual reason; the Catholic Church declares, and has always declared, that individual reason is inadequate to judge rightly and that resort must be had to the inspired and transmitted wisdom of the Church to which, through St. Peter, Christ entrusted the dissemination and interpretation of his teachings. And seeing how imperfect human reason and judgement are, and how many disastrous decisions and acts have flowed from them, there is obviously a great deal to be said for this view. Having, like most Englishmen, been brought up as a Protestant, my instinctive reaction is to apply the test of reason to any issue where faith by itself does not provide an answer. Yet reason also tells me that the discipline and guidance of the Catholic Church has been throughout the ages a tremendous and salutary force for civilizing and making wise and gentle the life of the world. Without it and its transmission of the Christian truths, Christianity itself might have perished.

In times of stress and peril there are virtues in uniformity, in theological and religious matters as in material and worldly ones. "Any Church," wrote my great predecessor of this page, G. K. Chesterton, "must be able to answer quite definitely when great questions of public morals are put. Can I go in for cannibalism, or murder babies to reduce the population, or any similar scientific or progressive reform? Any Church with authority to teach must be able to say whether it can be done . . . I have no use for a Church which is not a Church militant, which cannot order battle and fall in line, and march in the same direction."

> The duty of a church to exercise its authority as teacher in times of stress.

Yet there is a corollary to this truth. The direction must be the right one. The Gadarene swine fell into line and marched in the same direction. And though there should be no compromise with known and certain evil, those entrusted, whether by God or man, with the destinies and fate of a great moral institution, are under an obligation to plan the direction and course of that institution with worldly prudence and care. Otherwise, in their pursuit of abstract good, they may take a false step which endangers its well-being and even existence. A Catholic may be precluded from questioning the decisions and injunctions of the Pope,

> Dangers, however, in such conformity and obedience to religious authority which has not been subjected to "the test of individual reason and judgment"—the chief difference between Protestantism and Catholicism which caused the sufferings of the Reformation.

and applying to them the test of individual reason and judgement. A Protestant is not; it is because he claims such a right that he is a Protestant. This is what, stripped of the ephemeral, the Reformation of the sixteenth century was about. The Catholic Church of western and Roman Europe—the greatest educative force for good the world had ever seen—in its bureaucratic rigidity and arrogance insisted on the sanctity of propositions against which the reason and, consequently, conscience of sincere Christians rebelled. And, with the help of thumbscrew and flame, it turned those outraged and protesting Christians into schismatics. It was for mankind a profound and terrible tragedy.

Christ's answer to the eternal dilemma of idealists faced by harsh facts such as the cataclysmic suffering which will result if man is so irrational as to declare immoral the use of available scientific means of preventing overpopulation.

"Render therefore unto Caesar the things which are Caesar's; and unto God the things that are God's." So Christ answered the dilemma which faces every idealist who seeks to prescribe for himself and others a pattern of conduct in the harsh world of material fact. Through medical and hygienic knowledge man has found the means of prolonging the lives of countless millions who prior to the present century would have perished in infancy. As a result of this immense humanitarian achievement the population of the world is increasing at such a rate that within the next few decades universal famine, and probably pestilence and war, seem almost inevitable. Unless, therefore, man by the exercise of his reason can limit the extent of the population explosion that, by the use of the same reason, he has caused, there will ensue, not a diminution of human suffering, but an immense and cataclysmic increase of it. The only way to prevent this without doing injury to the living is for man to refrain from creating life beyond the point at which, with the material resources at his command, he can ensure a full life for all. It seems, therefore, irrational to renounce as evil the scientific means which can enable him to do this without either taking life or repressing too harshly the instinct which God has implanted in all his creatures to ensure that they reproduce and preserve their species.

Profoundly, therefore, as I respect the Pope, and the obviously deep and even agonizing sincerity with which he has wrestled with the dilemma confronting him and his Church, I cannot as a Protestant, who believes in the exercise of personal reason and judgment in matters of conscience, do otherwise than question his finding. The control of pregnancy is a matter which concerns both man's higher and spiritual nature and his terrestrial and material circumstances and necessities. It affects the formation and development of individual character, and the happiness, peace, and good order of human society. Above all, it affects the well-being, both material and spiritual, of women, whose right to express an opinion in such a matter seems to me to outweigh that of men. For it is women who have to pay with pain and suffering the price of each new life brought into the world, and for man to deny woman the right to choose freely for herself when she shall take up her cross seems to be a negation of that human dignity and freedom of choice which Christianity demands for every created being.

Conclusion
Repetition of thesis and further arguments appealing to "that human dignity and freedom of choice which Christianity demands for every created being."

OUTLINE

Thesis: The Papal Encyclical on birth control is irrational and takes away the right of a man and a woman to decide for themselves in conscience and reason what methods of contraception they wish to employ, for

I. The Encyclical is in harmony with traditional but potentially dangerous Papal doctrine.
   A. That doctrine rightly commands "Thou shalt do no murder," and
      1. It has always held all prenatal life as sacred, and
      2. It applies even to human life before conception
   B. That doctrine requires obedience and acceptance, but
II. The Encyclical is not scripturally or rationally on firm ground for

A. It goes beyond Christ's teachings.
B. It is not consistent with good reason, for
  1. God made man the sole means of initiating life.
  2. Woman, as man's sexual partner, should have the right to decide when that means should be employed.
  3. No Christian doctrine rules man must always create life.
  4. It is not easy to "see the moral distinctions" between one means of preventing conception and another.
III. The Encyclical intrudes upon the rights of the individual conscience, for
  A. The Church declares human reason is inadequate.
    1. This authority has been a tremendous and salutary force in preserving Christianity, yet
    2. This rule of authority may be dangerous.
  B. The Protestant rightly applies the test of individual reason to matters "where faith by itself does not provide an answer."
  C. The tragedies of the Reformation were occasioned by the Catholic Church's insistence upon the "sanctity of propositions against which the reason . . . rebelled."
IV. The Encyclical can have dangerous consequences, for
  A. It goes contrary to Christ's realistic teaching: "Render unto Caesar. . . ."
  B. It may undo what reason and science have done to prolong life.
  C. It may encourage further overpopulation, and
    1. Worldwide famine would result.
    2. Millions more will needlessly suffer and die.
V. The Protestant principle regarding birth control is preferable on all counts, for
  A. Reason shows the irrational aspect of the Encyclical, for
    1. Science cannot be evil in having found needed contraceptives.
    2. These means do not cause man to suffer.
  B. Reason shows the control of pregnancy is important to man's spiritual and material necessities.
  C. Above all, it provides women with the great right of choice in this important matter of childbearing.

COMMENTARY: ARRANGEMENT BY COMPARISON-CONTRAST

In examining this essay, we cannot help noticing that its author constantly kept two different things in mind throughout. As the word "dilemma" in the title tells us, he wrote keeping his eyes fixed first on one possibility and then on another. In all their aspects, he compared and contrasted two distinct views: the official Catholic position and the individual Protestant attitude on birth control.

Point by point he contrasted the authoritarian stand of the Catholic Church with the Protestant attitude of freedom of conscience on this highly controversial matter: the use of contraceptives to prevent the initiating of life. And this presenting of first one side and then the other gave him his "pattern of arrangement." We can note this pattern of contrasts begin to emerge in the second paragraph when, in the opening sentence, he tells us how a "reasoning individual" like himself must judge the matter. He concludes that the Papal Encyclical lacks any Biblical support in the recorded words of Christ in the New Testament. He compares respect for all human life, "the necessary corollary of Christ's philosophy of love to all men," with the doctrine that it is man's duty to "create life whenever he has the opportunity to do so."

A listing of these contrasts in parallel columns as they occur throughout the essay would reveal the effectiveness of the pattern and its usefulness to any writer.

Roman Catholicism	*Protestantism*
Belief in inspired wisdom	Reliance upon individual reason
A useful guard against disastrous decisions	Faith unable to provide all needed answers
Preserver of Christianity	Reason a necessary check on faith
Defender of absolute ideals	Advocate of reasonable worldly prudence
"Greatest educative force for good"	Preventer of religious persecution
Tradition over Scriptures	Advocate of Christian "realism"
Faith over reason	Defender of reason and science
Requirer of obedience	Protester against deadly overpopulation

The author's *stance* as an appreciative but critical observer adds greatly to the effectiveness of the essay. It should gain a good reception for him from both Catholic and Protestant readers, for his attitude is always respectful and mindful of the historic importance of the Catholic view but at the same time politely opposed to it. In fact, on a first reading the points of contrast listed herein do not appear with the blunt shock that they do in a bare, prosaic outline. His *tone* is suggested in his reference to the Reformation and the historic conflict it produced: "It was for mankind a profound and terrible tragedy." Also, throughout, he maintains stress on the values of human freedom and dignity involved in this painful dilemma.

WHAT DOES IT SAY?

1. What mental pictures does the phrase "the Papal Encyclical on birth control" suggest to you? What does *encyclical* mean?

2. How do you interpret this sentence: "Unless he [man] hitches his wagon to a star he is less than the meanest brute. . . ."?

3. How possibly can the Pope be said to represent "the greatest of all man's ideals"?

4. Can you state or explain what "Christ's philosophy of love" is? And why is "respect for all human life" its corollary? (Define *corollary.*)

5. As Sir Arthur Bryant uses the term, state in your own language the meaning of "the Protestant attitude."

6. In G. K. Chesterton's terms, on what national moral questions should "a Church militant" take a firm stand today?

7. Historically, what is the meaning of "The Reformation"?

8. How can Christ's counsel—"Render therefore unto Caesar the things which are Caesar's, and unto God the things that are God's"—be called "a pattern of conduct in the harsh world of material fact"?

9. What is the allusion to "the Gadarene swine"?

WHAT DO YOU THINK?

1. If you are familiar with it, write a defense, or an attack, on the only methods of "birth control" that the Papal Encyclical and the traditional stand of the Catholic Church permit.

2. Do Sir Arthur Bryant's views correspond with those of Dr. Berry in his "The Rhetoric of Conscience"? (p. 65). Explain your support, or criticism, of the rational attitude as defined by these two authors, and apply comparison-contrast to one of the following topics as viewed by an authoritative and a nonauthoritative sect or group.

Conscientious objectors	Nudity
"Mixed" marriages	Drugs
Integration	"Adults Only" movies
Organ transplants	Premarital sex

3. Come down the "abstraction ladder" with one of the following topics, and write an essay having a comparison-contrast organization or pattern of development.

The good marriage	Contraceptives and overpopulation
Christian marriage	Legality and abortion
Trial marriage	Sex education in the schools
Sex and the Bible	"Wanted" versus "unwanted" child

4. On reading the following pairs of statements, you will find that (1) and (2) in each pair represent two opposing views on the same controversial issue. Select one of these statements and write an essay telling why you think it is the more acceptable viewpoint. (You will have to include objections to the opposing statement.)
   a. (1) The Pope is making too big an issue of the question whether birth control devices can be used as means of preventing conception.
      (2) The Pope has to take the firm stand he has because the Church has always considered the use of contraceptive devices as immoral.
   b. (1) Far from being a social leper, the ex-priest now may become a hero.
      (2) Cardinals and bishops are right in disciplining priests who refuse to support the Encyclical.
   c. (1) "After spending 15½ years of marriage trying to believe that the Pope and the bishops knew what they were talking about, I will not let others be misled and nearly destroyed as we were."
      (2) "Have faith and God will provide."

Can We Bridge the Racial Gap?
Only if Whites Can Dig Black Power
by PATRICIA COFFIN

BLACK POWER IS BEAUTIFUL! Does that shock? If so, you are one of millions of Americans, black and white, who haven't a clue to what is happening here. Does it puzzle you? Then you do not comprehend that the black man inherited the American dream with Lincoln's Emancipation Proclamation. For more than 100 years now, this dream that he was dreaming has not come true. His disillusion is deep. "The new black American dream has got to be a better life than what we have," a Black Power student told me. "And we are going to get it. Reeducating the whites is one of our major tasks." The black man has come far since the first Negroes were sold by a Dutch shipmaster at Jamestown 350 years ago. His rebellion against the great white putdown, his insistence on his rights spring from a newfound pride. White unawareness is the most serious barrier to easing the racial crisis.

We all take our first steps alone before we can stand on our own two feet. The white American is going to have to let go of his black brother; give him massive economic support, technical advice, scholarships, but leave him to make his own mistakes, learn his own lessons. Nor does he want belatedly offered white friendship—yet. He needs to find his own identity, reconstruct his own past, before he is psychologically free to meet the white man on an equal footing.

Try as they will, most well-meaning whites cannot shed a paternalistic attitude toward blacks. Take the lady who shares her suburban swimming pool with Negro kids. Big deal. The only time she

Can We Bridge the Racial Gap?
Not if Blacks Have to Turn White
by GEORGE GOODMAN

CAN WE BRIDGE THE GAP? I am not sure. Do Americans understand the nature of the breach or what bridging it means? The question takes me back to Washington, June 19, 1968. It was Solidarity Day in the Baptist rhetoric of the Southern Christian Leadership Conference. It was a long day of soaring oratory about new wars on racism. But words didn't work any magic.

There were the assassinations. They stuck in the mind, blood-spattered reminders of the violence in this nation, while phony politicians worked the voters with flimflam about law and order. There was the Poor People's Campaign—13 weeks of feeblish protest for sweeping social change to which the Government responded with shoddy, piecemeal gestures. The public demanded no more than tokenism. Disillusionment was in knowing nothing more was coming.

Five days later, riot police clattered into Resurrection City. It only took them hours to clear the park. Dr. King's successor, the Rev. Ralph D. Abernathy, was arrested trying to lead 300 meek protesters onto the U.S. Capitol grounds. Worn and harried, Abernathy went willingly with the police. By now, it was clear even to defenders: the Nonviolent Protest Movement had fizzled to a close.

For a time, there will be no black Gandhi to rally his people with calls of "black and white together. . . ."

Two months after Washington, blacks gathered in Philadelphia. But the conveners of the third annual National Conference on Black

(*continued from* p. 102)
ever sees the ghetto is from her train window. The whites have a lot to learn, but the black man has too. He is entitled to that bag full of chips on his shoulder, but it unbalances his judgment. Why do the bad men in Westerns wear black sombreros? asks a Negro author darkly. So how come the basic black dress is always in fashion? say I. TV commercials are still almost all "white," even though six percent of the total spent on consumer goods in 1967 was by Negroes. That is $25 billion. That is black buying, or boycotting, power. Actually, the demand for black talent from advertisers is such that the complexion of our TV screens will get darker daily. That's Black Power at work.

This issue of LOOK is designed to reveal many more faces of Black Power to white America.

Black Power is a term that has caught the imagination of the activist black (that minority within a minority) as well as the liberal white. But it is much more than rhetoric. It is the beautiful answer. It is the Negro's control over his own destiny, it is economic self-help such as Operation Breadbasket in Chicago and the black farmers' co-operative in Alabama. It is the political muscle to elect Richard Hatcher mayor of Gary. It is enough pride in his past to get an Afro-American major into the undergraduate curriculum at Yale next fall. Hopefully, it is the beginning of black-implemented reform that will wipe out our present welfare system and transform the urban ghetto into a cooperative community. It does not stand for violence, but it means self-defense instead of turning the other cheek.

For generations, the Negro has rejected his own facial features. The discovery of his blackness as a source of pride makes "black is beautiful" mean much more than a shade of skin. It refers to a quality of spirit. Daily, we are startled by the elegant vitality of a Negro girl walking down the street—head high, hair cropped, looking like an Ife sculpture. The idiom of much of our music, dance, speech and food is thanks to the Negro. He calls it "soul."

When Dr. Martin Luther King, Jr., was shot last April, I felt shock, and the urge to put my arms in sorrow around someone black. My reaction was not unique. Then I went to work on this issue, and in my naïveté, I felt it might be a step toward "closing the gap." With three counts against me—being a woman (emotional), a WASP (white Anglo-Saxon Protestant) and over 30—I sought balance in a coeditor who was my opposite: a 29-year-old black man. He is George Goodman (see page at right). By talking and listening to him and to others, I soon learned that my missionary work belongs among my white friends. My black friends suggest I go home and clean my own house. That I will. But I'll come back and try at least to bridge the chasm. For I am my brother's keeper, be he white or black.

(*continued from* p. 103)
Power didn't come together for litanies on interracial love. They talked about survival and liberation, not civil rights.

They paid homage to the memory of Dr. King but expressed no grief over losing a petitioner to the moral conscience of white America. Even before the murder, blacks were censuring King for being too enchanted with dreams to deal with reality.

For an increasing number of blacks, the foremost reality about this country is white racism. To coexist instead of trying to overcome, black America is cultivating a racism all its own. It amounts, pretty much to what whites have going, but it's newer and thus less subtle.

Black is the new religion, and converts are made when the search for identity results in discovery. The walls of caste are crumbling—at least inside black America. Bourgeois blacks are integrating today with the products of the nigger caste—the faceless hoard of gnome-like people who have cowered for centuries in the shadow of whites. They are visible now and clearly audible: "We're black and beautiful." It can be a soft incantation or a Red Guard roar.

What is black? "What ain't white," says Philip Coran, a musician-philosopher of the Black Arts on Chicago's South Side.

"You begin with Whitey's system of separatism. If you look Negro, then Whitey's provided the ghetto where you live.

"Blacks end up with a commonality that lays the ground for unity with blacks in every city of the country."

The marks of bondage have become articles of sacrament. Blacks talk to blacks about the food they eat and the music they like and even about the rhythms of their walk. There is a black mystique.

There is a sense of collective responsibility too. For Black Panthers and Black Muslims, responsibility is preparing for Armageddon.

For others, less fatalistic or more naive, responsibility rivets to the here and now. Some who left the ghetto are dashing back. Many have found themselves, and a lot who claim they have are still looking.

Ghetto issues are crucial, and targets of oppression get bigger all the time. So, in Harlem today, militants bypass a white-owned liquor store to go after the university that's gobbling up parkland. Blacks raise hell about who teaches what to black children, and if black history isn't included, then even the children get pummeled in fractious debates and strikes.

History is important to blacks for the same reason it is to all people—it raises their enthusiasm for themselves. Blacks insist their heroes, including Nat Turner, be granted the infallibility that whites so unreasonably demand for their own. Can whites see this?

Can we ever bridge the gap? If it still means turning black people white, then the answer is no, probably never.

COMMENTARY: ARRANGEMENT BY DEDUCTION

"Nobody does much good, hard thinking if he doesn't have to. But when you're hard up against a tough nut of a problem, you do your best to crack it because you must." This comment is a general one (*generalization*); that is, it formulates a pattern of behavior that most of us would accept as an accurate observation. (Such general statements when taken for granted as being true are also called *assumptions*.) It is from such general statements that we *deduce,* or *infer,* certain conclusions when we apply the generalization to a particular situation.

The two *Look* Magazine editors who wrote these editorials on the subject "Can We Bridge the Racial Gap?" used this deductive procedure in their discussions of racial antagonism. Their mutual problem was to explain to their millions of readers the significance of the present Black movements and pressures and how these might or might not resolve existing racial hostilities. They both began by accepting the same assumption: that under certain conditions the racial gap might be bridged.

Beginning with that generalization, each editor goes on to apply the general "truth" to his own view of how the racial conflict might be solved. Patricia Coffin concludes that the racial gap can be bridged if Whites shed their paternalistic attitude and Blacks drop the chips from their shoulders. George Goodman, her Black co-editor, less optimistic, warns that the Nonviolent Protest Movement has failed and that bridging the gap involves acceptance of the "Black mystique," not the transformation of Blacks into Whites.

How both authors move from the general to the particular can be noted in the side-by-side summary below:

Patricia Coffin	*George Goodman*
Opening: White unawareness of the new Black pride is a serious barrier to bridging the racial gap.	Failure of Americans to understand the nature of the breach and what bridging it entails poses a serious difficulty to bridging the gap.
White America must shed its paternalistic attitude, must let the Blacks find their own identity.	A long succession of events has demonstrated that the Nonviolent Protest Movement has failed with its emphasis on interracial love.
Blacks must take the chips from their shoulders, for this attitude leads to an unbalanced judgment.	The new emphasis is survival and liberation, not civil rights; reality, not dreams.
Black power is real and, hopefully, will lead to black-implemented reforms.	Black racism, a reaction to White racism, is the new religion that is integrating the black community.

Blackness as a source of pride is gaining ascendency.	Collective responsibility is leading to attacks on larger targets than in the past.
Missionary work is needed among White Americans, but we must try to bridge the gap, for man is his brother's keeper, white or black.	Bridging the gap means accepting the Blacks as Blacks, not turning Black people White.

Following the pattern of the argument in this fashion fails to call attention to the details that each editor presents in applying the generalization to the particular situation. Miss Coffin and Mr. Goodman both call attention to the cause (a new-found pride) that is leading to an effect (the emergence of Black racism). Both make copious use of illustrations of paternalism: the Poor People's campaign, led by the Rev. Ralph D. Abernathy—an illustration of the fizzling out of the Nonviolent Protest Movement. Both make use of definition: What constitutes Black Power? What is *Black*?

And as one would expect of professional writers, both have made sure that their editorials have unity, stick closely to the topic, and avoid a common fault of beginning writers: discussing irrelevant de-

Courtesy of United Press International

tails that lead the reader off on a tangent, and thus destroy the force and effectiveness of the argument. Although each author chooses to rely upon a different paragraph style (What seems to be the principle underlying George Goodman's scrappy sentence paragraphs?), both essays have coherence—a logical movement from beginning to end.

WHAT DOES IT SAY?

1. George Goodman asks, "Do Americans understand the nature of the breach or what bridging it means?" Define this *breach* (or *gap*) and *bridging* to show that you understand.

2. What "assassinations" does he refer to, and what do they portend or symbolize for Black people?

3. Why can the late Martin Luther King, Jr., be described as "a petitioner to the moral conscience of white America"?

4. "We're black and beautiful." Under what conditions would this statement be "a soft incantation?" When would it be "a Red Guard roar"?

5. Identify the following: Armageddon, Black Panthers, Black Muslims, Nat Turner.

6. What does Patricia Coffin mean in saying the white American must let his "black brother" first become "psychologically free"?

7. Both authors refer to the "rhetoric" of Black Power. What do they mean?

8. Why is being a WASP considered to be a handicap in dealing with racial conflicts?

WHAT DO YOU THINK?

1. Employing *deductive order,* apply a general statement (assumption) to a particular situation of racial conflict. Some generalizations and particulars are listed here to suggest possible combinations.

Generalization	*Particular*
(a) We're all in the same boat.	General unrest at _____
(b) "We all take our first steps alone before we can stand on our own two feet."	Hair and dress styles

(c) In English, all terms having the word "black" in them have unpleasant meanings.

The meaning many people have for "The Black Student Union"

(d) Nobody likes to be "a minority within a minority."

Being a peaceful activist

(e) It takes one to recognize another one.

Students for a Democratic Society

(f) Violence breeds violence.

Police and demonstrators at _____

(g) There can be no true communication without a dialogue.

The college president and the recent "sit-in" at _____

2. Formulate a suitable general statement from the information provided by the following report, which is one typical for January 1969. Then apply your general statement to a particular situation now making news.

Campus troubles, including seizure of a college building by militant Negro students, kept students and administrators in various degrees of uproar at four institutions Friday.

At Brandeis University in Waltham, Mass., 65 black militants occupied a campus building for the third day despite a court order and a threat of expulsion.

The group, which claimed it had enough food stockpiled to last four days, occupied Ford Hall which houses the university's telephone switchboard and a $200,000 computer. They demanded hiring of Negro professors and establishment of an independent African studies department.

President Morris B. Abram met with representatives of the militants, and then said they would be suspended if they refused to leave the building.

At Queens College in New York City, Joseph Mulholland, director of a program aimed at providing higher education for Negroes, offered to resign if those involved in the program would give him a chance to defend himself and then vote for him to resign.

The college's 26,000 students returned to classes peacefully Friday, after student demonstrations forced cancellation of classes for two days.

They were protesting reports that the college planned to absorb SEEK—Search for Education, Elevation and Knowledge—into its regular program. The college denied the reports.

In California, police opened the way for students to attend classes at San Francisco State College, where the American Federation of Teachers defied a court order against striking or picketing.

At San Fernando Valley State College near Los Angeles, Academic Dean Delmar T. Oviatt lifted a ban on public meetings and unauthorized visitors on campus, and agreed to let black representatives make classroom presentations with the permission of instructors.

Nearly 300 students and their supporters were arrested during a rally Thursday after the Black Student Union demanded more Negro teachers, a Negro Studies program and amnesty for 28 students indicted for taking over the administraton building Nov. 4.

Peace returned to three other colleges in the Los Angeles area where demonstrations flared Thursday.[1]

3. Write a 500-word essay applying deductive order to what you have to say on one of these general statements:

(a) All students profit from physical education courses.
(b) The Peace Corps teaches you there is more to life than just making money.
(c) Good fences make good neighbors.
(d) Lend a friend money and you lose a friend.
(e) Astronauts are heroes.
(f) Every earth tremor is a warning.
(g) "Ghetto" is a state of mind.
(h) The "Pepsi Generation" is going to "pot."

[1] Reprinted by permission of the Associated Press.

A New Vision: A Better Tomorrow
by JULIAN BOND

The greatest change in the lives of most black people in the 1960's has occurred because we have become, with the rest of the United States, an urban population. We have moved from the country to the city. In Richmond, Nashville, New Orleans, Jacksonville, and Birmingham we are over 40 per cent of the population. In addition to having gone through that geographical change, black people in this country have gone through another change as well. For some of us, a great number of things have got better. We can now eat in places we could not eat in before. We can go to school at places we could not before. We can get jobs in places we could not get jobs in before. We can vote in places where we could not vote before; we can hold elective offices in places where we couldn't hold elective offices before.

But in many ways, a lot of things have got much worse—and to substantiate this statement let me cite a speech by America's greatest authority on race relations, Lyndon B. Johnson. Johnson said in this speech, delivered at Howard University a little over two years ago, that in 1948 the 8 per cent unemployment rate for Negro teen-age boys was less than that of the whites. By 1964 the rate had grown to 23 per cent as against 13 per cent for whites. Between 1949 and 1959

Reprinted from *The Humanist,* January-February, 1969. Reprinted by permission of *The Humanist* and the author.

the income of Negro men relative to white men declined in every section of the country. From 1952 to 1963 the median income of Negro families as compared to whites actually dropped from 57 per cent to 53 per cent. Since 1947 the number of white families living in poverty has decreased 27 per cent, while the number of nonwhite families living in poverty has decreased only 3 per cent. The infant mortality rate for nonwhites in 1940 was 70 per cent greater than for whites. In 1962 the infant mortality rate for nonwhite children was 90 per cent greater than for whites.

When you discuss poverty in the United States, you have to be honest and admit that not all poor people are black people. There are lots of poor white people as well. Poor white people, however, enjoy the dubious distinction of knowing that they are not poor because they are white but are poor in spite of their whiteness. From this we have to assume that there are two kinds of problems in this country; there are problems of race and problems of class. There are 357,000 black men and 419,000 black women who tomorrow morning will be looking for jobs they can't find. There are another 300,000 to 400,000 black women and men who have given up looking for work and are therefore no longer counted as being unemployed by the Labor Department. Unemployment among young black people between the ages of 16 and 21 runs six times as high as that for white people in the same age group.

If you were to take all those statistics and mold an average black man in this country, this would be what you would find: First, there is better than a 50 per cent chance he would have dropped out of high school. He would not only be unemployed but by current standards would be unemployable. He would have no saleable skill. Neither of his parents would have gone beyond the eighth grade. He would have entered school at six but because of overcrowding would have had to attend halfday sessions. During his six years in elementary school he would have attended four different schools.

In discussing this average young slum dweller one has to ask oneself what kind of efforts were made in his past and what efforts will be made in his future to improve his life. Since 1954 there have been various sorts of methods and techniques directed at solving the race problem. These have included the sit-in demonstration and the nonviolent march, the pursuit of education as a barrier breaker, the use of violence as an inducement to change, the challenge in the courts of segregation by law, and the thrust for power through political action. Each of these very obviously has its own successes and its own failures, its own strengths and its own weaknesses. Legal action, for instance, brought black people one of the greatest legal victories of the 20th century—a statement from the Supreme Court in 1954 that segregation in the public schools was illegal. But 15 years later, in 1969, there are more black children attending more black schools north of the Mason-Dixon line than there were in 1954. The sit-in demonstrations and nonviolent marches have obviously had their successes also. They won for southern black people the integrated lunch counter, the integrated bus and train station, the integrated toilet, and the right to vote. Now these first victories, integration of places of public accommodation, have had little meaning for most black people; and the last victory, the right to vote, has yet to win a bread-and-butter victory for them.

A great many people seem to think that education is the answer to the problems of race in this country, but education as a means of breaking down racial barriers dies as an effective means of social change every day that black ghetto children are taught that whiteness is rightness. The young slum dweller was told that poverty would be defeated, diminished, and finally removed from the United States. But by 1967 it had become obvious that the war in Vietnam had rendered that promise almost useless, if it ever was really meant. Violence has been the official policy of the United States Government in settling her disputes with other nations, and that belief has seeped into the police stations and the slums across the land. War has brewed anger in the black community and has given birth to the belief that nonviolence is only a joke.

There are some people still who believe that nonviolence and nonviolent confrontation will force this government to turn its attention towards a real solution of the race problem in America. There are those who believe that progress of a sort is being made today, and who believe like Scarlett O'Hara that tomorrow will be another day. There are those who are convinced that nothing good will come tomorrow until the structure of today is changed; and there are those who believe that giving small amounts of power, like control of neighborhood schools, will hold off the day of judgment. Now all of these sorts of things have their place, nonviolent confrontations among them, but one ought to remember that the success of nonviolence in India depended on the English having a conscience, while this government is thought to have none. A measure of the amount of conscience in the United States Congress was that only 36 out of all the congressmen could be found to support the recommendations of President Johnson's Committee on Civil Disorders.

Now it is true that better days have come for some black people and that perhaps in some far distant future true equality is coming for us. We have to be careful what kind of equality it will be, however, because we may be winning an equal chance to be poor instead of the more than equal chance we have now. If that is democracy, I would suggest that it is a little too much of a good thing. We need to examine and dissect the democratic system, and discover ways of directing it towards benefiting those who are presently its victims. We need to examine and change the job system, the welfare system, the police system, the housing system, the education system, and the health system. These systems need to be controlled by those who are now controlled by them and need to be responsive to the needs and desires of people whose needs and desires are presently now being recorded.

President Johnson's Commission on Civil Disorders asked for 500,000 new jobs for blacks. His Administration responded by requesting only 100,000 new jobs. The Commission on Disorders asked for 6 million new housing units for low- and moderate-income families. The Administration responded by asking for only 2½ million. The Commission said that unemployment was the major cause of summer disorder. The Administration responded by cutting 35 million dollars from the emergency summer programs of 1968. Poor education, the Commission said, is a persistent source of grievance and resentment in the black community. President Johnson responded by cutting Federal aid to education. Now if that's the kind of response that we can expect from government, then quite obviously changes must be made.

We await with anticipation the programs of the new Congress and the Nixon Administration to see if our expectations can be realized— though at this moment we are dubious. Our decision is between allowing America to continue as she does now, continuing racism, continuing poverty, continuing despair, continuing war, or having the country adopt a new vision of a better tomorrow.

COMMENTARY: ARRANGEMENT BY CAUSAL ANALYSIS

As a member of the Georgia State Legislature and one of the founders of the Student Nonviolent Coordinating Committee, as well as a nominee for the vice presidency at the 1968 Democratic Party Convention in Chicago, Julian Bond is widely recognized as a young civil rights leader. In this essay he has set for himself the task of answering a basic question that can be framed thus: "Why in this country, despite important legislation, do black people not yet enjoy equal opportunities with white people?" His analysis of the causes for the continuation of such injustices provides the answer.

To be fair and to disarm any readers who might rush to protest, "But look how far you black people have come!" he admits in his opening paragraph the many changes that have taken place through civil rights legislation. It may seem surprising, however, that he does not consider these advances in living and working conditions as the major change now having a bearing upon his people. As he states in his opening startling fact, "The greatest change in the lives of most black people in the 1960's has occurred because we have become, with the rest of the United States, an urban population." This move of blacks from farms to city slums has created the desperate situation which he sees as the basic cause of continuing racial and class disturbances in the United States.

In the second paragraph, to show how "in many ways, a lot of things have got much worse," he cites statistics indicating that the incomes for black people have not improved at all in ratio to whites who also live in poverty. His shocking figures of infant mortality among nonwhite people dramatically illustrates the case he makes for poverty as the prime cause of trouble between whites and blacks.

This mass movement to the cities has caused, he says, great flaws in our present social and economic order to reveal themselves; they show up in the two basic problems confronting the country: "problems of race and problems of class." Under the circumstances, black people will, naturally, suffer the most from these problems. He cites more figures to indicate this disparity, and to make these abstract figures specific and concrete he draws a composite portrait of "an average black man in this country." His paragraph of details spells out the desperate life and situation of "a young slum dweller."

Such are the causes producing the conflicts, tensions, and outbreaks of violence márking our times. In almost matter-of-fact language he lists the various methods and techniques black people have employed in attempts to solve the first of their problems—that of racial inequality. Their successes, though at first seeming to hold much promise, have turned out to be disappointments; the rights won to live as human beings have done little to improve the crippling conditions of poverty under which the typical young slum dweller is expected to make his way to social equality with his white neighbors.

His plight is made more painful by the promises made him but not kept. His bitterness and disillusionment continue to increase as he sees hopes for breaking racial barriers fade with the expenses of the Vietnam war and the adoption of violence as a means of national policy for dealing with troubles abroad and at home. In his view of the history of the black man in the United States, Julian Bond sees some good results possibly arising from both the violent and nonviolent strategies and actions so far undertaken by his desperate people. He admits that in time black people may come to enjoy a "true equality" (racially) with white people, but he fears that this equality will mean only the right to share a common poverty with the poor whites.

Since it is poverty that underlies all our problems, he urges examination and reform of all our basic systems—jobs, welfare, police, housing, education, and health. He further implies that those who are now most adversely affected by abuses in these systems should have some say in their transformation. In his conclusion, he recites the failures of the Johnson administration to meet the recommendations of the Commission of Civil Disorders, and in closing he expresses the hope that the Nixon administration would "adopt a new vision of a better tomorrow."

This *arrangement* of details reflects Julian Bond's *stance* as a spokesman who is quietly pleading with his predominantly white reader-audience to face the harsh facts confronting his people. He assumes his restrained cause-and-effect analysis will arouse the conscience of all fairminded thinkers, making them recognize that if old policies and practices do not give way to new and just ones, "then quite obviously changes must be made." How these changes are to be brought about if white people fail to respond to rational appeals, Julian Bond does not explicitly say, but his concluding statements express an appeal for a vision of hope.

WHAT DOES IT SAY?

1. Statistics and sociological terms generally are too abstract to create emotional effects. In his opening, Mr. Bond states that black people in the 1960's have become "an urban population" and in the cities he mentions "we are over 40 per cent of the population." What pictures of living conditions and daily problems do these abstractions suggest to you?

2. How might a less modest writer state the fact appearing in the last sentence of the opening paragraph?

3. How do you react to this statement: "In 1962 the infant mortality rate for nonwhite children was 90 per cent greater than for whites"? How might an emotion-arousing writer have exploited that fact?

4. What does it really mean to be "no longer counted as being unemployed by the Labor Department"?

5. How do you interpret this statement: "and the last victory, the right to vote, has yet to win a bread-and-butter victory for them"?

6. Can you explain the meaning of this statement: ". . . black ghetto children are taught that whiteness is rightness"?

7. Can you come up with any evidence that the "black community" holds "the belief that nonviolence is only a joke"?

8. In practical terms of everyday living what do you think Julian Bond means when he speaks of "true equality"?

WHAT DO YOU THINK?

1. What in your experience and personal background makes you strongly approve or disapprove of *one* of these Julian Bond assertions as it appears in its context:

   (a) "From this we have to assume that there are two kinds of problems in this country; there are problems of race and problems of class."

   (b) "Now these first victories, integration of places of public accommodation, have had little meaning for most black people. . . ."

   (c) "Violence has been the official policy of the United States Government in settling her disputes with other nations, and that belief has seeped into police stations and the slums across the land."

   (d) "But one ought to remember that the success of nonviolence in India depended on the English having a conscience, while this government is thought to have none."

   (e) "Our decision is between allowing America to continue as she does now, continuing racism, continuing poverty, continuing despair, continuing war, or having the country adopt a new vision of a better tomorrow."

2. Analyze in writing some of the causes you see at work in daily life producing one of the following problems:

   Runaway children   Abandoned automobiles

   High school dropouts   Litter in public places

   Desertion of families   Unwanted "junk" mail

3. How does the "image" of Julian Bond—his role, tone, views—in the following newspaper report compare with the one you have of him after having read his essay? Write an analysis stating your conclusions and explaining why you hold them.

"Will I run for president in 1972?" This was Julian Bond parrying a question. "Not that year. I'll be too young. Forget 1976. Try 1984."

The audience loved it.

Largely college students, they had crammed the University of Portland's Howard Hall to hear the reed-thin, 29-year-old Negro politician who had become a national figure with his icy cool and deft turn of phrase at the Chicago Democratic Convention.

Bond, who spoke Friday at the school, has other claims to distinction.

He was a founder of SNCC (Snick) in 1960 after graduation from Morehouse College. At 26 he became the first Negro to win a seat in the Georgia House of Representatives.

Barred from taking his seat, he won election twice again and the U.S. Supreme Court ruled unanimously he be allowed to take his post.

At the Chicago convention he was chairman of the contested Georgia delegation, seconded the nomination of Eugene McCarthy for president and was himself nominated for vice president. He withdrew because of his age.

Life magazine and other national publications have tabbed him a young man to watch on the national political scene.

Charisma? Slouching easily at the lectern, Bond had it and to spare.

"My God he's gorgeous," said a long-haired Oriental girl near the podium.

"I must go and say hello to Julian," said a middle-aged Milwaukie female politician.

Bond's politics or brand of political theory is less easy to identify. He quoted John Jay but drew tactics from Machiavelli. He made solemn reference to Dr. Martin Luther King, Jr., but warned that violence is "an alternative."

"The black experience in America differs only from the experience of other minorities in this country in degree and severity," he said.

"The root of minority problems," he continued "is that this is a country founded by white men and has remained in the eyes of white men a country for white men.

"The black man's struggle is part of that historic struggle against the concept that Providence has ordained the white man to take the land from the red man, sell the black man into slavery, convey by other more subtle means the white man's supremacy."

What is the answer? Moderation or confrontation?

Bond answered the question with fine historical irony.

"I will quote from a conversation on this very problem in 1812. The speaker is the Indian Chief Tecumseh and he says, 'Shall the Indian wait until the white man forces us into the corn field to work and chain us to posts to whip or shall we resist?' "

Bond continued: "There was a good moderate red man present and he answered, 'Let us submit our grievances for a just and equitable solution.' "

"You know and I know just how 'just and equitable' that solution was."

Nixon Blasted

He concluded "Black power must become more than rhetoric." He said that "Representative democracy has brought us limited victories," and then went on to blast the Nixon administration for its record on minority problems.

Bond said at the airport and again in Howard Hall that "Nixon's plan for 'Black Capitalism' cannot succeed because white capitalism has not succeeded for the white man."

He called instead for something he called "community socialism." This would call for federally funded organizations with ownership vested in those "who live in the area." The profits would remain in the area and go into reinvestment for the benefits of the people who live there."

Would this be like cooperatives? he was asked.

"Let's just call it 'community socialism,'" he answered.

What will be the tack of the civil rights or black movement in the future?

Bond said he thinks the time of massive sustained violence "such as Detroit and Watts is over."

"There will be violence," he said. "But today the police methods are too sophisticated and too efficient. Besides this kind of thing has proved to be counter-productive for the black community."[1]

[1] Reprinted from The Oregonian, March 29, 1969 with permission of the publication.

A Civil Religion
NEWSWEEK ESSAY

"We acknowledge Thy divine help in the selection of our leadership every four years," Billy Graham earnestly prayed from the podium. "We recognize, O Lord, that in Thy sovereignty Thou hast permitted Richard Nixon to lead us at this momentous hour in our history."

Evangelist Graham undoubtedly assumed more divine complicity in the election of his close friend as President of the U.S. than did Democrats at the Inaugural ceremony last week. Yet the presumption that God somehow keeps His hand in the politics of the U.S. did not originate with the vibrant preacher. Rather, it is one of the traditional beliefs that support what Berkeley sociologist Robert Bellah has aptly labeled the "American civil religion." According to Bellah, this civil religion is neither Christian nor Jewish, but an appropriation of the major symbols of both faiths as a way of understanding and honoring the history and destiny of the American people.

From the time of the Founding Fathers, he points out, American political rhetoric has employed Biblical symbols to describe the United States as the promised land created by a chosen people after their exodus out of European bondage. The trauma of national crucifixion was added after the Civil War and found its focus in the almost Christlike suffering and death of Abraham Lincoln. Since then, he observes, reconciliation has been a major theme of Inaugural Day rhetoric. Thus the assumption that God is somehow involved in America's continuing quest for wholeness adds a sacred dimension to the otherwise secular U.S. political process.

Solemnity: "The inauguration of a President," Bellah believes, "is an important ceremonial event in this religion. It reaffirms, among other things, the religious legitimation of the highest political authority." Graham's prayer last week went even farther: in his thundering pulpit voice, he besought God to "so guide Richard Nixon in handling the affairs of state that the whole world will marvel and glorify Thee." Still, the most solemn moment of the ritual came when the new President placed his hand on the Bible and swore his oath of office before the Chief Justice of the United States—thereby effecting a kind of sacramental union between God and the laws of His newly chosen people. And, true to tradition, the Inaugural Address that followed had all the pitch and promise of a sermon.

Not surprisingly, much of Mr. Nixon's speech took its inspiration from his two favorite preachers, Graham and Dr. Norman Vincent Peale. Prior to the election, Graham had announced that in his view the major issue of the Presidential campaign was "the spiritual issue." Mr. Nixon echoed Graham's concern at the rhetorical summit of his address. "To a crisis of the spirit," said the new President, "we need an answer of the spirit. And to find that answer, we need only look within ourselves. We can build a great cathedral of the spirit."

Optimism: But Mr. Nixon departed from Graham's vision precisely where the evangelist is wont to preach the need for repentance. Instead, the President turned to the uncluttered optimism of Dr. Peale, who recently preached a sermon on "A Wonderful Time in Sixty-Nine." Mr. Nixon's words, of course, were more restrained. "I know the heart of America is good," he reassured the nation. "Our destiny offers not the cup of despair but the chalice of opportunity."

If the President's appeal for moral rearmament was typically Protestant in its emphasis on inner renewal, the Inauguration as a whole added a wider, ecumenical dimension to the central ritual of the civil religion. At a pre-Inaugural gathering at the State Department, nearly 750 worshipers of all faiths joined in the first official prayer service since George Washington's Inauguration in 1789. There, Peale asked, among other gestures of faith, for all citizens to "reevaluate the principles and practices of their institutions that this may become a period of spiritual and moral renewal."

Oddly enough, this is precisely what dissident clergy and laymen have been doing in opposing the war, the draft—and the churches themselves. But, as in the selection of his Cabinet, Mr. Nixon failed to include on his Inaugural platform any voices from these restless sectors of the church. Instead, he picked figures from the beleaguered religious Establishment: Bishop Charles E. Tucker of the African Methodist Episcopal Zion Church, long a conservative voice in black church circles; Los Angeles's 78-year-old Rabbi Edgar Magnin, who in his Inaugural prayer condemned "immorality and dissension"; and two prelates whose selection by the President seemed to be "ex officio"—Greek Orthodox Archbishop Iakovos and Roman Catholic Archbishop Terence Cooke of New York, the successor to the late Francis Cardinal Spellman.

Regression? At bottom, however, it was the roles played by Graham and Peale that gave the Nixon Inaugural its specific religious coloration. Raised a Quaker, Nixon's religious posture was shaped largely during the Eisenhower years when faith seemed simpler, surer and eminently more successful. Those were also the years when Graham and Peale made their greatest impact on American religion. To many observers, it appeared last week that the Inauguration had permitted the torch of civil religion to be passed back to a previous generation. Complained the *Christian Century* in a lead editorial: "We seem to have entered upon a time of increasing polarization between a re-established establishment piety—epitomized by the steady companionship of our new President with Norman Vincent Peale and Billy Graham—and the anti-establishment cults of the new Christian left."

In truth, the easy identification between God and the political judgment of the American people no longer seems credible to even those Christians of the moderate middle. Quite inadvertently, the Nixon Inauguration may have furthered the contemporary schism in the civil religion. Nonetheless, the new President seems determined to give his brand of faith a strong place in the White House. At the weekend, it was announced that Graham would preach at a special Sunday service for the Nixon family and Cabinet members in the East Room. The featured hymn selected for the service: "All Hail the Power."

COMMENTARY: PERSUASION BY INDUCTIVE ARRANGEMENT

This *Newsweek* essay on the religious aspects of President Nixon's inauguration ceremonies provides an excellent contrast in stance and style to the one on the same subject published in *Time* and appearing as a companion article in this book (p. 125). *Newsweek* places great stress upon the roles of Billy Graham and Dr. Norman Vincent Peale in the new administration, and among other things, it points out the repercussions these figures and events have had upon the dissident clergy, who do not share the optimism keynoting the inauguration.

Although much of this essay is given to a definition of the term serving as the title, *a civil religion,* its main message, or thesis, appears to emerge only in the final paragraph, wherein it is pointed out that "Quite inadvertently the Nixon Inauguration may have furthered the contemporary schism in the civil religion." This statement, like the one just preceding it, bears the full import of the essay. All that has been said regarding the clergymen and their contribution to what *Newsweek* editors call "a civil religion" leads to this important fact of a split between the various religious establishments.

Seen in this light, the essay builds to the point being made in the final paragraph and has, therefore, an *inductive* arrangement of its parts: the central idea, or generalization, comes *after* all of the relevant data have been presented. Looking at the essay as a whole, we find that the three editorial headings—*Solemnity, Optimism, Regression?*—indicate three main divisions. The first part defines "civil religion" and its role in American history. The second—"Optimism"—traces the influence of Billy Graham and Dr. Norman Vincent Peale on Mr. Nixon's speech and then introduces the nature of the opposition raised against these conservative viewpoints. The third main division —"Regression?"—deals with the reactions of the dissident clergy and laymen to the character of the incoming administration. This third part starts with the paragraph beginning, "Oddly enough, this is precisely what dissident clergy and laymen have been doing in opposing the war. . . ." and takes up the differences in traditions and attitudes existing between the conservatives and the dissenters.

As exemplified in this essay, the *inductive* arrangement provides a very effective means of presenting a stand on a highly controversial subject such as this one. It permits the presenting of facts and ideas from both sides without at first offending either party. Next, while giving additional details, it permits by means of comparison and contrast—either spelled out or implied—a gradual move toward the conclusion the writer has had in mind from the very outset. And then when the readers have been prepared for it, comes the thesis as a logical conclusion to all that has been said earlier. Psychologically, the inductive method of development can be an adroit and effective means of eliminating the initial hostility that the *deductive* order tends to arouse.

WHAT DOES IT SAY?

1. Reading between the lines of Billy Graham's prayer found in the opening paragraph, what do you think he takes for granted?

2. Which are some of "the major symbols of both faiths"—Jewish and Christian—that civil religion has appropriated?

3. In context, how do you interpret President Nixon's assurance: "We can build a great cathedral of the spirit"?

4. Why did Mr. Nixon speak of "a cup of despair" and then of "the chalice of opportunity"—what connotations do "cup" and "chalice" have?

5. What kind of public acts and declarations must the author have had in mind when he referred to "the beleagured religious Establishment"? Why "beleagured"?

6. In its context, does the expression "Nixon's religious posture" imply any lack of sincerity?

7. Do you know of any religious group of the kind *The Christian Century* calls "the anti-establishment cults of the new Christian left"?

8. Is there any special significance to be found in the final sentence: "The featured hymn selected for the service: 'All Hail the Power' "?

WHAT DO YOU THINK?

1. Write an essay explaining your views and observations on one of the following often controversial subjects. In order not to lose your possibly hostile readers, try to imitate the *Newsweek* kind of use of inductive arrangement.

   (a) Should clergymen take active part in everyday problems growing out of social and racial injustice?

   (b) Should prayers be permitted to be said at presidential inaugurations but not in public school classrooms?

   (c) Does God "interfere" with presidential elections and influence the events that lead to the election of a Republican or a Democrat?

   (d) Was it appropriate for the first astronauts who circled the moon and returned to earth to take turns in reading from *Genesis,* the first book of the Bible?

   (e) Does prayer aid in the preparation for final examinations?

   (f) The leaders of the French Revolution who executed King Louis XIV and Queen Marie Antoinette and then established "The Rule of Reason" said that if God did not exist, it would be necessary to invent God. Do you agree?

2. Looking at the record of the first months of Mr. Nixon's administration, write a report on his use of this "civil religion."

Are the Wasps Coming Back?
Have They Ever Been Away?
TIME ESSAY

It is a low-key intuition, not spiteful or malicious, but pervasive: in the minds of most Americans the incoming Nixon Administration seems to represent the comeback of the Wasp: the white Anglo-Saxon Protestant. True enough, the new President's Cabinet, with three Roman Catholics, is statistically no more Waspish than most in recent decades, even though it stirred comment for including no Negro or Jew. But people sense about Nixon's appointments, and his style, a tone of reassuring Wasp respectability and good manners. The forces that elected Nixon—those who most avidly supported him—are Wasp to the core; the "ethnic blocs" voted for Humphrey. With Nixon's accession, noted Norman Mailer, it is "possible, even likely, even necessary that the Wasp enter the center of our history again."

Exactly who it is that will take over the center is a problem of definition. Wasps are not so easily characterized as other ethnic groups. The term itself can be merely descriptive or mildly offensive, depending on the user and the hearer; at any rate, it has become part of the American idiom. In one sense, it is redundant: since all Anglo-Saxons are white, the word could be Asp. Purists like to confine Wasps to descendants of the British Isles; less exacting analysts are

Reprinted from *Time,* January 17, 1969, by permission from *Time,* The Weekly Newsmagazine; Copyright Time, Inc. 1969.

125

willing to throw in Scandinavians, Netherlanders and Germans. At the narrowest, Wasps form a select band of well-heeled, well-descended members of the Eastern Establishment; at the widest, they include Okies and Snopeses, "Holy Rollers" and hillbillies. Wasps range from McGeorge Bundy and Penelope Tree to William Sloane Coffin, Jr., and Phyllis Diller. Generously defined, Wasps constitute about 55% of the U.S. population, and they have in common what Columnist Russell Baker calls a "case of majority inferiority."

A Quiet Retreat

Sometimes Wasps are treated like a species under examination before it becomes extinct. At the convocation of intellectuals in Princeton last month, Edward Shils, professor of social thought at the University of Chicago, announced: "The Wasp has abdicated, and his place has been taken by ants and fleas. The Wasp is less rough and far more permissive. He lacks self-confidence and feels lost." Other observers feel that the growing dissension in American life is a clear sign that the Wasp has lost his sting, that his culture no longer binds. The new radicals and protesters are not in rebellion against Wasp rule as such, but they deride the Wasp's traditional values, including devotion to duty and hard work.

Although it is possible to exaggerate the decline of the Wasp, who has never really left the center of U.S. power, he is indisputably in an historical retreat. The big change came with the waves of migration from Europe in the 19th century, when many of his citadels—the big cities—were wrested from his political control. In a quiet fallback, the Wasps founded gilded ghettos—schools and suburbs, country clubs and summer colonies.

Lately, the non-Wasps have pursued them even there. A few years ago, Grosse Pointe, a Wasp suburb of Detroit, was notorious for rating prospective homeowners by a point system based on personal characteristics; Jews, Italians and "swarthy" persons almost invariably got so few points that they could not buy houses. Now all that has been abandoned, and Grosse Pointe has many Roman Catholic and Jewish residents. Downtown private clubs remain bastions of Wasp exclusiveness, but doors are opening. One recent example: Jews gained admission to the Kansas City Club in Kansas City, Mo., after an uproar over exclusionary policies; a rumor got out that the Atomic Energy Commission refused to locate a plant in the city because of private-club discrimination.

Non-Wasp groups are far better represented in Ivy League schools than they used to be: Jews, for instance, constitute about 25% of the student bodies. So traditional an Episcopal prep school as Groton now includes some 25 Roman Catholics, a dozen Negroes and three Jews. Jews stand out sharply in the nation's intellectual life, and Jewish novelists are beginning to overtake the fertile Wasp talent. Scarcely a single Wasp is a culture hero to today's youth; more likely he is the bad guy on the TV program, where names like Jones and Brown have replaced the Giovannis and O'Shaughnessys. The banker who made Skull and Bones is no model for undergraduates, writes Sociologist Nathan Glazer in *Fortune*. "Indeed, often the snobberies run the other way—the white Anglo-Saxon Protestant, generally from a small town or an older and duller suburb, is likely to envy the big-city and culturally sophisticated Jewish students."

Proper Wasps still rule in tight little enclaves of high society that are rarely cracked by newcomers. Yet anyone with a will—and money—can find a way to outflank Wasp society, which is often haunted by a sense of anachronism. Such is the hostility to the Veiled Prophet parade, an annual Wasp event in St. Louis, that the queen and her maids of honor last year had to be covered with a plastic sheet to protect them from missiles tossed from the crowd.

A Certain Security

But the Wasp retreat has by no means gone so far as to destroy his basic power—particularly strong in business and finance, considerable in politics, battered but tenacious in the social and moral field. Irishmen, Italians and Jews may have established themselves in construction, retailing, entertainment, electronics and light manufacturing, but big business and big banks belong to the Wasp. Almost 90% of the directors of the 50 largest corporations are Wasps. Similarly, about 80% of the directors of the ten largest banks are Wasps.

Wasps dominate the governing bodies of the richest universities in a ratio of four to one. More than four-fifths of the directors of the largest foundations are Wasps; of the 37 officers and directors of the Council on Foreign Relations, only one is non-Wasp. Under pressure of law and of the meritocratic "cult of performance," Wall Street law firms and brokerage houses are making room for more Jews and Catholics, but they are still overwhelmingly Wasp-controlled.

The Federal Government has always been the domain of the Wasp. Until John Kennedy, every U.S. President was a Wasp, and so was every Vice President except Charles Curtis (1929–33), who was the son of an Indian. Last fall's candidates, Nixon, Hubert Humphrey and George Wallace, were quite predictably Wasps. Although the civil service has been a traditional path of advancement for non-Wasps (half of Post Office workers in the large cities are Negroes), the prestigious departments, such as State, are still run by Wasps. Congress is a Wasp stronghold: the newly elected one consists of 109 Catholics, 19 Jews, 10 Negroes, 3 Greek Orthodox, 4 Orientals and almost 400 Wasps. Committee chairmanships are largely in the hands of Wasps. Enlisted men in the armed services are an ethnic mix, but the officers are heavily Wasp. Even in the cities they no longer control politically —Chicago or Cleveland—Wasps have much behind-the-scenes power. In several cities, Wasp business leaders have mobilized to aid the blacks, including the militants in the ghettos. Other ethnic politicians fear the erosion of their own power as the result of Wasp-Negro deals.

A Divided Majority

As for the Wasp's moral authority, it is clearly waning, but he still has an inimitable asset: the inner security inherited from his Protestant background and his expansive American experience. "If you are a Wasp, you have the confidence that the Establishment is yours and that you are on the top," says Novelist Herbert Gold. "There is the feeling that the love of a horsy woman comes to you as a birthright." Hollywood may be filled mainly with non-Wasps, but they still usually take Wasp names and act out Wasp fantasies in films. In Jewish novels, the central character is often driven to live a Wasp-like life. Herzog finds his ultimate solace in a little bit of land he owns in the Berkshires: "symbol of his Jewish struggle for a solid footing in white Anglo-Saxon Protestant America."

Wasp power is obscured by the divisions natural to a majority, which keep Wasps from coalescing into the kind of cohesive blocs that other groups have formed. The Republican Party is preeminently Wasp; yet it has been rent for generations by deep-seated disagreements. Norman Mailer characterized the alienated delegates lusting for liberal blood at the 1964 convention. In a typical Mailer caricature, he evoked a "Wasp Mafia where the grapes of wrath were stored. Not for nothing did the white Anglo-Saxon Protestants have a five-year subscription to *Reader's Digest* and *National Geographic,* high colonics and arthritis, silver-rimmed spectacles, punched-out bellies and that air of controlled schizophrenia which is the merit badge for having spent one's life on Main Street. Indeed, there was agreement that the war was between Main Street and Wall Street."

To some extent, Wasps are presiding over the dissolution of their own dominion, and they are proud of it. In a book he wrote four years ago, *The Protestant Establishment,* Sociologist E. Digby Baltzell criticized upper-class Wasps for establishing a caste system in many places. Today, he gives them credit for being neither "arrogant nor insensitive. They are the least prejudiced people as far as intermarriage is concerned. Catholics are much more prejudiced and Jews are the worst of all." The great assimilating Presidents of this century—the two Roosevelts—were quintessential Wasps.

The well-bred Wasp who rebels against the snobbishness and starchiness of his background is an almost classic figure in American life. Prominent Wasp families have contributed to the ranks of the current youthful revolutionaries.

Ultimately, Waspism may be more a state of mind, a pattern of behavior, than a rigid ethnic type. Some non-Wasps display all the characteristics normally associated with the most purebred Wasps. Consciously or not, they are Waspirants. Many people were surprised to learn that Edmund Muskie, who talked and looked like a Down East Yankee, was actually of Polish descent. Edward Brooke, who was successfully promoted for the U.S. Senate by civic-spirited Wasps, has all the attributes of a well-bred Wasp, as does Whitney Young, Jr. One doesn't have to be white, Anglo-Saxon and Protestant to be a Wasp in spirit. The Wasp aura is created by the right education, style, social position, genealogy, achievement, wealth, profession, influence or politics.

Thus Roman Catholics like William Buckley, Sargent Shriver and Ted Kennedy are pushed toward Waspdom by their associations, professions and life styles. Though German Jewish, Walter Lippmann is still a Waspirant. His clubs (Metropolitan, Cosmos, River) and his influence on opinion give him undeniable Wasp power. Wall Street Dynasts John Schiff and John Loeb may qualify, if they want, as honorary Wasps. So may Walt Whitman Rostow, who has been a top aide of Lyndon Johnson and beats most Wasps at tennis.

"The perfect candidate," wrote Harvard Professors Edward Banfield and James Wilson, "is of Jewish, Polish, Italian or Irish extraction and has the speech, dress, manners and the public virtues—honesty, impartiality and devotion for public interest—of the upper-class Anglo-Saxon."

A Sense of Public Service

Ironically, it was a member of a Roman Catholic dynasty, John F. Kennedy, who added new luster to Wasp ideals. He was such a model Wasp with his dry humor, his laconic eloquence and his lack of sentimentality, that he set a style which encouraged many authentic upper-class Wasps to take heart and to run for political office. John D. Rockefeller IV was one. He was followed by George Bush in Texas, William L. Saltonstall and John Winthrop Sears in Massachusetts and

Bronson La Follette in Wisconsin. "In previous times, you had to be born in a log cabin to be elected to office," notes John Jay McCloy, who has been called the board chairman of the U.S. Wasp Establishment. "Now, to be born with a silver spoon in your mouth often means you have a distinct advantage. This would seem to indicate that the tradition of the Adamses, Elihu Root and Henry Stimson is perhaps even greater today."

At his worst, the Wasp has been too repressive and rigid. At his best, he has stood for a certain selflessness, a sense of public service, a disinterestedness in the face of brawling passions. A feeling is growing that in this time of ideological rancor these are qualities worth reviving.

COMMENTARY: DEFINITION AS ARRANGEMENT

Who, what, and where are "the Wasps"? The *Time* essayist stresses the importance of these terms of recent coinage by linking them in his opening sentence with the Nixon administration. Highly aware also that he cannot leave his readers-on-the-run puzzled for even a moment, he also immediately spells out "Wasp" as being the initial letters of "White Anglo-Saxon Protestant." He does not stop there, however, as one might do if he were tossing the term about in a social conversation. He continues for another 2000 words to analyze and demonstrate the connotations (associated meanings) that "Wasp" has as a word signifying power in the United States.

In the second paragraph, the widest and narrowest range of meanings for the term support the dominance which this essay gives it. Presumably readers will want to know whether they are included in this "power" group or are to be considered as remaining outside it for reasons of race, religion, or national origin. Note how the naming of celebrities gives the term concrete and specific *referents*— that is, providing particular persons or things to which the term applies.

In listing groups like "Holy Rollers" and "hillbillies," the author employs another form of thinking associated with the process of definition: classification, wherein certain bodies or groups having similar characteristics are identified as classes, divisions, or types coming under the terms of the definition. If, for example, we define *coward* as a person who lacks courage, we can by means of this definition readily identify as classes of coward those who lack moral courage and those who lack physical courage, in the same manner that the author herein has identified hillbillies as a class of Wasps.

The essayist also supplies his readers with a dramatic *transition,* or bridging device, to link his first paragraph to his second one. In the first, he ends with a quotation from Norman Mailer saying the Wasp may "enter the center of our history again." This key term, "the center," appears in the first sentence of the following paragraph as the key word of what proves to be the *topic sentence* (one stating the main or central idea or fact being explained in that paragraph). At the end of this paragraph, we find another prominent author cited, and again his words—"a case of majority inferiority"—lead us into the topic being discussed in the third paragraph. These and other *allusions,* or references, to prominent authors—several of whom are Jewish and, therefore, non-Wasp—also add significance to the import of the term being defined.

One way of defining is to give the history of the events or forces generally included under the term being defined. The essayist adopts this method in summarizing the history of conflicts between Wasps and those he calls "non-Wasps," and he gives specific references to places and events in relating aspects of this antagonism to be found in cities, clubs, and universities.

Another means of defining is the pointing out of the peculiar advantages and disadvantages characterizing members included in the terms of the definition. These are spelled out in this essay as the various forms of power enjoyed historically by Wasps: power in business, finance, politics, and "the social and moral field." Four separate paragraphs in turn deal with each of these powers.

This essay serves, furthermore, as a fine example of how an initial definition can take on wider meanings as its subject matter suggests or "generates" them. Following the discussion of four power aspects, we come upon this enlargement of the original definition of *Wasp:* "Ultimately, Waspism may be more a state of mind, a pattern of behavior, than a rigid ethnic type." Immediately the author employs again the method of giving numerous, specific examples to make this generalization clear and definite. He concludes by suggesting the value for present times of still another aspect of Wasp qualities: "a certain selflessness, a sense of public service, a disinterestedness in the face of brawling passions."

Looking back over the whole essay, we can now see how the definition of *Wasp* has moved from a somewhat restricted meaning to include a wider and wider scope of significance. As a model it serves also as an excellent example of how professional writers derive their general concepts from specific, concrete things and situations. In the same way, if a general meaning occurs to you, look to find what individual incidents or persons have suggested it to you. Then use these as supporting illustrations or applications of your definition.

WHAT DOES IT SAY?

1. What does the author refer to when he speaks of President Nixon's "style"?

2. How can "schools and suburbs, country clubs and summer colonies" be spoken of as "gilded ghettos" for Wasps?

3. "Scarcely a single Wasp is a culture hero to today's youth"—who in the past have been regarded as Wasp heroes?

4. Jews and Catholics can enter Wall Street law firms and brokerage houses only "under pressure of law and of the meritocratic 'cult of performance.'" What is meant by those "pressures"?

5. The word *ethnic* appears frequently in this essay in expressions like "ethnic blocs," "ethnic groups," and "ethnic politicians." What does *ethnic* mean?

6. How can "a little bit of land" become a "symbol of his [Herzog's] struggle for a solid footing in white Anglo-Saxon Protestant America"?

7. In saying that Presidents Theodore Roosevelt and Franklin Delano Roosevelt were "quintessential Wasps," what possible facts could the author have had in mind?

8. What images does the expression "The U. S. Wasp Establishment" suggest to your imagination?

WHAT DO YOU THINK?

1. Try writing an essay of definition, like the *Time* essay, wherein, after a brief introduction, you begin with a more or less *denotative,* or dictionary definition, and then in two or more additional paragraphs show wider meanings and connotations for the term being defined. Remember to give specific examples illustrating the qualities of the thing defined. Suggested topics:

Hippies	Yippies
Cool cats	The private sector
Swinger	Careerist
Uncle Tom	Management
Black militant	The now generation
The dissident	Pop culture
Tourist	The establishment

2. Write an essay attempting to define yourself and your position or role as a student among many other students.

3. If you are one who believes that in the United States we have "a sick society," write an essay defining and illustrating what you mean by the term.

4. Define "racial hostility" as you yourself have become acquainted with various forms or degrees of it in recent years. Be sure to give supporting examples and explain situations.

5. Define and illustrate by specific cases one of the following terms as you know it through daily experience:

Blue-collar worker   Unemployable laborer

White-collar worker   Employer

Vietnam:
Journey To Nowhere
by PETER R. KANN

"But why do you want to take the train?" persisted the stationmaster. "You could ride a helicopter. Perhaps you could even travel by car. But the train is very slow and very dangerous."

Trains in Vietnam tend to be these days. The country has some 1,100 kilometers of main-line track and about an equal length of spur line, but only one-fourth of the track is being used, some of this only sporadically, because of the fighting.

The particular train in question here is a convertible cog mountain railway that runs, spasmodically, between this former French resort city in the central highlands and Phan Rang on the coastal plain some 60 kilometers east.

One recent morning three Americans, duly warned by the stationmaster, boarded the train. They were armed with one captured Chinese AK-47 automatic rifle, two grenades, a bunch of bananas and a bottle of wine. It was an inauspicious day for an excursion; a typhoon had struck the South Vietnamese coast, sending high winds and rain squalls whipping through the highlands.

Reprinted from *The Wall Street Journal*, November 12, 1968, where it originally appeared as part of "Three Americans Find Train Ride in Vietnam Is Slow and Perilous." Reprinted by permission.

The Train

The train consisted of a 39-year-old German engine; a flatcar loaded with rocks and scrap iron and used as a buffer to detonate and cushion the impact of mines; a baggage car carrying a soggy mattress, a bicycle with one wheel missing and a cracked fluorescent light bulb; a tank car containing either oil, water, or vegetables, depending on whom one asked, and a second baggage car harboring two Hondas, three Vietnamese Popular Force (PF) soldiers and the train chief in a snappy white pith helmet.

What fuel powered the engine? This also depended on whom one asked: The engineer, who should know, said oil; the brakeman said wood; one of the PF soldiers said vegetables.

At 8:45 on the dot, with a blast of its steam whistle, the old train chugged off into the mountain mist.

"What do you suppose the Vietcong do on a rainy day like this?" said Peter Collins, a U.S. Embassy political officer.

"They try to find a nice dry train to get warm in," said Robin Pell, a railroad expert with the Agency for International Development.

In the rear baggage car, the PF troopers alternately chuckled at the foolish Americans riding the train and sought to reassure them. "Don't worry," said one PF, "we protect the train." The three soldiers had been riding the train for nearly an entire week, he explained, and never once had been attacked. Challenging the foe, a second PF discharged two carbine rounds into the air and his companions nodded thoughtfully, then grinned.

The train proceeded for three kilometers across pine-forested hills and rolled to a stop at the Trai Mat station, a three-walled cabin inhabited by a goose. The PF soldiers unloaded the Hondas, smiled at the Americans and hopped off the train. "This is the end of our area of responsibility," said one, mounting his motorcycle and heading back toward Dalat.

As the train continued to the next station at Da Tho village, four kilometers distant, Mr. Lai, the train chief in the pith helmet, recounted recent highlights of the run. The train, he said, had been making the Dalat-Phan Rang run for 25 years. But it has been meeting its schedule only sporadically since 1966 due to Vietcong harassment: Bridges blown, track mined, the train stopped and boarded. Passenger service was discontinued several months ago.

"The Vietcong put many mines on the track. Last month four people were killed and I was thrown off the train by an explosion. In May the Vietcong stopped the train and took away five Vietnamese soldiers," lamented Mr. Lai. The train, he said, is scheduled to close down soon.

Photographs on pp. 136 and 137 courtesy of United Press International

"The view from the train is very pretty," he added. "It is too bad the rain and fog obscure it."

The train pulled into Da Tho village, where the flatcar with rocks and scrap iron was uncoupled and positioned in front of the engine. Seven Vietnamese Regional Force (RF) soldiers, led by an aspirant (third lieutenant) in an oversized trench coat and a sergeant in a black frogman jacket crisscrossed with bandoliers of ammunition, climbed aboard.

Fifteen minutes later the train had switched to cog track and was puffing up a gradual incline when the brakeman brought it to a grinding halt. A massive pine tree lay stretched across the track. "VC blockade?" Mr. Collins asked Mr. Pell. "VC blockade?" Sgt. Thuo asked Aspirant Hun.

On cautious inspection it was concluded that the tree had been felled by wind rather than by the enemy. Nevertheless, Aspirant Hun and two of his men moved about 20 meters down the track and fanned out in wedge formation to form a neatly geometric, if potentially porous, security perimeter.

The engineer, brakeman, train chief and baggage master climbed off the train, examined the fallen pine, and then began alternately hacking away at it with small axes and arguing about the futility of this exercise. The husky Americans tried, with no success, to roll the tree off the track. Aspirant Hun's security forces meanwhile were busy trying to light cigarets in the rainstorm. The engineer finally produced a rusty cable with which he attached the tree trunk to the engine, put the train in reverse, and pulled the tree off the track. Cheers resounded from the second baggage car, where four RF troops had remained, snug and dry, throughout the operation.

Next stop, four kilometers ahead, was Cau Dat village, where the train was greeted by the stationmaster, a wizened old man, barefoot, towel wrapped around his head like a turban, hands clutching a red signal flag and a lantern. A long discussion with the train crew ensued, the gist of it being that many more trees had blown onto the track further on. Continuing the trip would be impossible.

So the engineer put the train in reverse and headed back toward Dalat. One of the Americans was riding in the engine, watching the engineer toot his whistle to clear water buffalo off the track, while automatic weapons suddenly began cracking at close range. The engineer blanched. The American ducked. Two RF troops leaned out of the baggage car up front and waved. "We shot so the Vietcong will hear us and be afraid," they later explained.

At five minutes after noon the train pulled into Dalat station. "Perhaps the train will be able to travel farther tomorrow," says Mr. Sac, the engineer, who has driven the run for 25 years. "But soon the train will not travel at all. It is very sad, is it not? The Vietcong want to damage and destroy our train."

COMMENTARY: CHRONOLOGICAL ORDER

What is the difference between an essay and a short story having a chronological order (one of time sequence)? Is "Vietnam: Journey to Nowhere" an example of exposition or of narration? We have by now some quite definite ideas of the nature of essays, but we have not previously encountered one that appears to resemble a short story. Peter R. Kann's report of a train ride in the summer of 1968 does seem to be a kind of story, and it certainly leaves the reader with a single impression, as a good short story is supposed to do. It makes us feel that as defenders of their country the South Vietnam military are in as bad shape as is their railroad.

However, although having some aspects of a short story, this article written for the *Wall Street Journal* is exposition. For one thing, it lacks a central character of the kind we look for in a story, one with whom we can identify as we read of his attempts to cope with his situation of conflict. Mr. Kann's "news story" creates an impression, but the incidents of action do not build to the customary climax, nor was the element of suspense foremost in the mind of the writer. In short, it relies upon the order of time—"what happens first and then what comes next"—but remains mainly a reporter's essay or explanatory report, wherein the narration serves mainly as an aid to description and explanation.

When the subject matter is "a natural" for the use of such chronological order, the writer does well to adopt it. We can rightly surmise that Mr. Kann arranged to take this train trip in order to see for himself what he could learn of the railroad's condition and the competence and morale of its crew and defenders. As an experienced journalist he was primarily interested in giving his readers the essential "who-what-when-where-why" details of this segment of the war, but like so many other reporters indebted to that great earlier newspaper correspondent, Ernest Hemingway, he also wanted to make his report interesting and dramatic. So instead of writing a detailed report summarizing the quantities of information he must have had access to, he chose to make his report an incident-by-incident account of what occurred on this one typical run.

He begins with a narrative-hook opening by introducing us at once to a fantastic situation, as stated in the words of the stationmaster, ending with the warning: "But the train is very slow and very dangerous"—a warning that arouses the interest of the reader. This device in fiction is called "the note of forewarning" or "foreshadowing," since it creates suspense by promising dramatic surprises.

Two brief, informative paragraphs explain the danger and the condition of this particular railroad and bring us to the beginning of the trip, but without any mention of the author's being one of the passengers: "One recent morning three Americans . . . boarded the train." The grim note about the typhoon adds to the sense of danger and also reminds us of the hazards of Vietnam climate that the fighting men there must expect.

Two more short paragraphs of descriptive details revealing ridiculous features of the train and the military show what an impossible venture the trip promises to be. The remarks exchanged by the author's two companions heighten the tension, but note that none of his own are added to the dialogue. He relies upon his *stance* as ironic and anonymous observer to speak for him through his selection of details, such as those describing the speech and acts of the soldiers who accompany the train as guards for a few miles.

Further incidents with other guards and the willing train crew are described as being equally pathetic and sadly comic. We infer that the American who was riding in the engine was the author. He ends his report with the ironic words of the veteran engineer and wants his readers to draw their own conclusions from them: "The Vietcong want to damage and destroy our train."

Within the chronological framework of this "news story" we can detect many features usually found in narratives: description, explanation, and suspenseful incident. On the whole, however, this piece is expository in that its purpose is to explain a state of affairs. Needless to say, it is an excellent example of its kind of journalistic report, but in your own essay experiments with chronological order do not hesitate to use the first person pronoun, "I," if you have difficulty in emulating the self-effacement of Mr. Kann.

WHAT DOES IT SAY?

1. How many miles of track is 1100 kilometers? What distance in miles was the train trip run of 60 kilometers?

2. What do you think was the purpose of the "soggy mattress" carried in the baggage car?

3. Wherein lies the irony of the PF who told the Americans, "Don't worry, we protect the train"?

4. From his comments, how would you describe the character of Mr. Lai, the train chief?

5. Why is the third lieutenant called "Aspirant Hun"?

6. What are we to conclude regarding the two RF troops who fired their automatic weapons and later explained: "We shot so the Vietcong will hear us and be afraid"?

7. Is there really anything appropriate in the closing quoted sentence: "The Vietcong want to damage and destroy our train"?

WHAT DO YOU THINK?

1. Relate in *chronological order* how feelings and attitudes—your own or someone else's near to you—regarding compulsory military service change and develop as the draft registration age of 18 nears and then finally comes.

2. If as a service man you have observed South Vietnamese soldiers in action, relate that experience in the light of your own judgment of their performance.

3. If you have witnessed, or participated in any protest action involving large numbers of people, describe in chronological order how the event developed and ended. Be sure to make your report convey your present judgment of the aims and results of that social action.

4. Among the current views on the Asian policy of the United States, choose the one that you consider the best under the present circumstances and defend it.

5. Relate in chronological order what you learned while undergoing a somewhat disturbing experience in doing one of the following:

Hunting	Hitch hiking
Driving late at night	Buying a car
Skiing	Walking at night
Skin diving	Having a wrong roommate
Bowling	Attending a festival
Losing a job	Physical conditioning
Being falsely accused	Being a stranger

Before Your Kid Tries Drugs

by STANLEY F. YOLLES, M.D.

Until quite recently, most parents of teen-agers were not especially concerned with facts about drug abuse. The use and misuse of new and ancient mind-altering preparations were largely matters of medical, pharmaceutical and, as regards control, legal interest. Any compendium on "what every parent should know" might comfortably exclude the subject.

No longer. Today our pill-oriented society is alarmed and confused over the growing abuse of drugs among young people. Waves of shock follow in the wake of reports of campus-wide pot. The word "marijuana" has, like it or not, infiltrated the nation's playgrounds.

And the problem is real. Drugs such as marijuana, the amphetamines, the barbiturates, the opiates, and LSD have become pot, speed, bennies, goofballs, junk, and acid in the world of youth whose innocence frequently blurs the distinction between being turned-on and turned-off.

As adults whose lives may include some acquaintance with drugs, such as alcohol, tranquilizers and other pills, we naturally desire to protect those who are too young to make mature and informed

Reprinted from *The New York Times Magazine,* November 17, 1968. © 1968 by the New York Times Company. Reprinted by permission of the publication and author.

decisions. The issues surrounding the use of dangerous drugs are many. Not the least of these is the law. The law-breaking use of illicit drugs can jeopardize not only health but the pursuit of careers. And for those youngsters whose curiosity may lead from experiment to regular use of mind-affecting chemicals, there are the potential threats of stunted development and alienation.

Fortunately, there is some evidence that the "Now Generation" holds a healthy respect for the facts and for the findings of science. While parental panic and admonition are little value as guidance and tend to stoke the fires of adolescent rebellion, knowledge of the facts may help. The current wane in the use of LSD, for example, may be traced at least in part to the reported possibility of genetic damage.

As the principal Federal agency responsible for stimulating research on drug abuse, the National Institute of Mental Health is vitally interested in strengthening our arsenal of knowledge and in helping to make the facts available to the public. Recently, the Institute published a series of leaflets which are being distributed widely throughout the country.[1] They attempt to answer some of the most frequently asked questions surrounding the use of marijuana, LSD, narcotics, barbiturates and amphetamines. Here are some of the points about drugs made in the N.I.M.H. booklets:

LSD

A powerful man-made chemical, lysergic acid diethylamide, generally called LSD, was first developed in 1938 from ergot alkaloids. A single ounce is enough to provide 300,000 of the usual doses. A mind-altering drug, LSD is legally classed as an hallucinogen, as are peyote, mescaline, psilocybin, DMT and STP. LSD is used legally only for controlled research purposes. It is illicitly produced in makeshift laboratories. Users refer to it as "acid."

An average dose of LSD, amounting to a speck, has effects that last from 8 to 10 hours. Users take it in a sugar cube, on a cracker, on a cookie or can lick it off a stamp or other impregnated object. The drug increases the pulse and heart rate, causes a rise in blood pressure and temperature, dilated eye pupils, shaking of the hands and feet, cold sweaty palms, a flushed face or paleness, shivering, chills with goose-pimples, a wet mouth, irregular breathing, nausea, loss of appetite, and distortion of the physical senses.

People who use LSD report a number of effects. The first effects,

[1] "LSD" (PHS 1828). "Marihuana" (PHS 1829). "The Up and Down Drugs" (PHS 1830) and "Narcotics" (PHS 1827) are available from Superintendent of Documents, U.S. Government Printing Office, Washington, D.C. 20402 for 5 cents each or 100 copies for $3.25 with the exception of "Marihuana," which costs $3.75 per 100 copies.

they indicate, are likely to be sudden changes in their physical senses. Walls may appear to move, colors seem stronger and more brilliant. They "see" unusual patterns unfolding before them. Flat objects seem to become three-dimensional. Taste, smell, hearing and touch seem more acute. One sensory impression may be translated or merged into another: music may appear as a color, and colors seem to possess taste.

A confusing yet common reaction among users is the simultaneous experience of strong, opposite emotions; they may feel simultaneously happy and sad, depressed and elated, or relaxed and tense. They report sensations of losing the normal feeling of boundaries between body and space and get the notion they can float or fly. Effects can be different at different times in the same individual. Responses, even in carefully controlled studies, cannot be predicted. For this reason, users refer to "good trips," or "bad trips," to describe their experience.

The LSD user loses his sense of time, though he may remain conscious. He is able to reason logically, up to a point, and usually remembers the effects after the drug wears off. He may report, for example, the fascination he felt over an object such as a chair or a vase. On larger doses, he may feel mystical and report a sense of rebirth or fresh insight. Studies fail to support the theory that LSD increases creativity.

Hospital studies report the following reactions: Panic—the user grows frightened because he cannot stop the drug's action, and he fears he is losing his mind. Paranoia—he becomes increasingly suspicious, feeling that someone is trying to harm him or control his thinking. This feeling may last some 70 hours after the drug has worn off. Recurrence (also known as "flashbacks")—days, weeks, or months after LSD use is stopped, sights and sensations may recur.

Long-lasting mental illness may result if a non-medically supervised experience becomes acutely disturbing. The strange sensations and clash of moods caused by the drug can be overwhelming even for a mature person. For young people who are undergoing emotional development and transition, the effects can be even more frightening.

Just how LSD works in the body is not yet known. But it seems to affect the levels of certain chemicals in the brain and to produce changes in the brain's electrical activity. Animal experiments suggest that the brain's normal filtering and screening out process becomes blocked, causing it to become flooded with unselected sights and sounds. Studies of chronic users indicate that they may continue to suffer from an overload of stimulation to their senses. Frequently, effects recur months after the drug is discontinued.

Long-term effects of LSD use are under close investigation. Short-term or immediate dangers include the user's sensation that he can fly or float with ease, and that he is invincible. Accidental deaths

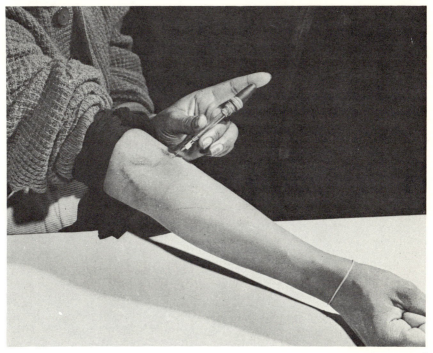

Courtesy of United Press International

have been reported. Users who suffer "bad trips" undergo temporary or longer-lasting psychosis. Chromosomal changes observed in LSD users have raised concern among scientists that these breaks may cause birth defects in the offspring of users.

Marijuana

A drug found in the flowering tops and leaves of the Indian hemp plant, *cannabis sativa,* marijuana grows in mild climates in countries around the world. The leaves and flowers of the plant are dried and crushed or chopped into small pieces and smoked in short cigarettes or pipes. It can be sniffed or taken in food. The cigarettes are commonly known as reefers, joints, and sticks. The smoke is harsh, and smells like burnt rope or dried grasses, with a sweetish odor. Its use is restricted and subject throughout the world to legal sanctions. There is no known medical use for marijuana. Pot, tea, grass, weed, Mary Jane, hash and kif are all names for marijuana.

The long-term physical effects are not yet known. The drug cannot yet, therefore, be considered medically safe. The research needed to weigh the effects of chronic use is in its earliest stages. Recent synthesis of the drug's active ingredient, *tetrahydrocannabinol,* now permits such investigation. The more obvious physical reactions include rapid heart beat, lowering of body temperature, and reddening of the eyes. The drug also changes blood sugar levels, stimulates the appetite, and dehydrates the body.

Effects on the emotions and senses vary widely, depending on the amount and strength of the marijuana used. The social setting in which it is taken and what the user expects also influence his reaction to the drug. Usually, the effect is felt quickly, in about 15 minutes after inhaling the smoke of the cigarette, and can last from 2 to 4 hours. Reactions range from depression to a feeling of excitement. Some users, however, experience no change of mood at all.

Sense of time and distance frequently becomes distorted. A minute may seem like an hour. Something near may seem far away. Any task or decision requiring good reflexes and clear thinking is affected by the drug. For this reason, driving is dangerous while under its influence. One of the more subtle results of regular marijuana use by young people lies in its influence on their personality growth and development—something that we have not determined as yet. Scientific findings, however, seem to point to rather deleterious effects.

Some investigators challenge the common belief that the drug is innocuous. In a survey reported in Boston last May, a group of West Coast researchers found that among 2,700 practicing mental health professionals, 1,887 patients with adverse reactions to marijuana were seen over a period of 18 months. At the same professional meeting, two researchers studying the "behavioral toxicity" of marijuana reported that their preliminary findings indicated that it may not be the "benign euphoriant" commonly alleged. Dr. Lincoln D. Clark and Edwin N. Nakashima of the University of Utah held that ". . . the very unpredictability of marijuana on different individuals and on the same individual at different times and under different conditions increases the risk to the user."

Stimulant Drugs

Amphetamines, first produced in the 1920's for medical use, are stimulants to the central nervous system. Best known for the ability to combat fatigue and sleepiness, they are also sometimes used to curb appetite. Under the supervision of a physician they may be used legally for medical purposes. The most commonly abused stimulants are Benzedrine, Dexedrine and Methedrine. Pep pills, bennies and speed are common names.

These drugs, Methedrine and Dexedrine, do not produce physical dependence. The body does, however, develop a tolerance which requires increasingly large doses. They increase the heart rate, raise the blood pressure, cause palpitations, dilate the pupils and cause dry mouth, sweating, headache, diarrhea and paleness. Action of the heart and metabolism is speeded up through stimulation of the release of *norepinephrine,* a substance stored in nerve endings, which then becomes concentrated in the higher centers of the brain. Exhaustion and temporary psychosis, which may result from abuse of stimulants, may require hospitalization.

The injection of Methedrine into a vein, a highly dangerous practice known as "speeding," has aroused medical authorities. "Speeding" may result in critical serum hepatitis. When injected in unaccustomed high doses, the drug can cause death.

Used without medical prescription, for kicks or staying awake for long periods, these drugs can drive a person to do things beyond his physical endurance that leave him exhausted. Heavy doses may cause a temporary toxic psychosis (mental derangement) requiring hospitalization. This is usually accompanied by auditory and visual hallucinations. Abrupt withdrawal after heavy abuse can result in deep and suicidal depression. Long-term heavy users are usually irritable, unstable and, like other chronic drug abusers, show social, intellectual and emotional breakdown.

Sedatives

These belong to a large family of drugs which relax the nervous system. The best known are the barbiturates, first produced in 1846, from barbituric acid. They range from the short-acting, fast-starting pentobarbital (Nembutal) and secobarbital (Seconal) to the long-acting, slow-starting phenobarbital (Luminol), amobarbital (Amytal) and butabarbital (Butisol). The short-acting preparations are the ones most commonly abused. They are called barbs and goof-balls.

Taken in normal, medically supervised doses, barbiturates mildly depress the action of the nerves, skeletal muscles and the heart muscle. They slow down the heart rate and breathing, and lower the blood pressure. In higher doses, the effects resemble alcoholic drunkenness: confusion, slurred speech, staggering and deep sleep. These drugs produce physical dependence. Body tolerance to them requires increasingly higher doses.

If the drug is withdrawn abruptly, the user suffers withdrawal sickness with cramps, nausea, delirium and convulsions, and in some cases, sudden death. Withdrawal must take place in a hospital over a period of several weeks on gradually reduced doses.

Large doses are potentially lethal. Any dosage may cause accidents because perception of objects becomes distorted, reactions and response are slowed. Barbiturates are a leading cause of automobile accidents, especially when taken with alcohol. Users may react to the drug more strongly at one time than at another. They may become confused about how many pills they have taken, and die of an accidental overdose. Barbiturates are a leading cause of accidental poison deaths in the United States, and are frequently implicated in suicides.

Narcotics

The term narcotics refers, generally, to opium and painkilling drugs made from opium, such as heroin, morphine, methadone, and codeine. These and other opiates are obtained from the juice of the poppy fruit. Several synthetic drugs, such as demerol and nalorphine, are also classed as narcotics. Cocaine, made from cocoa leaves, and marijuana are classed legally but not chemically as narcotic drugs. Heroin is the narcotic most used by today's addicts. It is often called junk, H, snow, stuff or smack.

Heroin depresses certain areas of the brain and other parts of the nervous system. It reduces hunger, thirst, the sex drive and feelings of pain. When a person addicted to heroin stops the drug, withdrawal sickness sets in. He may sweat, shake, get chills, diarrhea, nausea and suffer sharp abdominal and leg cramps. Recent findings show that the body's physical dependence on heroin lasts much longer than previously thought. Unexpectedly pure or large doses can and do result in death.

Typically, the first emotional reaction to heroin is an easing of fear and a relief from worry. Feeling "high" may be followed by a period of inactivity bordering on stupor. The drug appears to dull the edges of reality. Addicts have reported that heroin "makes my troubles roll off my mind," and "it makes me feel more sure of myself."

While medical treatments have been established to cure physical dependence on the drug, psychological dependence on heroin as a way to escape facing life may take extended rehabilitation.

The term "addiction" is most commonly applied to the abuse of heroin and other opiates. Authorities now think in terms of drug "dependence" rather than addiction. Dependence can be physical or psychological—or both. With true narcotics, the abuser suffers both. He is hooked as his body becomes physically dependent on the drug. Further, his body grows tolerant to the drug, which means that repeated and larger doses are required to achieve the same effects.

One of the points made to parents by pot-smoking youngsters concerns adult use of alcohol. "Well, you drink, don't you?" they are wont to respond, thrusting home with all the thrill of a newly discovered challenge. The analogy is pale. In the first place, the use of alcoholic beverages by persons over 21 is not against the law. Secondly, the immoderate use of alcohol as a crutch by some people does nothing to recommend this or other chemical means of "copping out." To the contrary, problem drinking and alcoholism are currently subjects of intensive medical and social research. Thirdly, the acceptability of moderate social drinking assumes that adults are mature enough to make mature decisions as to their behavior. And finally, there is the irrefutable fact that the fresh young years of personality growth and development are dangerously inappropriate for any chemical means of confounding reality.

As authorities well recognize, neither laws nor awareness of the medical facts can themselves secure drug abuse prevention. Nor can we stop people from using alcohol or cigarettes as support or as a bandage for their psychic wounds. Ours is a drug-oriented culture. From aspirin to sleeping pills, from tranquilizers to the "pill," Americans of all ages are ingesting drugs in greater variety and greater number than ever before.

It is not so much the phenomenon of use, however, but the mis-use and abuse of drugs that bears close investigation. Why do people choose to distort or to ward off reality through chemical means? Perhaps we deal with deep-rooted feelings of alienation. Alienation among the young has been characterized as "rebellion without a cause . . . rejection without a program . . . a refusal of what is without a vision of what should be." As scientists, we are left to probe whatever reasons can be found for this sad anomaly.

COMMENTARY: CLASSIFICATION AS ARRANGEMENT

After having characterized our society as being "pill-oriented," Dr. Yolles, in the third paragraph of his introduction, lists the kinds of drugs familiar to many young people by their slang names: "pot, speed, bennies, goof-balls, junk, and acid." Each of these drugs belongs to a class or general category, and these classes form the major divisions or parts of his article.

His general purpose and subject matter—to summarize the recently published National Institute of Mental Health booklets on drugs—pretty well dictated this kind of arrangement. But in adopting this pattern of development, he had to decide which one of these drugs he should discuss first and which one last. If we take a second look at that third paragraph listing, we can venture a guess as to why he arranged them here in this particular sequence. (Twice, later on he makes changes in this order.) Certainly the most familiar of these drugs is "pot," or marijuana; he says it has even ". . . infiltrated the nation's playgrounds." Pot is thus a logical choice to head the list, but for a good reason it is not the first discussed in the body of the essay.

Throughout this arranging in some kind of effective sequence, he can be seen striving for the psychological effect of *climax*. He ends this first list with "acid" probably for the reason that it is widely known as LSD and recently as a possibly dangerous, "mind-affecting" chemical. The order of climax presumes that readers, once their interest has been aroused, will keep plowing ahead with the anticipation that something of special interest awaits them at the end of the dramatic sequence. This essay builds and sustains interest by creating an air of suspense, and inducing readers to explore the dread fascination of this world of forbidden drugs. Once Dr. Yolles gets into the body of his essay, he runs the gamut from LSD to narcotics, a class of truly dangerous drugs.

As his *stance* and *thesis* clearly indicate, Dr. Yolles does not intend to exploit the melodrama inherent in his subject. Instead, he announces that he is giving the scientific facts about these drugs as found and reported by the Institute of which he is the director. Although in the opening he is addressing himself to the parents and identifies with them ("we naturally desire to protect those who are too young to make mature and informed decisions"), he strives to be totally objective. His language is always restrained and matter-of-fact, even in the introduction where writers tend to be somewhat shrill in dealing with such an explosive subject. His modesty is also apparent, for without an editorial footnote, we would not know that he is the director of the Institute.

As one would expect, he provides a great many details supporting the conclusions reached by the Institute on each of these various classes of drugs. He carefully defines each and relates such stimulant drugs as Methedrine and Dexedrine to their generic class of Amphetamines, and he does the same for various sedatives and narcotics. Throughout, until the conclusion, he remains factual, even in stating dangers and warnings.

In the concluding three paragraphs, he becomes somewhat "the counselor" but with very little change from the *tone* of his introduction. His final views and recommendations remain cool and properly objective as befits scientific explanation.

WHAT DOES IT SAY?

1. What kinds of behavior do you think of when you read that the "regular use of mind-affecting chemicals" may lead to "stunted development and alienation"?

2. Why is LSD classed as a "hallucinogen"?

3. According to this article, what constitutes "a bad trip"?

4. Does calling marijuana "pot," "tea," "grass," "weed," "Mary Jane," "hash" or "kif" make this drug more appealing?

5. If a drug like marijuana really is a "benign euphoriant," how "innocuous" a "behavioral toxicity" would it have?

6. Does calling Benzedrine, Dexedrine, and Methedrine "pep pills," "bennies," and "speed" make these stimulants sound less harmful?

7. What is meant by saying that the abusive use of stimulants may result in a "temporary toxic psychosis"?

8. To which class of drugs do the following belong: Nembutal, Seconal, Luminol, Amutal, and Butisol? How do they differ from "barbs" or "goof-balls"?

WHAT DO YOU THINK?

1. People who act in a manner considered "abnormal" or "strange" by others will probably exhibit certain habitual mannerisms and speech patterns. Write an essay classifying and describing in detail the types of such behavior you have noticed as being characteristic of *one* of the following:

Alcoholics	Salesmen
Smokers	Campus police
Beggars	Pill takers
Athletes	Dog walkers
Folk singers	Drag racers
Poets	Hairdressers
Car mechanics	Lifeguards

2. A few weeks after the publication of Dr. Yolles' article in *The New York Times Magazine, Time* published an article on the effects of marijuana, which begins with the following passage. Read it and then write an essay comparing its conclusions with those of Dr. Yolles and end by stating your own considered views.

> Practically everybody, whether doctor or layman, pothead or puritan, has been expressing dogmatic opinions for years about the effects of marijuana on its users. It therefore came as a surprise last week when a team of Harvard and Boston University investigators reported that

they had just conducted the first truly scientific tests ever made on the subject. Their findings, which appear in *Science* magazine, confirm some popular ideas about marijuana's effects and expose others as completely false. The drug, the investigators concluded, "appears to be a relatively mild intoxicant, with minor, real, short-lived effects." It seems to have a greater effect on thinking and perception than on reflexes and coordination.[1]

3. Write a letter of reaction to one of the speakers responsible for one of the following statements:

   (a) "I'd kill the sonofabitch if I ever found he was smoking pot."
   (b) "I smoke pot because it makes the world a beautiful place instead of a place filled with narrow-minded bigots like my father."
   (c) "Anyone who tries to say that fewer than half the students in any high school in Southern California have taken pot doesn't know what he's talking about."
   (d) "None of us know anything about it. It's so new, and I'm scared for my child!"
   (e) "The kids know more about drugs than their parents, and the kids know that they know more."
   (f) "Drugs are experimentation of the present, and if we are to prevent their misuse, abuse, and habitation in lieu of social participation, we must convince youth that, existentially, there is something worthwhile in the future."
   (g) "Facts and positive motivation are what young people need to help make a sound decision should they one day face the pressure of 'going along' with the drug-abuse crowd."
   (h) "I am willing to accept as fact that marijuana is not physically addictive, but based on what I believe to be considerable experience and direct contact with those concerned, I refuse to accept the fact that it is not psychologically and progressively addictive."
   (i) "I had not realized that once the decision was made, once I took LSD, I would never see the world quite the same again. At that time I believed E. E. Cumming's line, 'Once is never the beginning of enough'."

[1] *Time* Magazine, December 20, 1968.

SOME NOTES
ON THE
LIBRARY PAPER

As everyone sooner or later discovers, no matter how rich and varied his fund of experience and reading may be, it does not always provide him with sufficient information when he needs more facts and viewpoints to help him make up his mind on an important question. In such a situation the intelligent person seeks the aid of a well-stocked library and its staff of trained librarians.

Space here allows for only a brief introduction to this most important subject of the "library" or "research" essay. Let us begin by stressing that such a source paper differs from a sheer "opinion" paper in these fundamental points: (1) the "opinion" paper, or essay, usually represents "off-the-top-of-my-head" thinking and presentation of "facts," but the library paper at least indicates that an effort has been made to discuss the topic in the light of opinions and evidence obtained from several published sources; (2) the "opinion" paper usually is personal and highly subjective in tone, whereas the library one has the appeal of at least appearing to present conclusions which have been reached after consultation with other minds.

If the purpose of scholarship is to learn how to discover substantial facts, how to sort out and judge the validity of data, and then to present conclusions in an orderly manner, the library paper can be said to be the more "scholarly." Certainly it is the one college students are expected to master to some degree for their preparation of term papers and class reports.

The following essay, "The Old Police and New Violence," is an example of what a very cursory sampling of library sources can quickly provide on a current topic. It is not meant to be a study-in-depth, carefully and fully researched, as a scholarly paper should be. Rather, this short piece serves to show how any student can, in a very short time, find additional facts and views to support or balance his own views and experience.

Here are some of the basic library sources consulted in preparing this essay, the ones students come to know as soon as they learn their way around the library: *Readers' Guide to Periodical Literature, Social Science and Humanities Index, Essay and General Literature Index,* and *The New York Times Index.* Because of the timeliness of this topic, only very late supplements to these guides were used to find possibly helpful articles and chapters of new books.

Footnotes give the sources of quotations and any facts or ideas that lie outside the realm of common knowledge. They thus indicate and acknowledge the writer's debt to other authors and give the publications due credit in a form recommended by the documentary guide of the Modern Language Association (MLA). Whatever facts or views are considered to be known by anyone at all informed on the subject need not be credited with a footnote, for footnotes serve to give an individual source all due credit or else to add supplementary information.

The Old Police and New Violence
by ALEXANDER SCHARBACH

At one time, with its flashing light, siren, and two grim-faced officers, a patrol car was a symbol of authority and power. It represented the property-owning community and its values as a way and order of life never expected to change. But today, as they frankly admit, those same police officers ride in fear through city streets they once dominated. "You never can tell when you're going to round a corner and run into an ambush," commented one partolman over a television broadcast in December, 1968.[1] Probably never in the history of the United States has the authority image of the policeman been challenged more than it is today, or has the image of their law enforcement agencies been poorer among the populace.

In a country always mindful of its violent past, policemen have generally been marginal figures except in movie and television westerns, but the recent virulent attacks upon them seem to have come from their use of police dogs, electric prods, and general violence as witnessed by millions of television viewers during the Civil Rights marches. This has also brought into sharp focus the thin line between local law and moral rights. In addition, the helplessness of city police in dealing with riots in Watts, Newark, and especially

[1] "The People Are the City," NBC-TV broadcast, December, 1968.

Detroit further revealed the inadequacies and weaknesses of urban police forces. Accounts of police "brutality," such as John Hershey's *The Algiers Motel Incident*, added to the storm of indignation with its analysis of how "three of the young blacks—Carl Cooper, Auburey Pollard and Fred Temple—were savagely beaten and then killed by short-range shotgun blasts."[2] But it was what Alistair Cooke, the British journalist, called "The Chicago Shambles" in describing the police violence in that city during the presidential Democratic convention of 1968 that was most instrumental in arousing the general public against the police. Mr. Cooke, however, did not blame *all* of the Chicago police. Note the following passage:

> Several hundred youngsters—hippies, earnest, decent youngsters, well-known agitators, McCarthy idealists, hoodlums, a very mixed bunch indeed—were injured, and 40-odd were clubbed and wounded. We saw them, you saw them, everybody saw them on television: scenes of gallivanting brutality that chilled the blood. It seems that the mayor had made the decision to surround the main hotel with the toughest cops in Chicago. It was a disastrous decision, for it exposed to all of us a panicky, sadistic minority, while the 90-odd percent of the rest of the force tramped around the town helpless to say that they were another breed.[3]

It was this same minority of the Chicago police force that President Johnson's Comission on Violence branded as "rioters." Yet, it must be pointed out, a Gallup Poll showed that 56 percent of the American public approved of what Mayor Daley's police had done.[4]

Distrust of the police grows also out of a knowledge of their shirking their duty, as when readers of a national magazine encounter statements such as these: "Crime in the U.S. rose 19% in the first nine months of 1968 over the same period last year. . . . Yet the sorry fact is that while the cities sleep, so do a fair number of their on-duty policemen." So widespread is this catnap practice that it has different names in various cities. In Boston it is called "holing"; in Washington, D.C., "huddling," and in New York City, "cooping." Readers are not mollified to learn that these police are "all zonked out" because of having to "moonlight" to earn enough to support their families or because they cannot grow accustomed to rotating night duty shifts.[5]

For years the complaint against the police raised by the Black community of every major city has been "brutality" and "racism." A minor incident such as a routine traffic arrest can set off riots, and it is not only the militants among the Blacks who scorn and challenge

---

[2] *Ramparts* (August 10, 1968), 30.
[3] Alistair Cooke, "The Chicago Shambles," *The Listener* (September, 1968), 290.
[4] *Time* (October 4, 1968), 27.
[5] *Time* (December 27, 1968), 60.

the police. Acts such as the shooting of a 15-year-old boy caught looting during a riot brought forth bitter condemnation against the police, raising the question whether a human life was not worth more than property, yet when outnumbered police stood by and let the looting of stores and shops go unchecked, cries for "law and order" arose also against those same police. This last reaction provided the substance for former governor George Wallace's standard campaign speech: "I think the police ought to be allowed to enforce the law. I think they have to be allowed to use whatever measures are necessary to prevent the breakdown of law and order, and then if it does break down, they ought to be allowed to use whatever measures are necessary to stop it."[6] In his campaign speeches, President Richard Nixon also stressed the note of "law and order."

As a result of this kind of all-out support of the police, the residents of the Black ghettos came more than ever to identify "law and order" with further repression. As one Black peace movement leader protested: "It's a horrible phrase, a euphemism for racial repression. First you had slavery. Then you had Jim Crow laws. Then it was called 'separate but equal.' Now it is called 'law and order'."[7]

On university and college campuses across the United States students also have too often experienced the kind of encounters with police that *Newsweek* reporter Peter Barnes describes as follows: "In Berkeley, under cover of Governor Reagan's three-month-old 'state of extreme emergency,' police have also gone on a riot, displaying a lawless brutality equal to that of Chicago, along with weapons and techniques that even the authorities in Chicago did not dare employ: the firing of buckshot at fleeing crowds and unarmed bystanders, and the gassing—at times for no reason at all—of entire streets and portions of a college campus."[8]

Anthropologists and psychologists have their own explanations for the prevalent distrust of the police. They find that the man who wants to become "a cop" has "a tendency to be suspicious, act fast, take risks, be aggressive and obey authority." In Chicago, policemen are often eldest sons who are likely to have had harsh fathers; in Detroit, "they usually come from the bottom 25% of their high school class." In Berkeley, the policeman "pictures himself as the crime fighter standing alone against the Mongol hordes, without the support of the public, the politicians or the courts." Too many police are found to be "either-or" judges and resent bitterly the behavior of young people and Blacks who differ from their views of decency and propriety.[9]

[6] Associated Press interview (October 13, 1968).
[7] "The Fear Campaign," *Time* (October 4, 1968), 23.
[8] Peter Barnes, " 'An Outcry': Thoughts on Being Tear Gassed," *Newsweek* (June 2, 1969), 37.
[9] "The Police Need Help," *Time* (October 4, 1968), 26–27.

Their being compared unfavorably with the British police has further damaged the prestige of American officers. A British anthropologist describes the status enjoyed by the "Bobby" in these terms: "Increasingly during the past century, the English policeman has been for his peers not only a model of respect but also a model of the ideal male character, self-controlled, possessing more strength than he has to call into use except in the gravest emergency, fair and impartial, serving the abstractions of peace and justice rather than any personal allegiance or sectional advantage."[10] Perhaps another reason the British Bobbies enjoy such respect is that they do not carry guns or use chemicals or other weapons to control crowds.

Although violent crime is on the rise in England and demonstrations such as those against the war in Vietnam have become more militant, the police in Britain are not crying for weapons in order to maintain "law and order." One American reporter observed a recent attempt of 6000 marchers in London to storm the American Embassy. They were held off by 800 officers who stopped them by doing nothing more than linking arms and keeping cool while joshing good humoredly with those pressing against their line. When one student burned the British flag in front of them, a constable joshed him: "Now, it takes a university education to learn to do that." This reliance upon joking and teasing is a deliberate tactic taught the police as a means of reducing the tension and hostility of people who are demonstrating because they feel justified in doing so.[11]

Our police officers, however, cannot be blamed for the fact that the United States is not Great Britain. Anthropologists here maintain we cannot expect to enjoy a better police force unless we face up to some basic facts about our national life and traditions. Unlike Britain, we lack laws requiring the registration of all guns; there are no nationwide standards for the admission and training of police; our police are badly underpaid, and the lack of respect being shown to even the best of them by the general public is demoralizing. Also, as the mayor of New York City, John V. Lindsay, has pointed out, all police forces need funds to hire the best men and to equip them with new tools like voice prints, computerized information centers, and single-digit fingerprints. He also contends that increases in crime do not result from Supreme Court rulings giving crime suspects their fullest legal rights, but rather from "the complex pressures and forces which drive men to crime" in our deeply troubled society.[12]

[10] Lloyd Shearer, "What Would You Think of a Bearded Cop?" *Parade* (October 27, 1968), 5.

[11] Robert C. Toth, "Bobbies Keep the Peace with Jokes and Gentleness," *The Sunday Oregonian* (November 17, 1968).

[12] John V. Lindsay, "Law and Order," *Life* (September 27, 1968).

Too much has been asked of our police. Often they have been assigned the duty of determining just which magazines, books, and entertainment are in violation of local decency codes. They are supposed to remain uncorrupted when their superiors are known to accept bribes and close their eyes to the operations of crime syndicates; they are required to be welfare workers, psychologists, family counselors, and expert marksmen as well as experts on a multitude of conflicting laws. At any minute they are expected to make decisions involving their own personal safety against firearms in the hands of mad men and organized criminal bands. They are embittered by the delays and time-consuming preparations related to court trials and too often excessive leniency of overburdened judges. Being undertrained and underpaid, as well as much confused as everyone else seems to be, it is a wonder our police serve as well as they do.

All of these facts and circumstances lead to some quite obvious conclusions. Our communities require much better police systems and officers than they now generally have; they need also a more enlightened citizenry to support those very necessary reforms. Above all, the American people as a whole must agree upon what standards of behavior they consider permissive, what illegal. Thus, unless we clarify the role of our police, we stand a good chance of losing local control over agencies of "order" and risk the rise of what so far has been abhorrent to Americans—a national police system.

COMMENTARY: WRITING YOUR OWN ANALYSIS

Using the previous commentaries in this section as examples, write a commentary of your own for "The Old Police and New Violence."

WHAT DOES IT SAY?

Once more, following the practices found in other examples, compose eight semantic items for this essay.

WHAT DO YOU THINK?

1. We have, at present, state police systems, the FBI, United States Treasury agents, C.I.A. agents, and other law enforcement agencies. Why shouldn't all of these overlapping and competing enforcement agencies be incorporated into one national police organization? Write an essay developing your reply.

David J. Barrios

2. Taking one of the following suggested topics as a starting point for your thinking, write an adequately detailed essay on your personal experience and views regarding "law and order."

The local sheriff

Patrolmen in our area

Types of officers who give police a bad name

Kinds of policemen I respect

Daily problems encountered by a patrolman

"Order" in our city jail

Prostitution and the police

Drugs and undercover police

Local politicians and difficult laws

Traffic police and drunken drivers

"Order" in juvenile detention centers

Police behavior in city school areas

Justice of the peace courts

Police and firemen compared

3. What is your opinion of the National Guard or the Reserves? Here, as an example of a "library" source, are some quotations from "Our Restless Reserves" by Thomas Barry.[13]

"The Guard is our golf game."

"Suppose there won't be much call for us . . . but you never know."

"The nation's 390,000 guardsmen have a dual mission: backing up the regular Army overseas and helping keep peace at home."

"Paradoxically, riot duty makes more sense to young guardsmen than training for their remote Federal mission."

"Guard and Reserve officers agree that training inside their armories is worst, going overnight at a nearby base slightly better and summer camp best of all."

"If I handled my job at the bank the way this unit is run, I'd be fired in a day."

4. If your instructor recommends it, consult library sources, take notes, and then write a "library paper" on a topic such as one of these:

(a) Why not a professional army instead of a civilian one?
(b) Does Congress appropriate too much money for National Defense?
(c) Should county police be replaced by state police forces?
(d) Why ROTC programs (should, should not) be permitted to continue as at present.

[13] *Look,* July 12, 1969.

part V
THE MEDIA

SUASIVE STRATEGIES: HOW ARE YOU GOING TO PERSUADE THEM?

The slang expression "to get into peoples' minds" has come into wide use by student militants. Actually, this is simply another way of saying "to influence people," or, as Kenneth Burke, a modern rhetorician, has put it, a reliance on the strategies of *rhetoric* as the best means of persuading anyone upon a given occasion.

But the study of the means of persuading others involves far more than merely learning a list of devices and psychological gimmicks. As you have already noted in reading the essays in this text, a writer's effectiveness depends, in part, upon his personal ethics and values, and his judgment and skill in understanding the passions and prejudices of his reader-audience.

To persuade is to bring about a change. A recent study defines four kinds of changes a writer or speaker may have as his goal: (1) he may seek to change people's opinions, (2) he may seek to change people's perceptions, (3) he may seek to change people's emotional state, or (4) he may seek to change people's course of action.[1]

The difficulties that stand in the way of achieving this goal are great for the following reasons:

[1] Erwin P. Bettinhous, *Persuasive Communication* (New York, 1968).

1. Everyone has certain views and notions which make up his personal values as shaped by his family, his environment, his education, and so on (*frame of reference*).
2. Everyone is loathe to change those views and notions, because all change is disturbing and may even be painful.
3. As a result, everyone generally chooses to listen to or to read only those things that he already knows and has accepted (*selective exposure*).
4. He will hear only what he wants to hear, and no matter what he is told, he will generally come away more confirmed than ever that he has been right all along (*selective retention*).

Let us be under no illusions, therefore, with respect to how easy it is for the mass media of newspaper, magazine, film, radio, television, and such, to bring about a change, and to succeed in the attempt to influence. Because of the innate resistance to change of any kind, the difficulties are great. Long ago Aristotle recognized this truth in offering the following good counsel:

> That discourse may be totally effective, the audience must be well disposed toward the speaker; hence the speaker must appear affable, reliable, and the like, and he must adjust his discourse according to his estimate of the audience.

It may be helpful to list the four kinds of changes one might seek to bring about, along with the possible verbal means of doing so as follows: the specific end-results desired in one column and two possible verbal means of securing those ends (by "gentle" means and by "harsh" means) in a column opposite.

End-Result Desired	Verbal Means
1. *A change in emotional state*	*Gentle Means*
restore contentment	appealing
allay fears	promising
rebuild group loyalty	flattering
stir to anger	reassuring
regain trust	humoring
create fear	sympathizing
	cheering
2. *A change in opinion*	comforting
destroy a belief	setting up heroes
convert an unbeliever	joking
modify a policy	exhorting
demoralize a group	agreeing
	praising
	thinking

3. *A change in perception*   *Harsh means*
   make willing to listen   denying
   consider acceptance of a   threatening
   stranger   condemning
                                 warning
4. *A change in action*   shaming
   join a group   accusing
   leave a group   questioning
   vote as desired   humiliating
   fight for or against   satirizing
   remain peaceful
   surrender
   give money
   work harder

In the following essays, dealing with the mass media, you will find authors attempting to produce changes through verbal means and general *suasive strategies* such as these:

Connotative language: slanted words, "gentle" or "harsh," to control suggestion.

Climactic sequence: material arranged so as to produce a climax.

Testimony: statements of those whose words might well carry weight.

Repetition: emphatic examples to drive home the need for change.

Rhetorical questions: questions not directly answered which suggest an unquestionable concurrence.

Realistic detail: lifelike details that paint a picture.

Authoritative stance: an air of unquestionable knowledge or judgment.

Once again, the commentaries following each essay will try to point out and explain some of the particular persuasive strategies employed by the author.

Depth Reporting on the Road

by RICHARD G. GALLI

Introduction
Opening with a dramatic incident and the typical manner in which reporters write it up.

I had talked for only five minutes to the policeman at the scene, and already I knew just about how the story would go:

> "A 35-year-old Providence woman was seriously injured late last night when the car she was driving went out of control on Col. Rodman Highway, struck a guard rail, and careened into a utility pole. . . ."

Five paragraphs of vivid details representing the kind of facts that a report "in depth" would require.

That's how I imagined the story as I walked around the wrecked car, trying to focus the camera in the nervous glimmer of the policeman's flashlight. It was early September and a wet, cold night. An eleven o'clock moon was up there somewhere; down on the ground it was just dark. The wet pavement hid the skid marks, and the broken glass and metal fragments were lost in the roadside gravel and tall grass.

Reprinted from *The Quill*, May, 1968. Reprinted by permission of the publication and the author.

I looked across the road to the guard rail. There was no sign of the impact. But over here the small compact car was crumpled around the splintered pole. Not a single window was unbroken, the headlights were blown out, and the hood was sprung up in a grotesque sneer. The left front door was flung open and mashed against the car's flank.

The police had told me the car skidded sideways across the road, 100 feet or more, and hit the utility pole broadside. The woman had been thrown with great force against the pole, which had struck the car inches from her left elbow. They had found her lying on the ground, unconscious, bleeding badly.

I was thinking of that when I took a good look at the spot on which I stood. Near my right foot was her handbag, the flap open and the contents strewn around. The grass was drenched and speckled with blood. I had been walking through it.

I guess I was lucky, in a way, because deadline was less than half an hour away and the accident report was back at the police station, so it would take some determined hustle to get the story out on time. In this way I could concentrate on the form and the fact, without having to worry too much about what I was actually saying.

General thesis suggested: A reporter should write up an accident not in formula fashion, but in a report revealing the tragedy involved.

But that was two years ago, and there's been lots of time between: plenty of time to think it all over. I hadn't been merely writing up a story that night. I and my camera had gone sniffing into a real human tragedy.

Ever since that night, every accident story I've written has been an exercise in frustration. How do I put in words, in simple, concise, tepid words, the real facts of an accident?

"A 35-year-old Providence woman was seriously injured . . ." That's the form all right. It fits the style of the paper, it clues us in to the gravity of the story . . . but it doesn't really say anything at all. And the truth? The truth about the broken body, the smashed bones and

Body
Restatement of thesis idea as a problem. Why newspaper readers want the formula rather than reports in depth.

tattered flesh. . . .? That wouldn't set well with the breakfast-table reader.

> "A 25-year-old Coventry man was killed when his motorcycle skidded into a utility pole on Read Ave. . . ."

Six paragraphs stating another example with vivid details of the kind of facts needed to give the covering story its proper human "depth."

The body was gone, the cycle was unscathed. It wasn't even worth a picture, but of course I took one anyway. I called back from a neighbor's house what scraps of information I could work from the police. Back at the office, over the phone, the rest of the story trickled in: Young man, not very successful. Wife and two children. Roots deep in the community; relatives scattered all over town.

"Go out to the house and see if you can get a picture," the bureau manager said.

"Your husband's a traffic victim, you see," I could imagine myself saying to her, "and naturally people are going to want to know what he looked like. He's a celebrity of sorts. And besides, it makes the page so much more interesting—it breaks up the monotony of those great gray masses of print." But she wasn't at home, so both makeup and reader empathy suffered. I didn't mind.

The widow had fled to her husband's parents' home. She couldn't come to the phone— I could hear, almost feel her in the background —but the father gave me enough to go on. He couldn't give me the story though. I had to write that: Distance thrown from the cycle. Estimated speed. Description of injuries. Time. Direction. Witnesses.

But how could I explain the absolutely unfazed look of that cycle? How could I get across to people, in the finest journalistic style, the obscene way that empty helmet leered at me from the smooth leather of the seat?

The main reason why the reporter writes about accidents.

You had to be there.

Everyone should have been there, but everyone wasn't. So I had to tell them about it. And every year we tell them again and again, in language they think they understand.

Dead: 53,000. Injured: 4,000,000. One out of every thirty-six Americans who died last year did so in a traffic accident. One thousand Americans died Christmas weekend. Fifty-five thousand were injured. Oh yes, in the single month of October, 1967, the nation suffered an economic loss of $1,167,856,000 due to automobile mishaps.

"Most people dying on the highways are dying of smashed heads," says Dr. William Haddon, Jr., director of the National Highway Safety Bureau. ". . . each day over 10,000 people are injured in the United States in auto crashes. By any reasonable estimate, we're going to have thousands of crashes every day for the foreseeable future."

Each year, 25 out of every 100,000 Americans die in traffic accidents.

"Smashed heads. . . ." Tell the people the truth about Jayne Mansfield, about her hair spread out over the car's hood, blood and gold, stripped from her scalp as her head exploded through the windshield. Tell them this and they will curse your poor taste.

"Jayne Mansfield, actress and sex symbol to a generation of Americans, died today in an auto crash. . . ." That's the way they want to hear it. Simple, concise, readable, smooth.

Just what, exactly, is the reporter's job in covering traffic accidents? Why cover them at all? "It's news," the desk would say, "and besides, the story might induce others to be more careful."

Can a person appreciate chocolate layer cake merely by reading the recipe day after day? Or, at least once in his life, does he have to have a taste himself?

Can a person possibly appreciate the slaughter on the highways merely by reading the statistics—the recipes—day after day, or does he, too, need a more intimate, realistic, truthful appraisal?

Statistics of mortalities and damages. Dismal testimony by an expert.

Inadequacy of superficial reports on Jayne Mansfield's fatal accident.

Why reporters are sent to accident scenes.

An analogy.

Inadequacy of the formula news story on accidents: failure to report effects upon families and victims.

Why does depth reporting break down in the case of traffic accidents? Why is most of the story never covered? Columns are devoted to tire marks, damage estimates, estimated injuries—and then the story is dropped. The real essence of the piece—the effect on families and victims, the causes of the accident and the enduring results, the scars of the flesh and of the mind—all are forgotten. It's as if nothing happens prior to the first skid; nothing happens after the sponging and setting and stitching.

Conclusion
Realization of the impossibility of giving all fatal accidents the proper "in depth" reporting.

Thousands of reporters stand in millions of pools of blood and tell their readers of "serious injuries" and "critical injuries" and "fatalities." They tell of numbers and records and all manner of statistics. They tell of twisted metal and shattered poles and dollars lost. They cite the recipes, but never offer a taste.

Soon the words lose their meanings. The edge of truth is worn into a comfortable but totally deceptive familiarity. A serious injury is no longer a woman in agony—it's a category, to be noted and filed and later compiled. Some day someone will bury it in an almanac table.

There aren't enough reporters in the world to cover every accident the way it should be covered. There simply isn't enough room in the newshole to accommodate the whole truth.

Besides, people wouldn't like it.

Hypnotic effect of such formula reporting.

So they become hypnotized by the low-key drone of *accidentese*. Accident stories read like batting averages. A .290 is a .290. A serious injury is a serious injury. The phrases knead callouses in the public's understanding.

I sniff around with my camera and scribble with my pen, and the truth and the story are strangers. I glean the ingredients and serve up the recipe.

Another example. Closing repetition of thesis idea.

"A 35-year-old Providence woman was seriously injured late last night. . . ."

The story gets set in type. The truth just seeps into the ground.

OUTLINE

Thesis: "Ever since that night, every accident story I've written has been an exercise in frustration."

   I. As a reporter I am limited to giving only a few facts about any one road accident.
     A. Two years ago the violent death of the "35-year-old Providence woman" had to be reported in too brief detail.
       1. No mention was possible of grim details on how the accident happened.
       2. Lack of space prohibited description of the car and the body.
     B. Now after two years, I realize that as a reporter I was witnessing "a real human tragedy" I could not fully report.
     C. Breakfast-table readers would not relish such details.
     D. The death of a motorcyclist would have provided another tragic story but was reported without proper "depth."
  II. Newspapers have some public service motives in publishing death-on-highway reports, but are squeamish about including details.
     A. Statistics on the killed and injured are staggering.
     B. "Most people dying on the highways are dying of smashed heads."
       1. Jayne Mansfield's death was not described.
       2. It was reported in the usual stereotype story.
     C. Reporters are sent to accident scenes in hopes the news reports will help cut accident rates.
 III. Reporters continue to fail to report traffic deaths in depth.
     A. Their formula stories do not give readers the "taste" of the tragedies befalling the affected families.
     B. Reporters succumb to the hypnotic effect of such formula reporting.

COMMENTARY: PERSUASION BY REPETITION

As a reporter for the Providence, Rhode Island *Journal-Bulletin,* Richard G. Galli has written this moving essay for other journalists who, like himself, he says, "have spent a lot of time, ink, and sole leather at a task which is both odious and of questionable value." He laments the little-appreciated fact that reporters so completely fail to find and write about the personal and family tragedy aspects of highway deaths required for proper in-depth reporting. Obviously, he seeks to persuade his readers to stop writing such formula news stories and to change to reporting traffic fatalities in depth.

What is his strategy? Certainly the most obvious means he employs is the repeated use of dramatic examples—three in number—one more cruelly vivid than the other. In brutal terms he describes the appearance of the car in the first wreck as though it were a human being (*personification*): "the hood was sprung open in a grotesque sneer. The left front door was flung open and mashed against the car's flank." *Sneer* and *flank* personify the car in the same way similar terms describe the motorcycle accident: "the absolutely unfazed look of the cycle . . . the obscene way that empty helmet leered at me from the smooth leather of the seat."

Repetitions of the banal formula used to report such accidents also drive home the thesis message. We immediately recognize the trite, almost meaningless formula, as we can the reports: "A 35-year-old Providence woman was seriously injured late last night . . . A 25-year-old Coventry man was killed when his motorcycle . . . Jayne Mansfield, actress and sex symbol to a generation of Americans, died today in an auto crash. . . ." This constant pairing off of detailed, raw incidents and bland news stories purporting to report them should make even blasé newspapermen reconsider the whole matter of reporting accidents.

As the marginal notes and the outline indicate, Mr. Galli has taken care to supply supporting evidence and ideas for his thesis. He is no blatant propagandist who relies only on endless repetition of slogans, emotional appeals, and vague threats. Instead, as we can readily see, he digs and probes to find facts and raise questions that make us think. After the first incident he asks, "And the truth? The truth about the broken body, the smashed bones and tattered flesh. . . .?" After the second accident he asks, "But how could I explain the absolutely unfazed look of that cycle? How could I get across to people, in the finest journalistic style . . .?" And after the third incident comes the basic question: "Just what exactly, is the reporter's job in covering traffic accidents?" He asks still two more fundamental questions: "Why does depth reporting break down in the case of traffic questions? Why is most of the story never covered?"

Questions such as these raised in a speech or essay but not directly answered, are called *rhetorical questions,* and are examples of another suasive device. As they should be, these have a direct bearing upon Mr. Galli's fundamental thesis and purpose. Their repetition emphasizes the thesis.

Does he, in general, choose "gentle" verbal means or "harsh" ones? To begin with, he appears to have adopted a "confessional" stance and tone. He relies at first on expressions such as these: "I guess I was lucky, in a way. . . ." "But that was two years ago, and there's been lots of time between: plenty of time to think it all over." We identify with this unassuming reporter who is speaking candidly to us. His tone becomes more *exhortatory,* however, as he brings in the additional examples and laments the inadequacies of journalistic accounts that fail to tell the whole grim story of such accidents and all the terrible results concealed beneath the usual formula phrases.

In the concluding paragraph, his final statements seem despairing. Perhaps it has occurred to him that what we now can call "selective exposure" and "selective retention" are always at work, even among journalists. If so, can they be expected to begin reporting car deaths in depth?

Should they so report them? Has your opinion been changed?

WHAT DOES IT SAY?

1. In referring to the ineffectiveness of formula reports of road deaths as a deterrent, Mr. Galli makes the following comparison: "Can a person appreciate chocolate layer cake merely by reading the recipe day after day? Or, at least once in his life, does he have to have a taste himself?" What is the term given to this kind of comparison?

2. How can the way the motorcycle helmet "leered" at him rightly be called "obscene"?

3. Why or why not is the word *sniffing* appropriate in the context of this sentence: "I and my camera had gone sniffing into a real human tragedy"?

4. Can you give some of the connotations you have for phrases such as these trite ones: "serious injuries," "critical injuries," "fatalities"?

5. What does happen "after the sponging and setting and stitching" following a bad wreck?

6. Define "in-depth" reporting as found in the context of this essay.

7. Was the choice of the Jayne Mansfield accident effective? Why?

8. Explain the meaning of the concluding two sentences: "The story gets set in type. The truth just seeps into the ground."

WHAT DO YOU THINK?

1. Do you agree with Mr. Galli that the newspaper reports of fatal highway accidents should be reported in depth? Explain by means of specific examples, chosen from daily news accounts, why you believe he is right or wrong.

2. Using the strategy of *repetition,* try to change the behavior or opinion of a certain group regarding some aspect of one of the following subjects. Remember to be vivid and concrete in the details of your selected incidents.

   Physical education or "gym" classes

   Black studies classes or curriculum

   Smoking pot

   What about the hippies?

   Why or why not yippies?

   Pass or no-pass as a grading system

   "Greek" fraternal societies and "racism"

   Making 18-year-olds eligible to vote

   A guaranteed yearly income for every family

   A volunteer army

   Dormitory rule changes

   Parking on campus

   Sex instruction classes

   The Peace Corps

   More space exploration

3. By means of *repetition* try to convince the class that nightly news programs on television fail to report important events in depth.

4. By means of *repetition* persuade readers of your student newspaper that its news stories covering a certain subject lack in depth reporting.

5. On the basis of several of your own more or less painful experiences, try to persuade your classmates to accept your conclusions regarding one of the following:

   Telling the truth

   Ignoring overtime parking tickets

   Trying to be a "nice" person

   Believing you should try everything once

   Being a peacemaker

Being a consumer

Being a producer

Having a roommate

Renewing old friendships

Depending on friends

Following recommendations of friends

Being independent

Replaying old records

Going to church

Awaiting weekends

Viewing film "classics"

Listening to new music

What's Black and White and Pink and Green and Dirty and Read All Over?

by JOHN KRONENBERGER

If today's young have a message for the rest of the country, it is this: the inmates have taken over the asylum. They first rejected "outside" control of their music and their politics; now, as befits the first generation of the McLuhan Age, they have turned to the field of communications.

From the *East Village Other* in New York to the Berkeley *Barb* and the Los Angeles *Free Press,* and at innumerable way stations like Chicago's *Seed,* Detroit's *Fifth Estate,* Austin's *Rag* and Atlanta's *Great Speckled Bird,* youthful journalistic guerrillas have seized the hearts and minds of their peers. Two years ago, perhaps five "underground" newspapers existed. Since then, somewhere between 150 and 200 have sprung up—part of their subterranean nature being that no one really knows for sure just how many. They range from occasional sheets that number their readers by the hundreds up to the big three: the *EVO,* the *Barb* and the L.A. "Freep" have weekly circulations of 45,000, 60,000 and 85,000, and manage to pay most of their employees to boot. There is even an underground answer to the AP, the strife-buffeted Liberation News Service, whose schedule calls for thrice-weekly mailings of anti-Establishment news and features to 150 or so papers. Taken together, the papers probably have a circulation of close to two million. Their readers, like their cadres of writers and artists, are for the most part well under 30: high school kids and grad students, dropouts and social workers, hippies and activists are all part of the community both served and represented by the underground press.

In one recent month, casual skimming of various papers would have turned up, among others, the following stories: an account of police heavy-handedness during an allegedly "political" drug arrest ("One narco takes Jerry aside and punches him several times in the head, turns him around, and kicks him in the spine. Jerry falls."—New York's *Rat*); the trial and conviction of a draft resister ("Speaking softly, almost inaudibly, he asked the jury to render no verdict as he had made no plea, politely refusing to cooperate with the system which brought him into court."—L.A. *Free Press*); a Stock Market Report Analysis ("Minnesota Minding and Mescaline—colorful trading . . . Dandy Dan Dex—up, up, up, up . . . up."—*Seed*); a primer on bombs following an unsuccessful attack on a local draft board ("Experimentation by these hit and run artists will probably reveal some general lessons: An explosion in a confined space can do great damage. In an unconfined space it is good mainly for attracting cops." *Barb*); and the arrival of a *new* swami (". . . just as soon as the Beatles began to suspect that the Maharishi might not be altogether right in the head . . . word went out along the Astral Grapevine—'Where is there One among us so pure of mind, so sweet of soul, unsullied in the depths of his being and unburdened by the things of this world that he might become even a Great Shill?' And lo! from out of the vastness [of] the brooding Himalayas walked One, fresh from untold years' silent meditation. . . . He was seized . . . and thrust on a jet headed for the States."—*EVO*).

Less ingratiating is a general flair for conspiracy theories and rumors on everything from concentration camps to nerve gas. (The editor of one of New York's five—at last count—underground papers matter-of-factly says he knows his phone is tapped. But not by whom.) There are also great amounts of sharp, knowing criticism of music and films, weird comic strips that reflect drug highs and/or paranoid visions of violence and, last but hardly least, classified ads of an unclassifiable nature: "Girl wanted for girl with girl 3-year-old, object sex and swing," read a recent one in the *EVO*, though nobody at the paper could quite figure out who wanted whom for what. Some people always read the ads first.

All this comes wrapped in a bewildering fabric of scattershot (photomontages), eye- and mind-bending artwork, chaotic splashes of color. It is also laced with language until now deemed more or less unprintable, so hassles with authority crop up occasionally. Boston's elegant *Avatar,* whose formal perfection of typesetting and layout was for a time in a class by itself, found that its "conversational" use of certain four-, eight- and ten-letter nouns and verbs outraged the Cambridge City Council so much that street hawkers were being arrested in Harvard Square. The paper's solution to the problem was to make both the offending words and the salesmen more prominent; after one of the verbs had been drawn in letters four inches high, and 58 arrests had been made, a local court found the content not obscene. So the city finally relaxed, and an accommodation was reached: Cambridge agreed to cease bugging the salesmen if *Avatar* promised to avoid selling the paper to those under 18. But within recent months, underground word choice has led to arrests in Milwaukee and West Palm Beach. Peter Leggieri, a 26-year-old law-school student when he became the new editor of *EVO* last spring, feels that "there is no such thing as a free press in this country. There is a *permitted* press—but what is permitted depends on the locality."

Their job, as seen by most of the underground irregulars, is something much larger than reporting, so conventional newspaper standards simply do not apply. Few of the breed concern themselves with a strict recitation of events in the manner of the "straight" press. What's happened is not the point, "what's happening" is. *EVO*'s cofounder, Allan Katzman (at 31, older by far than most of his staff), prefers that his paper concern itself with transmitting "spiritual information"—by which he means what's in the air more than mysticism. "Twenty years from now," Katzman hopes, "people will be able to look back and understand this period, get a good feel for what it must have been like, by reading the *EVO*. . . . We're not based on perfection; we're based on our own reliable responses to what's going on. If at times we're extremely obscene, it's because we're *feeling* obscene. We're not afraid of expressing our feelings . . . it's journalism through your fingertips."

This attitude is echoed by Kip Shaw, who worked for Liberation News Service: "We don't pretend to be completely objective in our coverage, but we do try for an honest subjectivity that will convey a sense of what it's like to be on our side of the story. The events aren't as important as the *effect* of the events on us as human beings."

Concern for "our side of the story" is, of course, the major reason the underground phenomenon exists. In the last few years, an awakened awareness of American racism and the special menace of a war they alone are asked to fight have undercut young Americans' faith in the status quo. The chemical wonders of The Pill and psychedelic drugs have badly bruised traditional morality. And the advocacy of protest and pot has brought down upon the heads of the young a police toughness previously reserved for less educated and less articulate minorities. Unsurprisingly, it's become "us against them" for many restive adolescents and young adults—not just hippies.

Since the straight press belongs to the institutional America that outrages them, they can't or won't trust *it*, either. Therefore, the underground press: it makes no claim to absolute accuracy, but, as a counterweight to the Establishment media, corrects "mistakes" and "distortions," serves as a sounding board for the new mood and (at worst) propagandizes a bit for the coming revolution. When the New York *Times* all but ignored the injuries inflicted by the police during last spring's Columbia University insurrection, a number of impartial observers had to agree that underground suspicions had been somewhat vindicated.

Whatever the outcome of today's pitched battle at Generation Gap, the underground press seems unlikely to disappear tomorrow. The low cost of photo-offset printing (set your copy on a typewriter if you must, paste up any photos or art at hand, have 5,000 copies of your first issue printed for about $80) and the glut of volunteer labor are two reasons why practically no paper has folded for financial reasons. And for at least one underground editor, *Avatar's* Wayne Hansen, the papers represent something more important than a fad. "The twenties had Hemingway and Fitzgerald; the Beat Generation had Kerouac and Allen Ginsberg," he said not long ago. "But did you ever wonder where are the books of *this* generation? Today's writing is more immediate; you can't wait around for a publisher."

Smart people, he implies, should take a second look at the underground press. Sometimes sloppy or silly, often outrageous and obscene, it could be—he thinks—the true voice of the 1960's.

COMMENTARY: PERSUASION BY TESTIMONY

Does Mr. Kronenberger, who was writing for *Look* readers, approve or disapprove of "underground" newspapers? In the opening paragraph he says, ". . . the inmates have taken over the asylum . . . now, as befits the first generation of the McLuhan Age, they have turned to the field of communications."

On the face of it, he seems to have a poor opinion of our country, since he calls it "the asylum," obviously meaning a mental-care institution. In calling the young people of this generation "the inmates," he classes them also as being mentally sick. And in this opening statement he derides the young as being "the first generation of the McLuhan Age"—a remark having bitterly ironic implications. (See pp. 204 and 210.)

But aside from labeling youthful publishers of underground newspapers "journalist guerrillas," "underground irregulars," and "the breed," he is remarkably objective throughout the body and the conclusion of his essay in presenting quotations from the underground press as *testimony* in behalf of his contention that the young rebels are no more mad than the age in which they find themselves. His final sentence seems even to approve of their messages and method as being possibly "the true voice of the 1960's."

What is this *testimony* and how does it fit into his thinking? It consists of quotations gathered over a month from a number of the many publications he surveys in his second paragraph for their circulation and actual reader-audience. He presents five different subjects which he evidently considers representative, and he immediately follows each with a vivid quotation from one of the papers. Note how specific and concise these details are, showing careful selection and arrangement. It might be asked, "Aren't these typical statements quoted as *testimony* concerning what the underground press is like really only another form of *examples*?" The answer is that, of course, such items of evidence *are* examples.

What has been held by rhetoricians for centuries still applies: all forms of *example* can lead to inductive conclusions; that is, particular cases or instances lead us to make generalizations. Our author here has done just that; he has relied upon this method of presenting quotations which, when considered as a whole, lead the reader to accept the interpretation, or conclusion, he has himself drawn from them.

But his *testimony* included also a paragraph of what he calls "less ingratiating" items such as rumors and "conspiracy theories" also illustrated by representative quotations. In a subsequent paragraph he takes up the ever-sensitive topic of "language until now deemed more or less unprintable," and pins it down with a summary of conflicts involving the *Avatar* and the Cambridge police, with reference to similar troubles in Milwaukee and West Palm Beach. These incidents lead the author to these underground publications, and he quotes three different editors' views on the validity of their kind of publishing.

In what certainly appears to build up to a defense of these "journalist guerrillas," Mr. Kronenberger devotes two paragraphs listing the kind of events that have incited them to tell "our side of the story." And following this summary of issues of an "us against them" nature, he explains why the "straight" press is not trusted; he even provides his own *testimony* in the form of reference to the Columbia University "insurrection" and the failure of *The New York Times* to report injuries inflicted. He also warns that because of the low overhead enjoyed by the underground press, these publications can be expected to continue and flourish. And as already stated, he seems to regard them as very possibly being "the true voice of the 1960's."

Are you convinced by these carefully presented items of *testimony*, statements of fact, and warnings that the underground press is here to stay and should continue to flourish? Would *Look* magazine readers be impressed, if not convinced?

WHAT DOES IT SAY?

1. Identify Marshall McLuhan and explain what is meant by "The Mc-Luhan Age."

2. "Minnesota Minding and Mescaline—colorful trading . . . Dandy Dan Dex—up, up, up . . . up"—what manner of Stock Market Report Analysis is this?

3. Define the tone of *EVO* in the report on the arrival of a *"new swami."*

4. What are "scattershot photomontages"?

5. In context, can you define the difference between "a free press" and "a permitted press"?

6. Explain this statement: "What's happened is not the point, 'what's happening' is."

7. Is "journalism through your fingertips" the same as "reporting in depth"?

8. How do you interpret this judgment: "Today's writing is more immediate; you can't wait around for a publisher"?

WHAT DO YOU THINK?

1. If you have access to several issues of an underground newspaper, write an essay using the device of selected "testimony" from them to persuade . . . your classmates to accept your defense or criticism of some regular feature found in the issues. For example, the advertisements, a columnist, an editorial policy, the art work, or a series of articles on a controversial topic.

2. Write an essay wherein by means of selected quotations and summaries of representative articles, you support your criticism of the quality of reporting found in a certain department appearing regu-

larly in one of the weekly news magazines. A few suggested areas are:

Theater criticism	Education
Film reviews	Art news
Sports reports	Television
Medical advances	Newspapers
Financial news	Science news
Book reviews	National politics
International diplomacy	Urban problems

4. Through use of a number of very brief quotations, persuade your classmates to purchase a new long-playing album by your favorite singer or group.

5. Attempt to convey your deep feelings about some person by means of quoting that person's typical utterances on various occasions. (Try to be humorous if you think you can carry it off.)

TV: Reporting News or Making It?

by JACK GOULD

Television's coverage of the Democratic National Convention was a mixed bag of accomplishment under severely trying conditions and a wholly unnecessary electronic intrusion on a news event. Surely, the day is bound to come when TV will recognize more fully the basic journalistic distinction between observing a performance and becoming part of the act. . . .

Both the Columbia Broadcasting System . . . and the National Broadcasting Company were so bent on staging their own show that the viewer was deprived of hearing the full range of disagreement over the Vietnamese war plank, to cite only one example. The set owner also was the victim of the propensity of the TV medium for spreading rumors in an ill-concealed attempt to generate excitement.

There is no need to quibble about the behind-the-scenes pressures that influenced in part what a viewer saw. Both NBC and CBS were locked in the quadrennial struggle for audience ratings. [Their news departments, which in the last analysis have the final say over what Walter Cronkite (CBS) and Chet Huntley and David Brinkley (NBC) do, were terrified by the prospect of prolonged lulls and sought their own means of compensation.] The upshot was that the two chains providing gavel-to-gavel coverage became rattled and relied excessively on their floor reporters, who interviewed and re-interviewed delegates to the exclusion of the business of the convention.

Courtesy of United Press International

Admittedly, the TV networks probably never encountered a story quite like the chaos of the Democratic convention. The stringent and oppressive security regulations had to be reported, and the dissent from Vice President Humphrey's influence in the preliminary balloting demanded full coverage. But since dissent usually makes more news than concurrence, the networks themselves overresponded to the slightest suggestion of divisive heat. . . .

CBS, for instance, referred for hours to the abortive boomlet for Sen. Edward M. Kennedy of Massachusetts and invited a viewer to decide that the movement was sweeping the convention floor.

Eric Sevareid, the CBS commentator, forthrightly observed that the TV medium—in this instance his own network—could be charged, at least in part, with incubating a development which, to all seasoned political reporters, clearly was not in the cards. To its credit, NBC did not jump into this particular fray, but rather waited until John Chancellor, its most seasoned representative on the convention floor, had the opportunity to place the boomlet in sensible perspective. It was Mr. Chancellor's type of reporting that reflected mature journalism, avoiding involvement in the immediate hysteria and giving the viewer a rounded judgment of what was both afoot and not afoot in a practical sense.

To the credit of television—and only the visual medium could make such a contribution—was the fascinating vignette of Mayor Richard J. Daley of Chicago virtually running the convention from his seat in the Illinois delegation.

But overshadowing and directly influencing the convention was the television coverage of the disorders in the streets of Chicago. Because of the electrical workers' strike and Mayor Daley's security precautions, the TV industry had to catch such filmed pictures as they could. Certainly, whatever provocations may have been directed against the Chicago police, the response of the helmeted officers was too vividly detailed in pictures to permit any doubt that there had been wanton clubbing and beating of individuals.

In a conciliatory interview with Mr. Cronkite after the night of violence, Mayor Daley made a point that TV had neglected to report abuse of the Chicago police and ignored injuries suffered by them. It was a pity that Mr. Cronkite did not more aggressively pick up the point that innumerable reporters and photographers had been beaten by the police, even though they identified themselves and were trying to do their jobs.

Sen. Warren G. Magnuson, Democrat of Washington, and chairman of the Senate Commerce Committee has been quoted as suggesting that TV's reportorial behavior at political conventions should be reviewed before 1972. If Congress proposes to intrude in such matters, it would be censorship and news management of the most blatant sort.

There should be, voluntarily and without government pressure, independent and separate studies by convention managers and networks alike. One direct cause of TV's frequent pursuit of trivia and its impatience with formal convention proceedings is the outmoded format of the convention itself. To pass a whole evening with minor parliamentary matters constitutes an open invitation to the networks to try to find stories brewing on the floor. . . . The attempts of both parties to delay embarrassing moments until after the prime evening viewing hours were indisputably obvious.

The networks themselves need to be more careful and restrained. For too many hours at a time, the viewer might easily decide that the anchormen and floor reporters are the substance of a convention, rather than the delegates and candidates. There is a bolt loose somewhere when the familiar faces of Mr. Cronkite, the Messrs. Huntley and Brinkley and Howard K. Smith are on camera more hours than the people ostensibly making the news.

The whole concept of omnipotent anchormen has had the effect of coming between the viewer and the event in which he is interested. TV's conceit that it is invariably more interesting than what is being said on the podium is simply not true. The viewer has some rights in arriving at these judgments for himself and the function of TV is then to provide unobtrusive background material.

Television's task is to mirror as accurately as possible the confusion or conflict that may exist, but not become a party to its growth or a studio substitute for the event itself. The dividing line is admittedly an extremely difficult one to walk, but after Miami Beach and Chicago the matter hardly can be ignored.

COMMENTARY: PERSUASION BY ETHICAL STANCE

Contrary to the somewhat ironic but cautious approach found in the previous article on the underground press, this one by Jack Gould, outspoken television critic for *The New York Times,* speaks out in a tone of absolute authority. Its opening sentence begins with a slight concession but ends with a blasting condemnation: "Television's coverage of the Democratic National Convention was a mixed bag of accomplishment under severely trying conditions and a wholly unnecessary electronic intrusion on a news event." Right after this blast comes a prophesy of change in policy and behavior by broadcasters in the future.

Then, as they should, come the particulars of the accusation fired at the two giant television networks. He attacks them first of all by attributing to them a noncomplimentary motive meant to account for their objectionable behavior—an old trick! He says they spread rumors and acted as they did "in an ill-concealed attempt to generate excitement." (This may have been one of the motives, but was it the governing one?) Mr. Gould then cites two examples showing the misguided direction to which the reporters and floormen were subject.

But to show he is fair, he gives, in the third and fourth paragraphs, some recognition of the unusual difficulties encountered by the news directors responsible for broadcasting the Democratic National Convention in Chicago in 1968. Also, in order to give the appearance of having considered all aspects of the policy and behavior he attacks, he anticipates possible points that the networks could raise in their defense against his charges. So he does acknowledge with approval the behavior of certain reporters, such as that of Eric Sevareid and John Chancellor, and the showing of Mayor Richard J. Daley's "virtually running the convention from his seat in the Illinois delegation."

Thereafter, however, he returns to taking the networks to task in the person of Walter Cronkite and even includes a United States senator in his castigations for threatening to introduce censorship procedures that would destroy freedom of the press.

Some social critics consider it unnecessary to provide solutions for the problems they analyze and the policies they condemn, thinking it meritorious enough to have named and defined the evil. This practice is wholly justifiable when the problem is a new one and not widely understood. But a critic like Mr. Gould, who has solid convictions regarding morals and taste, usually is not content with just lambasting what displeases him. Like all such persuasive people, he wishes to improve the lot of mankind and make human life happier. (Aristotle would have approved of him!) In this particular rendering of judgment Mr. Gould does offer solutions to the problems confronting television reporters bringing us important news events such as political conventions.

His concluding four paragraphs recommend specific changes—studies by convention managers and networks, care and restraint by networks, rights of viewer over anchormen—and ends with a restatement of the thesis as a practicable working principle. By making these positive proposals, Mr. Gould tempers some of his initial harshness and makes readers probably more willing to accept the legitimacy of the earlier attacks.

In case you are interested, this particular essay is a splendid example of one of the three kinds of persuasive discourse that Aristotle classified ages ago as "the deliberative or political discourse," wherein the adoption of a policy or an action of importance in public affairs is urged. Isn't this what Jack Gould is demanding—a change in the attitude and practices of television newsmen covering political conventions? And he argues on the highest ethical grounds: "The viewer has some rights in arriving at these judgments for himself and the function of TV is then to provide unobtrusive background material." Mr. Gould is against "sin"—a most persuasive stance in any argument.

WHAT DOES IT SAY?

1. Why, do you think, does Mr. Gould use the expression "a mixed bag of accomplishment" in his opening sentence? What kind of expression is it?

2. How would the networks probably have stated what Mr. Gould implies in this statement: "Both (CBS & NBC) were so bent on staging their own show that the viewer was deprived of hearing the full range of disagreement . . ."?

3. What is the tone you find in a sentence such as this one: "There is no need to quibble about the behind-the-scenes pressures that influenced in part what a viewer saw"?

4. What is "an abortive boomlet"?

5. How bland and characterless general and stock expressions can become! What specific, concrete events were referred to here: ". . . whatever provocations may have been directed against the Chicago police, the response of the helmeted officers was too vividly detailed in pictures to permit any doubt that there had been wanton clubbing and beating of individuals"?

6. Which features or practices would come under the general heading of "formal convention proceedings" and "the outmoded format of the convention itself"?

7. List three things in the behavior and manner of television "anchormen" that are responsible for their being called "omnipotent."

8. What happened at Miami Beach?

barrios 9-68

David J. Barrios

WHAT DO YOU THINK?

1. Using the *stance of authority* and proper ethical attitude, try to persuade your classmates to do one of the following:

   Stop smoking cigarettes

   Give up going on "beer busts"

   Stop putting off studying until examination time

   Halt drawing color lines

   Start sharing rides

   Develop more school spirit

   Give blood to the blood bank

   Join the band (or any extracurricular activity)

   Stop being so much the activist

   See what is most relevant

   Quit griping about _____

2. Attack a pattern of public behavior that you strenuously object to as being socially harmful, and propose more acceptable alternatives. Suggestions:

   Politicians' use of heavy make-up for television appearances

   Comedians who insult and put down everybody

   Do-gooders who see and hear no evil

   Door-to-door evangelists who will never take "no" for an answer

   Mail addressed to "Occupant"

   Unsolicited pornography

   Television popularity rating systems

   Student government procedures

   Treatment by townspeople

   Public transportation service

   Campus housing provisions

   Police protection

   Pollution

3. Assuming the *stance of authority* and proper ethical attitude, write a criticism pointing out in detail what you consider ill advised or even dangerous about what goes on daily around us. Here are a few suggestions:

Driving recklessly

Getting married too young

Dropping out of school

Going on welfare without good cause

Overemphasizing athletics

Moving to suburbs

Evicting for slum clearance without first providing a suitable place of residence

Careless handing out of credit cards

Constantly increasing the cost of living

Failing to pass gun registration laws

4. In many cities the leading newspaper and television station are owned by the same one owner. What are the dangers in such single ownership? If such is the situation in your local area, discuss some regional concerns wherein such control of the news media has been, or could be, beneficial or harmful.

5. Listen to local radio talk programs and then write an essay comparing the authoritative stance of radio hosts.

Up Tight About Hang-Ups

NEWSWEEK ESSAY

Walter Muir Whitehill, an author and the director of the august Athenaeum library in Boston, couldn't believe what he saw on the annual report from Colonial Williamsburg, Inc., which administers the restored village of Williamsburg, Va. "The title of the report," reports Whitehill, "was 'Williamsburg Tells It Like It Was'."

Groovy. Beautiful. Out of sight. The jargon of the alienated, the oppressed, the discontented is becoming the idiom of Middle—nay, Colonial—America. Television writers babble like acid-heads; newspaper columnists sound like black militants; and advertising copywriters echo the slogans of the teeny-boppers. "Turn on, before you turn in," read one advertisement in *The New York Times* last week, "with your own fun-at-home steam bath." "People used to want to grow up," notes *Times* columnist Russell Baker, dourly. "Now they just want to sound young."

The mainstream of language, of course, is always being refreshed by new sources of words and phrases, and only the most doctrinaire purist would argue that lively lingo should be banned from straight usage. "*Hang-up* is good, it replaces psychiatric text-book talk," says *Chicago Daily News* columnist Mike Royko. Adds writer and press critic Ben Bagdikian: "I think *The Man* expresses very succinctly the idea of the person of authority. It is a private language, a secret sort of handclasp." NBC commentator David Brinkley says he likes the term *up tight* better than earlier, less expressive terms such as tensed up.

Overkill: But what happens is that the innovators—blacks, young people and, as the sociologists would put it, other "out groups"—find that their cabalistic expressions are taken over by the square world and spoken and written to death. Journalists, too, overkill with jargon and pretentious usages because they come quickly to mind and substitute for thinking. Unfortunately, interment doesn't come fast enough. A chrestomathy of current phrases that a representative group of lovers of English offer up for burial:

"Tell it like it is," volunteers literary critic Philip Rahv. "It is the supreme cliché of the year. Certainly, the person saying it doesn't know what really 'is'. Who does? What an arrogant statement, a ridiculous request." British writer Katherine Whitehorn can do without *with-it* and *so-called*—"it doesn't mean the object is misnamed, just that the user doesn't like it."

Bergen Evans, professor of English at Northwestern University and a leading member of the permissive school of language, hopes he will never have to be confronted with the term *confrontation*.

Robert Manning, editor of *The Atlantic,* picked up a newspaper and focused on the phrase *sort of* as an expression he considers "useless, ambiguous and grating." Manning is disturbed also by the proliferation of obscenity. "I wish the problem would go away," says Manning. "The words won't. In some pieces they are essential to convey the point. But in others they are being used more and more for shock purposes only."

Louis Lyons, former curator of the Nieman Foundation at Harvard, and James Boylan, editor of the *Columbia Journalism Review* are exacerbated by *you know*—which both say they hear much too often over radio and TV. "What does it mean," asks Lyons. "What do I know? What is that expression? A nervous tic? A lack of vocabulary?"

Both Bagdikian and Baker believe that the value of *Establishment* has been debased. "It would be all right to keep the Establishment members," Baker says, "if we got rid of the word."

Washington newsmen are annoyed most by officialese. "The first expression that I want to go is *viable*," says Art Buchwald. "It dates back to the Kennedy Administration and it just isn't very viable any more." But he also objects to some of the phrases that Mr. Nixon has introduced. "In every speech," says Buchwald, "he throws in a line that goes: 'I want to make this perfectly clear' or 'I want to say this candidly'." Adds Russell Baker: "Republicans go in for Latin stems and roots a lot. We're bound to hear a lot about *definitization* and *implementation.*"

The problem has become an English one as well as an American one. William Davis, the new editor of *Punch,* says he "would like to dispose of—*crisis, taking into consideration, in the final analysis, within the framework of, at this time, other things being equal* and *alive and well and living in.*" Adds Bill Grundy, press critic for the weekly *Spectator:* "I could do without *participation; charisma* has lost its charisma for me; let's eliminate *teach-ins, sit-ins, live-ins* and any other bloody ins; and I'm sick of *in depth,* which usually means in length."

Newsweek would like to recommend early retirement for *it's what's happening, where it's at, up against the wall, doing (my, your, his, her) thing, generation gap, name of the game, piece of the action, relevant, commitment, culturally deprived, disadvantaged, value judgment* and *meaningful relationship* (instead of campus sex).

But Art Buchwald deserves to pronounce the final, meaningful, relevant, viable judgment: "Another thing I'd like to see go," he says, "is stories about words that are in or out."

COMMENTARY: PERSUASION
BY HUMOROUS AND CLIMACTIC REPETITION

One highly effective way to bring about a desired change is to make the present practice or policy appear ridiculous by piling up instances that show the incongruous gap between theory and practice. This critical article on media writers' reliance upon clichés, slang, and jargon exemplifies this method while serving in itself as an example of current journalistic style.

Before examining the humorous examples of this faulty language, let us define some terms. A cliché is a hackneyed, trite expression that once may have had the verve and bounce of novelty but has been worked to death by speakers and writers; for example—*tell it like it is, way out, in this modern age.* Slang includes all expressions that once were newly coined but failed to achieve permanent acceptance and usage; for example—*teeny-boppers, trick bag, where it's at.* Jargon applies to technical terms and phrases which were once found almost exclusively within the language of a certain profession or craft but which in time have become widely adopted with little regard for their original and limited meaning; for example—*generation gap, commitment, culturally deprived, meaningful relationship.* Words such as *viable, definitization,* and *implementation* make up what this author calls "officialese," but they are also another form of jargon. As Robert Waddell has well said, "The only sign of life in jargon is this unctuous, flabby, mush-mouthed eagerness that everything shall be, in a broad general way, smooth and well greased."

That journalists especially should be found guilty of such language faults is understandable. Writing news reports as they do under the pressure of meeting deadlines and having to interest readers-on-the-run, they tend to welcome the ready-made phrase promising to convey the meaning wanted. Also in hopes of appearing up-to-date and knowledgeable, they like to adopt colorful expressions popularized by others. How often this policy fails in practice is a basic point being made by this *Newsweek* writer.

In short, working journalists have somewhat the same language problems the rest of us have in trying to convey to others in typescript or ink on a white expanse of paper the flesh-and-blood ideas and impressions we consider important to us and, we hope, important also to our readers. We are all tempted to rely upon current or "popular" terms and expressions currently in vogue, even though we may suspect them of being clichés, slang, or jargon. If we make no distinction at all between the vocabulary of our everyday speech and that of our far more formal writing, we risk deadening rather than enlivening our writing style. Rarely does such a recently coined expression as David Brinkley's favorite one, *up tight,* attain any permanence. And what is generally more dead than last year's "clever" column?

The *Newsweek* author himself switches from one level of language to the other, as these two neighboring sentences show:

> The jargon of the alienated, the oppressed, the discontented is becoming the idiom of Middle—nay, Colonial—America.
> Television writers babble like acid-heads, newspaper columnists sound like black militants; and advertising copywriters echo the slogans of the teeny-boppers.

He has inserted the slang words *acid-heads* and *teeny-boppers* in with standard English expressions. (By *standard English* we mean usage recognized as having achieved at least a good promise of enjoying permanent acceptance.) He mixes these levels of language throughout the article: "cabalistic expressions are taken over by the square world. . . . Journalists, too, overkill with jargon." Expressions like "the square world" and "overkill" have not yet attained universal acceptance.

The article is a persuasive one, impressing us with the inadequacy of much of current journalistic language. Its sequence of one example after the other of the kinds of faulty language vividly shows that nonstandard English does not generally produce the effects journalists intend it to have. The opening emphasizes the incongruity between the dignified nature of "the restored village of Williamsburg, Va.," and the title of its annual report—"Williamsburg Tells It Like It Was." And as a concluding protest against clichés, following *Newsweek's* own list, comes the quotation from Art Buchwald to add the final authoritative blow and to serve as a means of making the article itself humorously ironic: "another thing I'd like to see go . . . is stories about words that are in or out." This ending is climactic, coming as it does with its final surprise twist to make this article on objectionable journalistic language itself a total cliché.

WHAT DOES IT SAY?

1. How do you classify *groovy, beautiful,* and *out of sight* when these are exclamations?

2. What is objectionable about the advertisement which is quoted: "Turn on, before you turn in . . . with your own fun-at-home steam bath"?

3. Why can *up tight* possibly be considered more expressive than a term like *tensed up*?

4. By its context what meaning do you give to the word *chrestomathy* in this quotation: "A chrestomathy of current phrases that a representative group of lovers of English offer up for burial. . . ."?

5. Why are expressions such as *with-it, so-called, sort of,* and *you know* considered objectionable in written language?

6. How is the term *the establishment* holding up as time passes?

7. Have some of the terms recommended for "early retirement" by *Newsweek* actually disappeared or do they still turn up in the language of harassed journalists?

8. What has happened to "groovy!"?

WHAT DO YOU THINK?

1. One reason why the habitual use of slang expressions is frowned upon is that terms like *groovy* and *way out* may quickly lose their effectiveness and become outdated. Prepare a list of slang expressions popular at present on your campus, and describe what they mean and how they are used and under what circumstances.

2. Sports writers pride themselves on finding "action" words to give their game reports dash and color. Examine the sports section of a daily newspaper, and compare the literal meaning of the descriptive terms with the actual events being described. Try to classify your findings and present them in an organized essay.

3. Without necessarily naming any names, list the language "hang-ups" of one or more of the following types and describe the circumstances when they are most evident.

Class lecturer	Tiresome acquaintance
Chiding parents	Well-meaning store clerk
Presumptuous relative	Neighborhood gossip
Opinionated employer	Barber or beauty operator
Clergyman	Disc jockey

4. Analyze a typical Art Buchwald or Russell Baker newspaper column, and show in detail, by references to the article, how the author has seized upon some word or expression very much in the news and ridiculed its application to some extreme situation.

5. Give a detailed description of an experience you have had with a term or expression such as one of the following and the reality which it now assumes in your memory.

Sit-in	Protest	Soul music
Live-in	Confrontation	Soul food
Love-in	Blood brother	Integration
Charity	Vacation	Weekend

The Children's Ghetto
by RICHARD GOLDSTEIN

Kids don't watch teevee the way the rest of us do. They sit right up there, mere inches from the screen, environmentalized from the start. They dig anything that "moves" (this week, watch a kid respond to a commercial, singing along with the jingle, or following the jump cuts with appropriate nods and gestures). They show a corresponding impatience with anything which is static, analytical or visually witless. Those who object to extensive viewing by the young (the hide-the-set-in-the-closet syndrome) miss the point of television: it doesn't destroy taste, but it re-orients it.

Right now, two kinds of programs seem to fascinate the kids (I took my own informal poll): syndicated cartoons and situation comedy re-runs. The "educational" format has by no means lost its impact on the young, but the heyday of the televised nursery school has passed, and the remnants—*Captain Kangaroo, Romper Room*—creak with age. They are particularly guilty of insensitivity to the esthetic of momentum which so captivates their audience. Next to the dizzying fluidity of children's action shows, they almost seem like radio. Only Misterogers (the spry, soft-spoken man who ends his late-afternoon puppet show by telling his audience, "You make every day a special day") transcends the limitations of his environment. Though he some-times seems effete to me, when I overcome the Mickey Spillane in my innards, Misterogers makes me understand why a kid will turn to teevee for love, when his folks are busy.

As for those eternal re-runs which dominate a child's afternoon, I think the appeal lies in their pulse—an almost uninterrupted stream of slapstick—coupled with a mode of presentation which seems nos-talgic to those of us who remember these shows from their first run, but must seem oddly stylized to anyone seeing them for the first time today. A kid who watches *My Little Margie* in 1969 is going to think he's at a costume party.

Finally, there are those cartoons. Dozens of syndicated packages compete for the attention of the very young—most sponsored by toy companies, but many associated with products tangential to a child's existence (the old training-bra theory of consumption at work). On any weekday morning, should you feel the urge to glimpse the face of American childhood today, and American adolescence tomorrow, you can sit through *Casper, Kimba, Krazy Kat* (offering little evidence of the original's charm) and *Underdog.* But Saturday is the traditional children's feast, with cartoons cutting a wide swath through the morning and afternoon.

What is so fascinating about these moving comic strips to a viewer raised in another generation is their tone and pace, which is distinct from anything else on television. These shows move in a continuous arc of color and sound, with little variation in anything but the locales and the costuming of the villains. Visually, they are uniformly flat, with sparsely detailed figures deliberately distorted to resemble comic books. There is no attempt to portray authentic motion; these super-heroes move in spurts, and when they stand still long enough to talk, it is often only their mouths and eyes which move. Their faces remain static. A popular technique is to graft real lips onto an animated figure, producing a mutant which is real in neither the "live" or "drawn" sense, but an authentic creature of make-believe.

About the violence: of course, it is disproportionately high, but no more so than anything on prime time teevee. What disturbs (and fascinates) me is not the frequency of violence in cartoons, but the sterility which surrounds it. Brutality is structurally essential to the contemporary cartoon. In a television action series, all elements of plot are reduced to a series of skirmishes, staged with virtually no reference to emotions which accompany violence. In a typical plot, a vast white whale, accompanied (naturally) by two child-sidekicks, is searching for a school of metallic fish, who are the villain's me-chanical henchmen. When the adversaries clash, the ensuing impact is illustrated with exploding fields of color. Violence is very trippy in a teevee cartoon. And when the show is over, what we remember most about these frequent clashes is not what they felt like, but how they looked.

As a kid, my access to violence on television was severely limited. But more important, the cartoon characters who often engaged in gratuitous brawling were highly personalized creations. When Bugs Bunny beat up on Elmer Fudd, you damn well felt the effect of those encounters on the characters involved. Even in a cinematic cartoon like *Road Runner,* the perpetual conflict between the loser-coyote and his oblivious assailant provides a genuinely poignant tension for the audience.

But who can identify with a faceless hero, who moves mechanically through a landscape of unrelieved tonal intensity, and whose only true adventure comes in the barrage of brilliant colors which accompany his every assault?

I'm afraid the generation gap in televiewing extends even to the esthetics of revolt. Where are the anti-heroes of the children's ghetto? Certainly not out there shouting "kid power" at the mad wizard. In fact, the rule is strict (though loving) obedience, and unquestioning loyalty to the parental creature. Whenever children participate in these shows, they are the hero's helpmates, but I have never seen a cartoon in which the kid refuses to hang onto the dragon's neck or the white whale's tale.

COMMENTARY: PERSUASION BY CRITICAL ANALYSIS

Just as a physician in examining a patient looks for telltale signs his highly trained senses can analyze and identify as possible sources of illness, so can a skilled critic examine television entertainment and analyze its possible effects on the social wellbeing of the viewing audience. In "The Children's Ghetto," Richard Goldstein seeks to persuade us that he is such a highly competent critic and that his analysis of television programs aimed at children is a correct one.

Let us take a careful look at how an expert goes about establishing his competency as a critic so that his interpretation of certain trends in television programs for children will be accepted. Firstly, he presents evidence in his introduction showing his ability as an observer of how children react while watching their programs—"They sit right up there, mere inches from the screen, environmentalized from the start." Like a psychologist watching the reactions of mice in a maze, he notes the general behavior pattern of these young viewers.

At the end of this opening paragraph, he tosses in a startling generalization about the effect of television on taste: "it doesn't destroy taste, but it re-orients it." This kind of authoritative pronouncement, following his demonstration of ability as observer, at once bolsters his position as a competent critic who has something important to say.

His second paragraph begins with further evidence supporting his role as analytical observer: "Right now, two kinds of programs seem to fascinate the kids (I took my own informal poll). . . ." He also immediately thereafter establishes his familiarity with the history of children's programs, being sure to refer to two specific, outmoded programs—*Captain Kangaroo* and *Romper Room*. His analysis of the causes for their decline in popularity again is intended to demonstrate his reliability and high degree of perceptiveness. Who could refuse to give him credit for observing, in the final sentence of this paragraph, that somehow "a kid will turn to teevee for love, when his folks are busy"?

Once more, in his third paragraph, he builds the reader's confidence in his knowledge and skill by discussing the second of the two kinds of programs he has previously stated—the "situation comedy re-runs." And again he reveals the feature giving this program its appeal—"an almost uninterrupted stream of slapstick." He further shows his insight by noting that "A kid who watches *My Little Margie* in 1969 is going to think he's at a costume party."

Now all of these observations and details can be said to have been only preparation for the main analysis (diagnosis) and conclusion (prognosis) yet to come. For beginning with his fourth paragraph, he comes to the kind of program which most concerns him—"syndicated cartoons." In fact, his language underlines its importance: "Finally, there are those cartoons."

With the deliberate restraint of a social scientist, he turns his attention to the cartoons appearing daily on the small screen. As a note of forewarning, regarding the long range effects of watching these programs, he remarks that one needs only to look at the faces of youngsters absorbed in these cartoons to see what they will be like as adolescents.

He next focuses on the "tone and pace" of these cartoons, the comic book distortion of the figures, and the emotionless expression of the faces even while mouths and eyes move. Then, in the same dispassionate tone, he discusses the violence making up the action vividly portrayed in the cartoons. Where he does bring in another of his judgments, it is again in low key: "What disturbs (and fascinates) me is not the frequency of violence in cartoons, but the sterility which surrounds it." He identifies this "sterility" as the absence of show of emotion by the figures doing these acts of brutality, and he goes on to contrast this lack of emotional display with the kind of emotional identification he used to experience in watching *Bugs Bunny* and *Road Runner*—cartoons wherein the characters did register feelings.

It is only in his concluding two paragraphs that he raises his main criticism of these cartoons: the fact that children cannot identify emotionally with the "faceless hero," an identification he indirectly suggests should be the proper result of viewing such scenes of violence and brutality. As something of a corollary to this conclusion, he notes that none of these cartoons ever show the children who are the "hero's helpmates" in rebellion against their masterful hero—nor do they ever leave their all-powerful hero.

Throughout the analysis, we can detect his clinical tone, but he persuades us to go along with him because he seems to present good evidence as to his fitness to make such a study and to arrive at the modest conclusions he offers. Do you now share his uneasiness regarding the long range effects upon children who watch these cartoons?

WHAT DOES IT SAY?

1. What are the connotations of the title, "The Children's Ghetto," as applied to the kind of television programs being offered to children as entertainment?

2. How can a child be "environmentalized" by the programs he habitually watches?

3. What are *jump cuts* and *jingles* as they appear in commercials?

4. What does the author mean when he insists that television "doesn't destroy taste, but it re-orients it"?

5. Who is Mickey Spillane and why is his name linked here with children's programs?

6. What kind of comedy antics do you associate with *slapstick*?

7. Why is the term a *mutant* appropriate as a description of the typical cartoon superhero?

8. What is the author trying to tell us when he describes television violence as being "very trippy"?

WHAT DO YOU THINK?

1. In a hurried reading of Richard Goldstein's highly persuasive article, you may have unthinkingly accepted some of his really very controversial statements. Here, as possible subjects for an essay expressing your agreement or disagreement with him, are a number of such observations. Choose one, and discuss it in the light of your own experience with these programs.

   (a) "It [television] doesn't destroy taste, but it re-orients it."
   (b) "A kid will turn to teevee for love, when his folks are busy."
   (c) "But Saturday is the traditional children's feast. . . ."
   (d) "Brutality is structurally essential to the contemporary cartoon."
   (e) "Violence is very trippy in a teevee cartoon."
   (f) "What disturbs me is not the frequency of violence in cartoons, but the sterility which surrounds it."

2. Try to recall the kind of pleasure you had in watching one special program series for children that you greatly enjoyed. Describe your anticipation of its appearance, your home surroundings where you viewed it, your feelings on seeing it begin, its chief characters, their typical actions and outcome, and what effect—if any—this program may have had on you as you now look back upon it.

3. If convenient, make your own study of the tastes and behavior of children (possibly in your own family) while they watch current programs broadcast for them. (You might want to imitate the approach and manner of Richard Goldstein.)

4. For "adults," re-runs of old situation comedy series like *Lucy* continue to appear "eternally" on home screens. View one of them, if possible, and report on your reactions to one of the episodes. Are you more "sophisticated" in your tastes now than you were when you saw such an episode years ago? Describe the typical features of the program and your reactions to the parts and the whole.

5. Almost everyone grows nostalgic recalling the events and movies seen on the Saturday mornings of his childhood. If you have some vivid memories of such incidents and pictures, try to recreate for your readers one of those memorable Saturday mornings. (You may find chronological order helpful in organizing your essay.)

Fashion: A "Bore War"?
by MARSHALL McLUHAN

Many people have commented on clothing as weaponry, as Carlyle did on institutions as clothing, but there are a good many unexplored facets of the topic of clothing and fashion.

For a century, to take one example, the French had made strenuous efforts to induce their Arab colonials to strip off the purdah. In the Algerian "troubles" of 1954–1958, things were reversed. The Arabs themselves actually had their women take off the purdah so that they might infiltrate the enemy ranks in European guise. Without the purdah these hapless females were not only unable to infiltrate European precincts, they were unable to cross the street. The stark, staring confrontation with motorcars and buses induced hysteria. Even worse, when they resumed the purdah and returned to their old surroundings, they discovered that they had become alienated from them and had undergone a radical sensory change.

At a quite different level, Africans attempting to acquire literacy have found it expedient to wear European costume for the simple reason that it retains a great deal more bodily heat and energy than their native costume. The act of reading printed matter drains off a huge proportion of human energy, as any convalescent knows. Anthropologists are well acquainted with the fact that the scantily clad native cannot go without food and water for more than 24 hours because of the rapid dissipation of his energies over the entire surface of his exposed body. On the other hand, the heavily clad Eskimo in a most inhuman environment can last for six or seven days without food or water. In contrast to the Western function of clothing, desert dwellers wear heavy clothing to exclude the heat.

These are all simple cases of clothing as weaponry designed to combat hostile conditions, and an inventory of such weaponry could easily be extended. Clothing as an extension of the human skin is as much a technology as the wheel or the compass. Strangely, the world of fashion has never been approached from this point of view. Is it merely a "bore war"? Is it merely an attempt to add a bit of spice and variety to the monotony of life? Possibly the fact that there is no such thing as fashion in native societies may provide an approach to this question. In these societies clothing indicates age and status and serves complex ritual functions that relate the energies of the tribe to cosmic forces, as much as we relate our energies to tanks and airplanes. Clothing is power and the organization of human energy, both private and corporate. In tribal societies they prize the integral power of the corporate far above the variations of the individual costume. In fact, when all members of the tribe wear the same costumes, they find the same psychic security that we do in living in uniform, mechanized environments. Since our environments are so drastically uniform, we feel we can afford a wide play of private expression in behavior and costume. However, when we seek to rally the corporate energies for sharply defined objectives, we do not hesitate to impose uniforms. Both the military costume of the citizen as robot and the ceremonial costume of the elite at dignified functions are exact parallels to the tribal use of costume. It is somewhere between the military uniform and the fixity of formal attire that the world of fashion falls.

Is then fashion the poor man's art? Is it an attempt to adjust the sensory life to a changing technological environment? It would seem very likely that this is the case. The teen-agers have begun to experiment with clothing as an artist does with his pigments. Many of the hippies make their own clothes, and many of the clothes worn by teen-agers look as though they've never been made by anybody. There is, nevertheless, an unmistakable rapport between the shaggy and disheveled garments of the teen-aged male and the sounds of the music and the look of the art to which he also gives his loyalty. After 2,500 years of visual culture the violent switch to the audile-tactile stress, and resulting indifference to visual appearances, is a fact that concerns all our institutions and experiences. The world of fashion, whether at the level of the slob or the snob, now has the same textural qualities that express rebellion against the departing visual values.

Colors play a very large part in this rebellion. Color is apprehended not by the periphery of the eye but by the central macula, and the shift from the outer to the inner area of the eye is as much a part of the information implosion as television.

Considering clothing, then, as an anti-environmental gesture, whether physical or psychical, it becomes fascinating to study this language. The study of armor as a clothing related to the stirrup makes a nice correlation with the clothing of the cowboy or of the motorcar as clothing. The rapid change of car styles reveals it as a form of human clothing.

The mini-skirt, of course, is not a fashion. It is a return to the tribal costume worn by men and women alike in all oral societies. As our world moves from hardware to software, the mini-skirt is a major effort to reprogram our sensory lives in a tribal pattern of tactility and involvement. Nudity itself is not a visual so much as a sculptural and tactile experience.

Whereas clothing is the enclosed space of Western literate man, the attire of the medieval or Renaissance page boy and gentleman strongly stressed a world of contours. Again, if the enclosed attire of literate man strove for individualist and specialist effects, dichotomizing the attire of male and female, the exact opposite now seems to be true. A recent Associated Press story provides some examples:

"As women begin to look like and in a sense become men, the men, freed of the responsibility of running things . . . become more flamboyant," James Laver, British fashion historian, recently told an interviewer.

"Man is trying to get women to notice him," Mr. Laver said, "and I don't think his interest in clothing and colognes and so on is necessarily going to make him effeminate."

So what has he been doing lately to make women notice him, now that his wife is bringing home half the rent money?

He's wearing:

—Turtlenecks. Men have probably struck their hardest blow for fashion independence by snubbing the necktie, bowtie and a variety of other starched harnesses. Though the necktie industry swears it is not choked up over the trend, the turtleneck boom is still booming.

—Fur coats. Men are wearing rugged Persian lambs cut military fashion and moleskins in hardy trench styles. When the fur is mink, it is hidden unostentatiously as lining.

—Colored shirts. Television started it. Prominent people appearing on camera were asked to wear blue shirts because white bounces light. And since others wanted to look as though they were prominent enough to be asked to be guests on television panels, they wore blue, too. After blue, could yellow, green or even pink be far behind?

Perhaps fashion is a kind of macro-gesticulation of an entire culture having a dialogue or an interfacing encounter with its new technologies.

COMMENTARY: PERSUASION BY AUTHORITATIVE STANCE

As everyone knows, Marshall McLuhan is no timid, hesitant critic of the social-economic-moral environment in which we all live: a world, he argues, shaped by the media of the printing press, radio, and now television. He has taken upon himself the task of telling us in no uncertain terms what effects the media are having in determining the quality of our personal lives and character. He has said: "Since you cannot survive the effects of media if you huddle or hide, you must rush out and kick them in the guts—give them what for—right in the midriff. And they respond very well to this treatment. Media, after all, are only extensions of ourselves. The road to understanding media effects begins with arrogant superiority."

McLuhan's unique writing style grows out of that "arrogant superiority" needed to take on the multibillion dollar, omnipresent voices and faces of the media. His stance of absolute assurance appears in all of his highly controversial books such as *The Mechanical Bride, Understanding Media,* and his recent *War and Peace in the Global Village.* His self confidence shows itself in the series of one-sentence judgments characteristic of his style, sentences like those found in the essays of Ralph Waldo Emerson and Henry David Thoreau. Our selection here, "Fashion: a 'Bore War'?" has many such universal statements. Here are a few of them:

> Without the purdah these hapless females were not only unable to infiltrate European precincts, they were unable to cross the street.
> Clothing as an extension of the human skin is as much a technology as the wheel or the compass.
> Clothing is power and the organization of human energy, both private and corporate.
> After 2,500 years of visual culture the violent switch to the audile-tactile stress, and resulting indifference to visual appearances, is a fact that concerns all our institutions and experiences.

Those who agree with McLuhan consider such pronouncements, however unsupported by detail, in the same light as McLuhan does himself—that is, as *probes.* "That's why," he says, "I feel free to make them sound as outrageous or extreme as possible. Until you make it extreme, the probe is not very efficient. Probes, to be effective, must have this edge, strength, pressure. Of course they *sound* very dogmatic. That doesn't mean you are committed to them. You may toss them away."

Puns, or word-play, are also a feature of his "probing" style as can be seen in the title of one of his books: *The Medium Is the Massage,* a pun on "the medium is the message." In our essay the question whether fashion is a "bore war" centers on a pun, in that "bore war" alludes to the Boer War (1899-1902) in which Great Britain defeated the descendants of Dutch colonists in South Africa. (To explain all of the implications of this pun and its relation to fashions of clothing requires more space than a commentary allows. But consult an encyclopedia or history of this war and decide for yourself the relevance of the pun. McLuhan, you see, demands very literate readers!)

It is small wonder, then, that he has been called a wide variety of names by his critics—names such as these: "King of Popthink," "Electronic Man," "Oracle," "The Fake Social Scientist," "The Shoddy Scholar," and "The Prophet." His "message" and style continue to evoke wide response. Before making up your mind about him, read at least one of his books and consider criticisms such as those appearing in the following essay. You can expect controversy, but this is not unusual since McLuhan is the man about whom Tom Wolfe, the well known social critic, raised this significant question: "Suppose he is what he sounds like, the most important thinker since Newton, Darwin, Freud, Einstein, and Pavlov—what if he is right?"

WHAT DOES IT SAY?

1. Who is the Carlyle referred to in the opening sentence, and what was his view "on institutions as clothing"?

2. What is "the purdah" and how could Arab women deprived of it for a time and then made to assume it again have "undergone a radical sensory change"?

3. In what sense can clothing be called "an extension of the human skin"?

4. Try to translate into scenes and pictures all that McLuhan is telling us in this sentence: "Both the military costume of the citizen as robot and the ceremonial costume of the elite at dignified functions are exact parallels to the tribal use of costume."

5. How possibly can fashion be called "the poor man's art"?

6. What meaning do you give to this statement in the fifth paragraph: "After 2,500 years of visual culture the violent switch to the audile-

tactile stress, and resulting indifference to visual appearances, is a fact that concerns all our institutions and experiences"?

7. In what sense can he correctly say, "The mini-skirt, of course, is not a fashion."

8. What in the world can be meant by calling fashion "a kind of macro-gesticulation of an entire culture . . ."?

WHAT DO YOU THINK?

1. Want to try your hand at being a McLuhan? Write an essay of *probes* (insights and "hunches" thought out to their extremes). Some possible topics:
   (a) Wearing Levis "of course, is not a fashion" but instead a new way of looking at life.
   (b) Why should women's skirts grow shorter during periods of a nation's prosperity?
   (c) "Nudity itself is not a visual so much as a sculptural and tactile experience."
   (d) Do clothes make the man?
   (e) Do women dress for other women?
   (f) Long hair is a sign of _____
   (g) Not bathing regularly means _____

2. Here are some "McLuhanisms" from Gerald E. Stearn's *McLuhan: Hot and Cool.*[1] Write an essay trying to define one of them and your view regarding it.
   (a) "I don't explain—I explore."
   (b) "I am an investigator. I make probes."
   (c) "I have no point of view. I do not stay in one position."
   (d) "As people become more involved they know less and less."

3. McLuhan insists that it is not the quality of what we see and hear on television that influences us, but rather the medium of television itself ("The medium is the message"). He advocates, therefore, that all television broadcasting should be banned for one year in order that we could learn just what television is doing to us. Since you, or younger people in your family, are of the "TV generation," what do you think this medium is doing to us? What do you advocate regarding it?

4. Describe human beings as "a stranger from another planet" might characterize them after having nothing more than a week of television watching by which to judge human beings.

[1] Dial Press, 1967.

McLuhan: The Soft Machine
by THOMAS R. EDWARDS

Though it's hard to believe that people really read or talk much about Marshall McLuhan these days, he and his critics keep electing him man of the decade. Frank Kermode remarked in 1963 that "in a truly literate society [*The Gutenberg Galaxy*] would start a long debate," but no one has waited for so improbable a millennium; McLuhan goes on writing new books and republishing old ones, but it hardly matters, since the debate about him now seems to have become self-generating. In *McLuhan: Hot and Cool,* an intriguing new olio of things by and about the master, we are assured of his importance by ad men, hip Jesuits, Susan Sontag and various Canadians, assured of his folly by Dwight Macdonald, George P. Elliott, Christopher Ricks and other Urizenic tyrants of typographical law, assured of his mixed value by judicious Centrists like Harold Rosenberg, Jonathan Miller and George Steiner.[1] But no one, least of all McLuhan himself, doubts that he has

Reprinted from *Partisan Review,* Summer, 1968. © 1968 by *Partisan Review.* Reprinted by permission of the author and publication.
[1] Marshall McLuhan: *The Gutenberg Galaxy: The Making of Typographic Man* (paperback), University of Toronto Press, 1966. $2.25; *The Mechanical Bride: Folklore of Industrial Man* (paperback), Beacon Press, 1967. $2.95; Marshall McLuhan and Quentin Fiore: *The Medium is the Massage: An Inventory of Effects,* Random House, 1967. $10.00; *Keep in Touch,* McGraw-Hill, 1968. $5.95; Marshall McLuhan and Parker Harley: *Through the Vanishing Point,* Harper and Row, 1968. $6.95; *McLuhan: Hot and Cool,* ed. G. E. Stearn, Dial Press, 1967. $4.95.

to be dealt with somehow. What is his fatal fascination? How has a mind that is by any known test slipshod and derivative, a style that so relentlessly cultivates the tasteless and the banal, occupied so much critical space? How can a man who solemnly assures us that "the word parody means a road that goes alongside another road" be trusted with any harder science than Greek etymologies?

It is I think best to assume that *what* McLuhan says is the least important thing about him. McLuhanism is not a message but a medium, a rendering of the uneasy excitement about contemporary culture that grips thoughtful people of a certain age. To my knowledge none of the contributors to *Hot and Cool* is under thirty, and for the people who are creating the new state of things or will have to live longest with it, McLuhan himself is nearly irrelevant. The Lumpen-youth, in whom his prognostics seem best realized, don't read much and don't need him to tell them where they are, while their more clerkly peers, still provisionally interested in print and rational operations, find him superficial and old hat. (For them the electronic culture is also a paperback culture, and they read or at least carry Lévi-Strauss and Fanon, not *Understanding Media*.) McLuhan's audience consists mostly of people like himself, middle-aged souls formed by the literary culture of the twenties and thirties but anxious to feel up to date and touchingly sure that an intelligent reader of Joyce and Eliot can grasp just about anything if he sets his mind to it. There are no essays in *Hot and Cool* by psychologists or communications scientists—the wise, apparently, are saying nothing till they see.

McLuhan is *our* sage, alas. Like us, he can apprehend technical innovation only through analogy. Like us, he can do "research" only by pasting up other people's discoveries. Like us, he wants badly to have a sense of humor, keep cool and witty in the face of seeming nightmare, respond openly to the new without quite yielding to its seductions, remain critically objective without holing up in pedantry and moral fogeyism. His task has been to find a style, an expressive medium for his predicament and ours, and it's his style, in the largest sense, that here concerns me.

He's at his worst when he plays the sage, pronouncing organized conceptual plenitude upon a world that would otherwise be unbearable in its randomness, a Virgil in search of other Dantes than just himself. But if we would locate our infernal regions elsewhere, in just that consciousness of personal and collective failure he so insistently excludes from his scheme, we might do well, in dismissing his pretensions, not to dismiss the phenomena he calls to our attention. He himself, in his literary presence, is a modern phenomenon, and a particularly pleasant one. He's not a serious man—indeed it's one of his virtues that in some moods he would take this as a compliment, as I mean it to be. Rather he's a modern type of the Enthusiast, the man

who (like some Swiftian Projector) has found the right "approach" at last
and wants very badly to share his great secret with the world. He
loves the sound of words like *absolutely, totally, perfect, exact, entire,
complete,* as well as ones like *Fantastic, amazing, tremendous;* and we
all know that voice and have felt inner dismay as it approaches across
the noisy room, grips our elbow and solves the universe before our
eyes. If the solutions change from moment to moment, that is only
because the problems do too, and there are possibilities of delight as
well as dismay in the spectacle of perpetual mental motion and an
amiable indifference to one's own comic value. It would be miraculous
if a "surround" as fragmented, discontinuous, irrational as he says ours
is *could* be adequately explicated by a mind so infatuated with historical
patterns and universal correspondences, and so innocently committed
to instrumental solutions. But the McLuhan style, with its suprarational
agility, its hunger to know just enough about everything to escape
ever having to shut up, its saving power to forget what it just said,
does in a funny way convey the feel of experience nowadays and
demonstrates some of the skills it takes to keep going.

Indignation or horror is not the best response to McLuhan. He
once dismissed hostile critics by observing that "many people would
rather be villains than nitwits," and one suspects that he quite enjoys
the lurid roles he's so often cast in; but his own literary presence
is hardly that menacing. He would be at home in a Dickens novel
or a play of Shaw's, and there you would never mistake him for
a *villain.*

COMMENTARY: PERSUASION BY RIDICULE

Since the classical times of Aristophanes, one of the favorite means
of discrediting important or popular figures has been that of making
them appear ridiculous. We can see this intent in Mr. Edwards' skillful
use of the device of *irony* to portray Marshall McLuhan and his fol-
lowers as being interesting but misguided people. Irony makes up
both the substance and the manner of this "message."

Traditionally, a writer or speaker relies upon irony to say one thing
but mean its *opposite,* or at least to mean something *other* than what
he says. He also tries to make good use of the two basic methods
found at work in almost all ironic statements: *blaming by praising*
and *praising by blaming.* Irony thus is a very sophisticated form of
expression and requires the writer to keep his target and language
always clearly in mind.

Let us consider first some examples found in this essay of *blaming
by praising.* In the opening paragraph, McLuhan is called "the master"
but in a context which implies that McLuhan does not deserve such

a title. In that same sentence, as in the very first one of the opening, Mr. Edwards goes out of his way to belittle those who consider McLuhan important. Another paragraph opens with apparent praise: "McLuhan is *our* sage, alas," and the irony is spelled out when in the beginning of the next paragraph we read: "He's at his worst when he plays the sage. . . ."

As might be expected, we find fewer examples of *praising by blaming,* but here is at least one: "He's not a serious man—indeed it is one of his virtues that in some moods he would take this as a compliment, as I mean it to be." Most of us would probably consider it a compliment to be called a "serious" person and so would not appreciate being described as "not serious."

The examples so far cited illustrate traditional irony, statements which *say* one thing but *mean* exactly the opposite. A somewhat different kind of irony is found in the very first sentence of the opening paragraph: "Though it's hard to believe that people really read or talk much about Marshall McLuhan these days, he and his critics keep electing him man of the decade." Here Mr. Edwards means something *other* than what he is saying, although not its direct opposite. He knows very well how much McLuhan continues to be a controversial figure. The six recent books listed in the footnote attest this interest, as does the later admission—however sardonically stated—"But no one, least of all McLuhan himself, doubts that he has to be dealt with somehow."

The author then proceeds to show how he is going to deal with this controversial figure. He employs another ironic form of speech, the *paradox,* to state his thesis sentence in the opening of the second paragraph: "It is I think best to assume that *what* McLuhan says is the least important thing about him." This statement seems to contain a self-contradiction. How can a man be considered important if what he says is of no importance? But as the rest of the essay shows, it is the phenomenon of "McLuhancy" and not the man himself that Mr. Edwards deems important. So the apparent contradiction between what is said and what is really meant makes this statement a *paradox.*

On the whole, as the concluding two paragraphs repeatedly demonstrate, the irony is of the *blame by praising* kind. Sentences begin with apparent praise but end ridiculing the very qualities they initially extol, as for example does this fine *periodic* one, wherein the main idea emerges only at the end: "But the McLuhan style, with its suprarational agility, its hunger to know just enough about everything to escape ever having to shut up, its saving power to forget what it just said, does in a funny way convey the feel of experience nowadays and demonstrates some of the skills it takes to keep going."

But despite all of these ironies, Mr. Edwards' stance reveals a sneaking admiration for the "phenomenon" he considers Marshall

McLuhan to be. And this tone of begrudging respect and affability makes the reader—as the author surely desired—smile and admit the worth and the wit of both the attacker and the one attacked.

WHAT DOES IT SAY?

1. In the opening paragraph we find terms such as the following used ironically. Explain the irony you find in one of them:

   A truly literary society

   A millennium

   Hip Jesuits

   Urizenic tyrants

   Parody

   Judicious Centrists

   Greek etymologies

2. When Edwards maintains that "To my knowledge none of the contributors to *Hot and Cool* is under thirty," and that McLuhan's "audience consists mostly of people like himself, middle-aged souls," what is he arguing?

3. Who are "the Lumpen-youth" Edwards refers to?

4. Can you identify Lévi-Strauss and Fanon? If you can't, would Edwards consider you one of "the Lumpen-youth"?

5. Do you agree with Edwards that because psychologists and communications scientists "apparently are saying nothing till they see" "they" are "wise"?

6. According to Edwards, what features characterize McLuhan's style?

7. In what sense is McLuhan probably correct in calling our social environment "a surround"?

8. Why would McLuhan never be mistaken for "a villain" in a Dickens novel?

WHAT DO YOU THINK?

1. Write an essay wherein you *blame by praising* one of the following that you consider a worthy target of irony:

   An overrated athlete

A once-popular political figure

An irritating columnist

A too-well-known talk-show performer

A neighborhood pest

A drive-in theater manager

A used car dealer

A car insurance salesman

A revolutionary film director

A writer or poet you dislike

A most tedious class

A comic strip hero

2. Mr. Edwards' essay appeared in *The Partisan Review,* a periodical proud of its "intellectual" tone and subject matter. Study several issues of this journal and write an essay discussing its intellectual appeal and content.

3. If you are familiar with any of McLuhan's books, are you in agreement or disagreement with the following summary of Hugh Kenner's views on McLuhan as found in a new book of essays, *McLuhan: Pro & Con,* reviewed by Dudley Young.[2]

> There are three souls dwelling within McLuhan's breast: a pop artist and thinker of considerable genius, a wildly irresponsible funny-man addicted to inaccurate generalization, and the ultimately sinister oracle whose prophecies may hasten the arrival of the millenial nirvana he contemplates.

4. Here are typical McLuhan questions. Choose one for an essay discussion:
   (a) What was the effect of the radio on movies? On newspapers? On magazines? On language? On the concept of time?
   (b) What changes occurred in radio listening and programming after television?
   (c) Why does the twelve-year-old tend to turn from the television set to radio?
   (d) Is it only coincidence that young people are currently interested in astrology, clairvoyance, and the occult?
   (e) What is the real use of the computer in the future?

[2] *The New York Times Book Review,* September 8, 1968.

part VI
SCIENCE AND THE FUTURE

LOGIC AND COMPOSITION: STRAIGHT THINKING, VALID JUDGMENTS

The art of persuasion, sadly enough, does not exclude the possibility of being illogical. Indeed, people have often been swayed by arguments that are far from sound, whether those arguments are deliberately misleading or not. What is more, if you are unskilled in the techniques of logical reasoning you might well, unconsciously, find yourself guilty of irrational, false arguments and leave yourself open to the charge of being either a fool or a fraud. And no one, we suspect, wants to regard himself in these terms.

Clearly, it is important, therefore, to consider the nature and quality of what passes for most of us as "thinking," because what we say and write puts us on trial in the eyes of others. The image one has of himself is important to his self respect and, therefore, to his self confidence. And the impression one makes on others is important, especially when it reveals that he possesses excellent judgment, implying, among other things, his ability to appraise facts and thus to make relevant inferences and deductions from them.

The science that deals with the criteria of valid thought—what is loosely referred to as "correct thinking,"—is called *logic*. Ever since the days of Aristotle the study of *rhetoric* has been tied in with logical reasoning by means of the *syllogism*, which is a form of argument that reaches a conclusion on the basis of two premises. The first premise, called the *major premise,* is always a generalization accepted as valid, presumably, on the grounds of common experience. This premise may also be called an *assumption.* The second premise is less broad, and states a particular instance that comes under the head of the major premise. It is called the *minor premise.* The *conclusion* is the inevitable inference drawn from the two premises. Here, for example, is a syllogism:

> Major Premise: All heavy cigarette smokers run a considerable risk of getting lung cancer.
> Minor Premise: My sister is a heavy cigarette smoker.
> Conclusion: My sister runs a considerable risk of getting lung cancer.

In this syllogism, as in all syllogisms, if you accept the validity of the major premise and the accuracy of the minor premise, there is no escaping the conclusion. The *reasoning,* we say, is valid.

Syllogistic arguments, however, are seldom phrased with such completeness, and the major premise, the assumption upon which the argument rests, is often concealed. The above syllogism, for instance, would most likely be stated as follows:

> My sister is running a considerable risk of getting lung cancer because she is such a heavy smoker of cigarettes.

Here the major premise is taken for granted, as it is in statements such as these:

> If you drink, don't drive. (Assumption: Drivers who drink are dangerous.)
> Fail the final exam and you'll fail the course. (Assumption: Anyone who fails the final exam in this course is certain to fail the course.)

These shortened syllogisms are called *enthymemes.*

Recent studies in *semantics* call attention to the fact that there are at least three kinds of statements that make up our spoken and written utterances, whereby we communicate with one another:

1. Statements of easily established facts; for example: The smog today makes your eyes smart.

2. Statements of judgment or evaluation; for example: Driving on the freeways through the city is becoming dangerous.

3. Statements of emotion; for example: Me ride a bus? Nothing doing!

Of these three statements the first is rather easily confirmed or disproved. It is a question merely of the testimony of one's senses. The second statement, however, is clearly an *assumption,* an idea taken for granted by the speaker. This is the type of statement that makes up the major premise of a syllogism and obviously requires supporting evidence in the form of details and possibly illustrations. The third statement is a mere expression of feeling, and is normally accepted for what it is. It could, of course, lead to an *argument* should someone who has strong feelings to the contrary take exception to it, and ask questions such as these:

> What do you have against buses?
> Do you think it is cheaper and less troublesome to drive your own car through a crowded city going and coming from work?
> And what about the parking problem?

It is the assumptions that we are asked to accept which present the difficulty in agreeing with a proposition. We demand answers to fundamental questions such as these:

> What can I know for certain?
> How can I verify the truth of this assumption?

The problem is complicated by the nature of language. Words have often been described as "slippery." The reason for this is that words are merely *symbols,* standing as the name of a thing or an idea. Consequently, they are nothing but sounds or written forms to which people speaking a certain language have given various meanings. These meanings change with the times and the circumstances. Remember that *the word is never the thing itself.* The word only *means,* or points to, whatever it may happen to represent.

Semantics is the study of the meanings that words have as symbols, whereby we communicate our judgments and emotions to one another. And, in general, word meanings are classified into two kinds: *denotation* and *connotation.* The denotation of the word *book,* for example, indicates that it is a term applicable to almost any bound collection of printed or written sheets. But notice some of the transformations the word *book* undergoes, and the meanings it takes on, in the following contexts:

> Two racetrack gamblers were arrested for *making book* in Columbus, Ohio. They were *booked* by the police on charges of gambling and fraud. The judge later *threw the book* at them when it came out that they had been *booked* by a syndicate to handle the betting at the state fair. Maybe now they wish they had lived by the *Good Book.*

These many different meanings are *denotations* of the word *book;* their variety and range suggest the misunderstandings which can arise if someone lacks familiarity with our language. The *connotations* of *book* will include all the experiences, the places, the things anyone associates with that word. Connotative meanings are private, often making the word a symbol of a complex situation. Under certain circumstances, for example, on hearing or reading the word *book,* you may be reminded of a particular library, a particular person who read to you or who gave you a book, or almost any other experience in which the word made a deep impression upon you.

Open to misunderstanding as words often may be, we are forced to depend upon the meanings that words have for us as a result of our experience, both "in the world," as it is sometimes referred to, and from our reading. Unfortunately, as our examination of suasive strategies suggests, not all those who try to persuade us to accept a proposition are ethical; writers and speakers can deliberately attempt to sway us by playing upon our emotions with the words that they use, or by presenting deliberately misleading statements under the guise of valid reasoning.

It is well, therefore, to be alert to the possibility of being taken in by tricksters, or being misled by unintentional mistakes in reasoning. To check on your own reasoning as well as that of others, you may find the following lists helpful:

Approved	*Fallacious*
Ample verifying evidence	Unsubstantiated claims
Relevant examples	Insufficient, inadequate examples
Clear, unambiguous definitions	Vague, undefined terms
Valid appeals	Unfounded generalizations
Coherent arrangement of parts	Irrelevant conclusions
Considered assumptions	Assuming a point has been proved
Regard for moral values	Name-calling, unfounded attacks on character
Support from recognized authority	Unsupported testimonials

Computerocracy
by FREDERIC NELSON

Nobody's perfect, as "Candy" Mossler is supposed to have remarked during her trial for the
murder of her husband. So, when I opened
my bank statement a few months ago and
noted a deposit of $76,000 which I had not
made, my first split-second, just barely sub-
conscious thought was that a fellow could get
on quite well in Majorca or somewhere like
that on the income from $76,000. Had I known
at the time that Dr. Louis T. Rader of General
Electric had said that the electric computer
has a more beneficial potential for the human
race than any other invention in history, I
should have remarked "How True!"

However, Sober Second Thought soon
went to work, and I recalled that another bank
depositer in the area, confronted with a similar temptation, had taken Dr. Rader's judg-

Introduction
Opening with the author's
startling experience with
a bank computer that
made a gross error.

His memory of a similar
thing happening to one
who was jailed for try-
ing to profit by the mistake.

ment too personally and, after checking with his bank twice to be assured that the statement was correct, he drew out the bonus deposit, hid it away in another bank and prepared to live the life of Riley. Unfortunately for him, the Computer giveth but also taketh away, and, after a few months of pushing buttons and flashing red lights, the "system" caught up with him, and despite the bank official's earlier assurance that the bank's statements were always accurate, the poor wretched man is in jail.

His informing the bank of his decision "to act" the good citizen.

So, for one reason or another I decided to act the way good solid citizens, the backbone of America, are supposed to act. I called the bank and explained that, while I appreciated its generosity, I was a little worried about the fellow who thought he had deposited $76,000 and might be getting notices that he had overdrawn his account. The bank said something like "Thanks awfully."

Another bank error, probably by a computer, which had amusing and ironic results.

Banks like their clients to assume that papal infallibility is no better than a tie with computer infallibility. Once in a while, though, they meet their match. A Philadelphia bank was executor of a will which provided $100 for a mass to be said for the soul of the testator. Things went wrong at the bank, whether computer-wise or not I wasn't told, and the pastor in charge got the word that $1000 had been set aside for the mass. In this instance the bank caught up with the error fairly rapidly, and a flustered Junior Executive was able to telephone the pastor and explain that the bequest for the mass was $100, not $1000.

"How regrettable," said the reverend father, "That mass was said last Sunday!"

The fact that bank computers can make such errors introduces the wider topic of "computerocracy."

This error, I was informed, cost the bank $900. Had the alleged felon mentioned *supra,* who sought to profit from a banking error in his account, known of this episode, his defense might have been more aggressive. There does seem to be here a conflict of concept on a bank's responsibility for its own statements. The two episodes caused me to conjure up all sorts of might-have-beens.

Suppose that I *had* made the deposit of $76,000—well let's be realistic and make it $760—and that the amount had been credited to the account of somebody else. And suppose the bank sent me a notice that I had overdrawn my account, and suppose that the fellow who got my $760 was not a Boy-Scout-type like me but a chiseler who just kept his mouth shut. I tremble to think.

One of the painful effects such bank errors could have.

Leaving banks out of it, there is a lot to shake you up in the wonders promised for the future when the thinking machines really get in stride. Weather will be controlled: it doesn't say whether after a majority vote for fair and warmer, or an opt for a quick downpour at Aquaduct to give a book-making syndicate a muddy track. Genetics will be monkeyed with, "opening up the possibility of preventing the passing on of hereditary defects." Shall he take after Mummy or be cursed with Daddy's defective characteristics? The F. B. I. already has a computer system which can come up with a crook's record minutes after he has been spotted by a suspicious policeman. If computers can catch criminals a few jumps faster than Chief Justice Warren *et al* can spring them, more power to electronics!

The first clear statement of his thesis, or general purpose: "Leaving banks out of it, there is a lot to shake you up in the wonders promised for the future when the thinking machines really get in stride."

A Bell Telephone man is quoted in *U. S. News and World Report* as predicting the day when nobody will have to carry cash in his wallet. All he'll have to do is press a button and "a computer will automatically check his balance, debit his account with the proper amount and credit the seller's account at the same time!" That should be an end to forgery and bank hold-ups. All the crook of the future will have to do is buy a Cadillac, push his victim's computer number and drive away.

Body
Some spectacular and alarming things that computers will do.

More frightening possibilities that may come with the computer age.

How would he get the sucker's bank number? I don't know, but to judge from the list of lost and stolen credit cards posted in every restaurant, filling station or You-Drive-It agency (not to mention my $76,000 nondeposit), it is easy to assume that the problem won't prove insoluble.

Therefore it is hardly remarkable that some skeptics, including the American Civil Liberties Union, are more alarmed than overjoyed at the prospect of a gigantic computer complex which will "process" the facts about every citizen from cradle to coffin: income, sex life, membership in dubious organizations, (or organizations officially declared to be dubious), tangles with the police, political deviations, use of alcohol (LSD?) etc., etc. All this and countless other details of a man's life are to be available for inspection by whoever has access to the controls. Who knows, Drew Pearson and Jack Anderson, or their equivalents, might be able to persuade some civil servant to give them a chance to survey the career of some politician they were about to take after. This might prove a lot easier than talking the statesman's secretary into rifling his files after closing hours! To be sure, gossip writers will also be represented in the super-gadget's files, if that's a comfort.

It is terrifying to imagine all this information at the disposal of anybody—political opponent, tax official, blackmailer, vengeful ex-wife or ex-husband, shyster lawyer—who might have use for it. Suppose the calculating machine errs. Suppose Russell Baker's file gets mixed up with Bobby Baker's file, or that Gen. Clay gets credit for statements by Cassius Clay, or suppose the views of liberal Senator Eugene McCarthy of Wisconsin slip into the programming contraption reserved for "McCarthyism." Mistakes like these happen all the time as things are now. The possibilities for confusion

when this new ganglia of calculation gets going appear to be unlimited.

Once in a downtown building I rode the
elevator with a pair of serious-minded young
scientists who work on computers. One of
them said to the other, "A wrong punch destroys memory." At first I thought the reference
might be to the condition of a prize fighter
after mixing it with Mohammed Ali, but "A
wrong punch destroys memory" doesn't
sound like fight-fan talk. It wasn't. The two
earnest fellows were suggesting, probably un-
wittingly, that a wrong punch, temporarily at
any rate, might destroy a man's reputation, or
land him in prison, or persuade his wife to
divorce him or cause him to blow out his
brains.

Probably I exaggerate. There was a great
deal of bearing of false witness before computers were ever heard of, and it could be that
a more healthy skepticism will greet misinforma-
tion produced electronically than was aroused
by scandal spread by malicious individuals.
Anyway, this is the kind of thing we are already having to live with.

It could just possibly be that, in the dizzy
excitement of "processing information at extraordinary speed," the "human element" will
begin to holler "Wait for Baby!" A few years
ago, when we were in Europe, I received a communication from a Federal Bureau requesting
information about some fact in my life. I replied that I was in Europe with no address
except c/o American Express here and there,
but would look up the item when I got home.
I did look it up, took the necessary papers
down to the proper office, showed them the
original demand and the result of my researches.
An efficient secretary took the whole "corpus"
off somewhere, stayed there for some time
and finally returned looking discouraged.

"When did you last hear from us about
this?" she asked.

Another of the author's
disturbing experiences and
the results he imagines.

His admission that per-
haps he exaggerates, his
repetition of his thesis:
"Anyway, this is the kind
of thing we are already
having to live with."

One instance in which the
machine was too fast for
"Man to keep up."

I explained that I had never heard any-thing since getting the original document.

"Then why don't you forget it?"

The machine had evidently become too eager in the chase for Man to keep up.

Another personal exper-
ience, one in which the
Machine proved too much
for the worker. Its inad-
equacy compared with a
human accountant.

Other times Man, confronted with the in-adequacy of the Machine, just gives up. Take an outfit for which I have done a little work from time to time. For tax purposes I called this office on the telephone and asked for a breakdown on whatever I had been paid dur-ing the calendar year.

"But," explained somebody, "We have computers here and it would take several weeks to dig out that information."

Eventually, of course, the information had to be supplied to the recipient and to the Internal Revenue Service, and I got it. However, I wanted the facts early so as to complete my tax return and get out of town. A little man in an alpaca coat and wearing a green eye-shade could have given me the information in ten minutes.

Ironic apology for at-
tacking the machines
ending with the ridiculing
of computer-dating.

In view of all the benefits supposed to be conferred on mankind by the simple device of giving him a number instead of a name, it is probably ungracious to denigrate computers. After all, most of my young friends sell com-puters, install computing "systems" or com-pute by them. Young people meet suitable mates by throwing into the hopper a complex of their own qualities, tastes, economic and social backgrounds, race (if not forbidden by law), religion, physical appearance and edu-cational achievements. Push the button and, after some whirling and grunting of the ma-chinery, out pops just the right member of the opposite sex. This is supposed to be more nearly foolproof than going to Christian En-deavor or introducing yourself to the prettiest secretary during the coffee break. On the other hand, a computer has no way of taking ac-count of halitosis or the use of expressions like "Goodbye now" unless these qualities are included in the mix to be "programmed."

Actually youth seems to feel that, whatever may be the advantages of programmed love, the computer has its limitations when it comes to education. One of the most frequently heard complaints by "alienated" students is that they seldom see a professor in action, not to mention having a heart-to-heart talk with one, because everything is done electronically. We are assured that soon we shall have a whole generation trained from infancy to obtain knowledge, not from daily contact with flesh-and-blood teachers, but by watching a board, something like the ones you see flashing mysterious digits and symbols in brokerage offices. The kids punch a button when they think they know the answer. This may be the way to get arithmetic into the little robots, but I can't see how it's going to cure their alienation.

There are people who feel better when they know that the ages, weights, racial antecedents, incomes and sex habits of millions of Americans, or Chinese for that matter, can be classified, re-classified and de-classified all in a few seconds, but I am the type who would feel better if, when wishing to question my bill for fuel oil in Philadelphia, I could discuss it with an individual in my own city instead of taking it up with a computer system in Kansas City. You should have seen what happened when we rented our house for a few months during our stay abroad. The tenant, who moved out two years ago, was at last accounts still getting bills, and so do I. The file of my appeals to the computer to for Heaven's sake forget about that tenant would be twice as thick as it is, if I had ever received any replies!

Melvin Kranzberg, writing in the New York *Times* recently, predicted that users would soon "communicate with the computer in a language approaching simple English." A cozy prospect but I'd still miss somebody from

Fear that machines will only increase the alienation that youth now protests.

Another of his bad experiences with computers.

His distrust of promised future machine efficiency.

whom you could get the answer to a civil question.

By this time it will be suspected that I am not exactly the progressive type. All right. Just the same I am glad that it is no longer necessary to have a leg amputated with no anesthetic but a stiff slug of Maryland rye. Also I imagine it was progress for electricity to release women from the drudgery of housework, even if the new leisure does make millions of wives so busy with committees on public affairs that the husband, after a hard day at the office, gets a TV dinner. It's also convenient to dial California direct, even if it means that the telephone bill is three times what it was in the days when we thought we had been robbed if the bill came to $8. And probably one can change the address on a magazine subscription more quickly in the computer age than when a roomful of girls disconsolately passed papers back and forth among themselves.

Nevertheless I suspect, in spite of the current idolatry of Science, that we could do without the rocket, certainly without the atom bomb and the electronic device that permits a cop or columnist to listen in on your confidential conversation from the pub across the street. There is no assurance that scientific achievement invariably works out for good. When the late Prof. Ernest Hooton, Harvard anthropologist, heard about the destruction of Hiroshima, he didn't join the chorus about how the advent of the Atomic Age promised a miraculously improved life for everybody. He said: "With a weapon of such power in the hands of a race with the intelligence of apes and far more malice, the doom of mankind is assured." Too pessimistic probably, but the odds against it shouldn't be prohibitive. After all, that obsolete bomb dropped on Hiroshima killed some thousands of people, and progress in that field continues.

Still, having buried ourselves beneath an unmanageable mass of paper work, largely the

List of possible benefits coming from machines.

Conclusion

His pessimistic fears of future results from these machines.

creation of our tax laws, I suppose it's a blessing that there are devices capable of sorting out
this material and making it appear to have some
purpose. William D. Smith, in the New York
Times, sponsors the opinion that "if computers
were suddenly withdrawn from service both
government and business operations would
come almost to a standstill," including stuffing
my mail-slot with unwanted junk addressed to
"occupant." Machines which can do complicated mathematical calculations in "nano-
seconds" (i.e., billionths of a second) operate
industrial plants formerly "manned" by hundreds of people, and give election returns before the citizens have even voted, are nothing
you can laugh off—except, in my case, sardonically. Presumably computers will speed our
arrival on the moon, if that's a legitimate am-
bition, and, as one enthusiast puts it, they will
undoubtedly be responsible for "abolishing
old ways and creating new ones in a constant,
upgrading shift of human effort." The key word
here is "upgrading," and with me it's on pro-
bation.

The principal reason for doubting that living
electronically will necessarily mean better living has been best stated by computer-minded
people themselves: "The computer can only
work with the material it receives from human
hands." A great many things can be accom-
plished by these gadgets in a few billionths of
a second, but whether they are worth doing or
not will still depend on individual human beings who, up to now, seem not to have improved over the past century or so *pari passu*
with the mechanical apparati they have con-
trived in the same period. In fact it could be
argued that the increasing dependence on
mechanical devices has brought with it an un-
wholesomely awesome attitude toward scientific triumphs and increasing distrust of individual performance. The skeptical philosopher
of yesterday has become the nut of today.

Main reasons why he
distrusts these "gadgets."

His final recommendation: the thesis elaborated.

What do I suggest, aside from a lot of unconstructive wringing of the hands? Nothing really, beyond an attitude of skepticism and resistance to the temptation to bow down and worship the Machine as if it were a new God. Like Aaron's Golden Calf, these dizzying machines have been fashioned by Man, and behind all their complex and bewildering operations are human beings, to be admired by us ignoramuses for their accomplishments, but with judgment suspended as to how Man the Master will manage to tame the demons that he has turned loose.

OUTLINE

Thesis: We should temper our admiration for electronic machines with skepticism and resistance until we see how "Man the Master will manage to tame the demons that he has turned loose."

  I. Computers in banks make serious errors.
   A. My bank account was mistakenly credited with $76,000.
     1. I was tempted to take the money.
     2. If I had, I could have been sent to prison.
     3. I decided to act "the good citizen."
   B. Another local bank computer made a similar error, and this time the bank lost out.
   C. Banks do not guarantee the accuracy of their machines.
     1. Bank computer errors can have serious consequences.
     2. They foreshadow the dangers of "computerocracy."
 II. The electronic machines produce more harmful than helpful results.
   A. They may do some useful things.
   B. But they may be exploited by illegal use of credit cards.
   C. I had other painful experiences with the Machine.
     1. One showed the Machine was too much for its staff.
     2. Another proved inefficient.
III. Machines will not really solve the problems of youth.
   A. They will only increase the present "alienation."
   B. Computer-dating does not assure good matches.
   C. I have good reason to distrust the machines.
 IV. Despite some possible benefits from them, I am pessimistic.

A. That they may "upgrade" our lives is doubtful.
B. They will always be operated by error-prone humans.
C. They have not yet been at all "mastered" by Man.

COMMENTARY: INFERENCES AND ASSUMPTIONS

Probably no one likes to admit even to himself that he is really afraid of what is going to happen in the future if present policies and practices are permitted to continue unchanged. And one who does venture to voice those genuine fears can well expect to be called everything from a cynic to a "fink."

Evidently Frederic Nelson knew what he was up against when he decided to take on the "brain machines" and attack them in *The Intercollegiate Review,* a magazine aimed at campus readers who either design such machines or teach how they are to be installed and operated. Mr. Nelson, as we can see, employed a very diplomatic approach to ward off immediate outcries from his possible readers: he began with an amusing but highly relevant personal experience, wherein, guided by the example of someone else's bad experience, he assumes the role of "good citizen" and "Boy Scout" moralist.

On the basis of a bank computer error which deposited $76,000 to his account and the error which sent a man to prison, he *infers* that computers are not to be trusted. This conclusion is an *assumption* that he seeks to strengthen with the ironic anecdote concerning the Philadelphia bank and the will. On the basis of three examples, or experiences, he *deduces* that we are living in the age of "computerocracy," a term he does not explicitly define.

As a former editor of the now defunct, but once very popular *Saturday Evening Post,* Mr. Nelson judged that his *evidence* would be accepted because of the manner in which it was presented and the specific examples. He then skillfully added an apparently offhand statement of his thesis idea, suggesting he had grave doubts about the advisability of ever letting the machines control human affairs. At this stage of his argument, the reader might be in the mood to smile and agree that Nelson knew what he was talking about—especially if the reader had ever questioned the checking account statements he received from his local bank.

But accepting such a wide, all-inclusive conclusion on the basis of only a few scattered instances would lead one into the error of making *a hasty generalization.* Now we probably are all more or less guilty of making "snap judgments" of this kind. One bad experience with a business establishment or public official may make us over-

react. In what we read, however, we are generally more wary and withhold such ready assent to sweeping generalizations. Mr. Nelson assumes that such may be our response, and so he goes on to support
his attack on the machines with various other statements.

But what kind of statements? Evaluating ones, expressing feelings
of judgment or convincing statements of fact? Or emotion-charged
opinions having a strong effect on those who hear or read them?
Let us look at just a few of our author's statements:

> Banks like their clients to assume that papal infallibility is no better
> than a tie with computer infallibility.
> Genetics will be monkeyed with, 'opening up the possibility of pre-
> venting the passing on of hereditary defects.'
> If computers can catch criminals a few jumps faster than Chief Justice
> Warren *et al.* can spring them, more power to electronics!

How valid is the first statement with its sweeping generalization
implying that *all* banks and their staffs *assume* (take for granted) that
the checking account balances issuing from their computers are to be
received with the same unquestioned acceptance expected of dogmas
proclaimed by the Pope for devout Roman Catholics? Mr. Nelson's
statement has, of course, the saving grace of humorous irony, but it
still is loaded with allusions and terms that are "slanted" against bank
computer reliability.

In the second statement, note again the choice of slanted language: "Genetics will be monkeyed with. . . ." Why "monkeyed with"
instead of "experimented with" or "subjected to careful scrutiny"?
Again, in the third statement, note the condemnation of the United
States Supreme Court as an agency which does nothing more than
free convicted criminals as fast as they are arrested. Also, in this context, the singling out of Chief Justice Warren approaches "character
assassination," for the *connotations* of the expression, "A few jumps
faster than Chief Justice Warren *et al.* can spring them" are decidedly
harsh and abusive.

Moreover, Mr. Nelson's essay is loosely organized, giving the impression of sporadic thought, not carefully and logically developed.
And the fact that it is humorous and bantering in its tone is no excuse for this looseness of construction.

On the whole, however, Mr. Nelson's manner of expression of
his emotional thinking inspired by his experiences and observations
is typical of all writers and speakers who are said to have been
"turned on" by their subject matter. In the other essays in this section on "science" we shall have the opportunity of comparing the
logic of Mr. Wilson with that of some eminent thinkers in science
and also of some other nonscientists.

WHAT DOES IT SAY?

1. When you read or hear the expression "to act the way good solid citizens, the backbone of America, are supposed to act," what images or specific acts pop into your mind?

2. Describe your picture of "a flustered Junior Executive."

3. Why does Mr. Nelson use the words and spelling he does in this statement: "Shall he take after Mummy or be cursed with Daddy's defective characteristics?" What is implied?

4. Here are synonyms the author used for *computer*: "thinking machines," "super-gadget," "calculating machine," "programming contraption," "new ganglia of calculation," "the machine," and "the Machine." How do the connotations of these expressions reflect the tone of his thesis?

5. Does this "current idolatry of Science" have any special meaning for Congressmen?

6. What meaning are we to attach to the author's remark: "By this time it will be suspected that I am not exactly the progressive type"?

7. Which emotions seem to have prompted this statement: "Still, having buried ourselves beneath an unmanageable mass of paper work, largely the creation of our tax laws, I suppose it's a blessing that there are devices capable of sorting out this material and making it appear to have some purpose"?

8. If computers eventually will be "abolishing old ways and creating new ones in a constant, upgrading shift of human effort," just what things could they possibly be doing?

WHAT DO YOU THINK?

1. Frederic Nelson's statements are often very controversial and have probably pleased or angered you. Select one of them, on which you have some firsthand information, and attack or defend his view. Here are some sample statements:

   Also I imagine it was progress for electricity to release women from the drudgery of housework, even if the new leisure does make millions of wives so busy with committees on public affairs that the husband, after a hard day's work at the office, gets a TV dinner.

   There is no assurance that scientific achievement invariably works out for good.

With a weapon of such power in the hands of a race with the intelligence of apes and far more malice, the doom of mankind is assured.

A little man in an alpaca coat and wearing a green eyeshade could have given me the information in ten minutes.

It is terrifying to imagine all this information at the disposal of anybody . . . who might have use for it.

. . . The electric computer has a more beneficial potential for the human race than any other invention in history.

2. The following comment was made in a recent interview by Harold C. Urey, Nobel prize winner in chemistry and consultant to the National Aeronautics and Space Administration. Choose one of his statements as the starting point for an essay.

Regarding President Nixon's proposed antiballistics missile system: It is doubtful if the system will be a satisfactory solution to the problem. It would be very difficult to make such a system 100 per cent fool proof if war should start. Some [enemy missiles] would come through. And there is the critical time factor involved. . . . There may not be time to reach the President—and certainly not time to get a congressional declaration of war. Would a computer be set to trigger our missiles and antiballistic missiles on a certain set of signals? This would put the computer in a position of declaring war for the nation.[1]

3. Anyone of these widely accepted assumptions is probably debatable. Take your choice for an essay supporting it or taking issue with it. Remember to be specific and concrete.

(a) See one and you've seen them all.

(b) The poor you always have with you.

(c) Home is where your heart is.

(d) Mother knows best.

(e) It takes one to know another one.

(f) There's a man for every woman, and a woman for every man.

(g) Turn on, tune in, drop out.

(h) Give a little and take a little.

(i) All the kids are doing it, so why can't I?

(j) The best things in life are free.

[1] *The Oregonian,* March 29, 1969.

4. An IBM advertisement maintains, "Machines should work. People should think." In the light of Frederic Nelson's "Computerocracy," what do you think about other statements in this same IBM persuasive advertisement?

In just the last fifteen years, the cost of a business letter has jumped from $1.17 to $2.54. And shows every sign of increasing further.

And this at a time when, more than ever, business needs to free the energies of its people for more important tasks than paperwork. Tasks such as thinking.[2]

[2] *Time,* March 28, 1969.

Next—The Planets
by ARTHUR C. CLARKE

It has been said that history never repeats itself but that historical situations *recur*. To anyone, like myself, who has been involved in astronautical activities for over 30 years, there is a feeling of familiarity in some of the present arguments about the exploration of space. Like all revolutionary new ideas, the subject has had to pass through three stages, which may be summed up by these reactions: (1) "It's crazy—don't waste any time"; (2) "It's possible, but it's not worth doing"; (3) "I always said it was a good idea."

As far as orbital flights, and even journeys to the Moon, are concerned, we have made excellent progress through all of these stages, though it will be a few years yet before everyone is in category three. But where flights to the planets are involved, we are still almost where we were 30 years ago. True, there is much less complete skepticism— to that extent, history has *not* repeated itself—but there remains, despite all the events of the past decade, a widespread misunderstanding of the possible scale, importance and ultimate implications of travel to the planets.

Let us start by looking at some fundamentals, which are not as well known as they should be—even to space scientists. Forgetting all about rockets and today's astronautical techniques, consider the basic problem of lifting a man away from the Earth, purely in terms of the work done to move him against gravity. For a man of average mass, the energy requirement is about 1000 kilowatt-hours, which customers with a favorable tariff can purchase for ten dollars from their electric company. What may be called the basic cost of a one-way ticket to space is thus the modest sum of ten dollars.

For the smaller planets and all satellites—Mercury, Venus, Mars, Pluto, Moon, Titan, Ganymede, etc.—the exit fee is even less; you need only 50 cents' worth of energy to escape from the Moon. Giant planets such as Jupiter, Saturn, Uranus, and Neptune are naturally much more expensive propositions. If you are ever stranded on Jupiter, you'll have to buy almost $300 worth of energy to get home. Make sure you take enough traveler's checks!

Of course, the planetary fields are only part of the story; work also has to be done traveling from orbit to orbit and thus moving up or down the enormous gravitational field of the Sun. But, by great good luck, the Solar System appears to have been designed for the convenience of space travelers: All the planets lie far out on the gentle slope of the solar field, where it merges into the endless plain of interstellar space. In this respect, the conventional map of the Solar System, showing the planets clustering round the Sun, is wholly misleading.

We can say, in fact, that the planets are 99 percent free of the Sun's gravitational field, so that the energy required for orbital transfers is quite small; usually, it is considerably less than that needed to escape from the planets themselves. In dollars and cents, the energy cost of transferring a man from the surface of the Earth to that of Mars is less than $20. Even for the worst possible case (surface of Jupiter to surface of Saturn), the pure energy cost is less than $1000.

Hardheaded rocket engineers may well consider that the above arguments, purporting to prove that space travel should be about a billion times cheaper than it is, have no relevance to the practical case—since, even today, the cost of the fuel is trivial, compared with the cost of the hardware. Most of the mountainous Saturn 5 standing on the pad can be bought for, quite literally, a few cents a pound; kerosene and liquid oxygen come cheap. The expensive items are the precision-shaped pieces of high-grade metals and all the little black boxes that are sold by the carat.

Although this is true, it is also, to a large extent, a consequence of our present immature, no-margin-for-error technology. Just ask yourself how expensive driving would be if a momentary engine failure were liable to write off your car—and yourself—and the fuel supply were so nicely calculated that you couldn't complete a mission if the parking meter you'd aimed at happened to be already occupied. This is roughly the situation for planetary travel today.

To imagine what it may one day become, let us look at the record of the past and see what lessons we can draw from the early history of aeronautics. Soon after the failure of Samuel Langley's "aerodrome" in 1903, the great astronomer Simon Newcomb wrote a famous essay, well worth rereading, that proved that heavier-than-air flight was impossible by means of known technology. The ink was hardly dry on the paper when a pair of bicycle mechanics irreverently threw grave doubt on the professor's conclusions. When informed of the embarrassing fact that the Wright brothers had just flown, Newcomb gamely replied: "Well, maybe a flying machine *can* be built. But it certainly couldn't carry a passenger as well as a pilot."

Now, I am not trying to poke fun at one of the greatest of American scientists. When you look at the Wright biplane, hanging up there in the Smithsonian Institution, Newcomb's attitude seems very reasonable, indeed; I wonder how many of us would have been prepared to dispute it in 1903.

Yet—and this is the really extraordinary point—there is a smooth line of development, without any major technological breakthroughs, from the Wright "flier" to the last of the great piston-engined aircraft, such as the DC-6. All the many-orders-of-magnitude improvement in performance came as a result of engineering advances that, in retrospect, seem completely straightforward and sometimes even trivial. Let us list the more important ones: variable-pitch airscrews, slots and flaps, retractable undercarriages, concrete runways, streamlining, and supercharging.

Not very spectacular, are they? Yet these things, together with steady improvements in materials and design, lifted much of the commerce of mankind into the air. For they had a synergistic effect on performance; their cumulative effect was much greater than could have been predicted by considering them individually. They did not merely add; they multiplied. All this took about 40 years. Then there was the second technological breakthrough—the advent of the jet engine—and a new cycle of development began.

Unless the record of the past is wholly misleading, we are going to see much the same sequence of events in space. As far as can be judged at the moment, the equivalent items on the table of aerospace progress may be: refueling in orbit, air-breathing boosters, reusable boosters, refueling on (or from) the Moon and lightweight materials (e.g., composites and fibers).

Probably the exploitation of these relatively conventional ideas will take somewhat less than the 40 years needed in the case of aircraft; their full impact should be felt by the turn of the century. Well before then, the next breakthrough or quantum jump in space technology should also have occurred, with the development of new propulsion systems—presumably fission-powered but, hopefully, using fusion as well. And with these, the Solar System will become an extension of the Earth—if we wish it to be.

It is at this point, however, that all analogy with the past breaks down; we can no longer draw meaningful parallels between aeronautics and astronautics. As soon as aircraft were shown to be practical, there were obvious and immensely important uses for them: military, commercial and scientific. They could be used to provide swifter connections between already highly developed communities— a state of affairs that almost certainly does not exist in the Solar System and may not for centuries to come.

It seems, therefore, that we may be involved in a peculiarly vicious circle. Planetary exploration will not be really practical until we have developed a mature spaceship technology; but we won't have good spaceships until we have worthwhile places to send them—places, above all, with those adequate refueling and servicing facilities now sadly lacking elsewhere in the Solar System. How can we escape from this dilemma? Fortunately, there is one encouraging factor.

Almost all of the technology needed for long-range space travel will inevitably and automatically be developed during the exploration of *near* space. Even if we set our sights no higher than 1000 miles above the Earth, we would find that by the time we had perfected the high-thrust, high-performance surface-to-surface transports, the low-acceleration interorbital shuttles and the reliable, closed-cycle space-station ecologies, we would have proved out at least 90 percent of the technology needed for the exploration of the Solar System— and the most expensive 90 percent, at that.

Perhaps I had better deal here with those strange characters who think that space is the exclusive province of automatic, robot probes and that we should stay at home and watch TV, as God intended us to. This whole man—machine controversy will seem, in another couple of decades, to be a baffling mental aberration of the early space age.

I won't waste much time arguing with this viewpoint, as I hold these truths to be self-evident: (1) Unmanned spacecraft should be used whenever they can do a job more efficiently, cheaply and safely than manned vehicles; (2) Until we have automatons superior to human beings (by which time, all bets will be off), all really sophisticated space operations will demand human participation. I refer to such activities as assembling and servicing the giant applications satellites of the next decade and running orbital observatories, laboratories, hospitals and factories—projects for which there will be such obvious and overwhelming commercial and scientific benefits that no one will dispute them.

In particular, medium-sized telescopes outside the atmosphere— a mere couple of hundred miles above the Earth—will have an overwhelming impact on Solar System studies. The recent launching of OAO II—the initials stand for "Orbiting Astronomical Observatory"— was a promising beginning. Until the advent of radar and space probes, everything we knew about the planets had been painfully gathered, over a period of about a century and a half, by astronomers with inadequate instruments, hastily sketching details of a tiny, trembling disk glimpsed during moments of good sighting. Such moments—when the atmosphere is stable and the image undistorted—may add up to only a few hours in an entire lifetime of observing.

In these circumstances, it would be amazing if we had acquired any *reliable* knowledge about planetary conditions; it is safest to assume that we have not. We are still in the same position as the medieval cartographers, with their large areas of *"Terra Incognita"* and their "Here Be Dragons," except that we may have gone too far in the other direction—"Here Be *No* Dragons." Our ignorance is so great that we have no right to make either assumption.

As proof of this, let me remind you of some horrid shocks the astronomers have received recently, when things of which they were quite sure turned out to be simply not true. The most embarrassing example is the rotation of Mercury: Until a couple of years ago, everyone was perfectly certain that it always kept the same face toward the Sun, so that one side was eternally dark, the other eternally baked. But now, radar observations indicate that it turns on its axis every 59 days; it has sunrise and sunset, like any respectable world. Nature seems to have played a dirty trick on several generations of patient astronomers.

Einstein once said: "The good Lord is subtle, but He is not malicious." The case of Mercury casts some doubt on this dictum. And what about Venus? You can find, in the various reference books, rotation periods for Venus ranging all the way from 24 hours to the full value of the year, 225 days. But, as far as I know, not one astronomer ever suggested that Venus would present the extraordinary case of a planet with a day longer than its year. And, of course, it *would* be the one example we had no way of checking, until the advent of radar. Is it subtlety—or malice?

And look at the Moon. Five years ago, everyone was certain that its surface was either soft dust or hard lava. If the two schools of thought had been on speaking terms, they would at least have agreed that there were no alternatives. But then Luna 9 and Surveyor 1 landed —and what did they find? Good honest dirt.

These are by no means the only examples of recent shocks and surprises. There are the unexpectedly high temperature beneath the clouds of Venus, the craters of Mars, the gigantic radio emissions from Jupiter, the complex organic chemicals in certain meteors, the clear signs of extensive activity on the surface of the Moon. And now Mars seems to be turning inside out. The ancient, dried-up sea beds may be as much a myth as Dejah Thoris, Princess of Helium; for it looks as if the dark *Maria* are actually highlands, not lowlands, as we had always thought.

The negative point I am making is that we really know nothing about the planets. The positive one is that a tremendous amount of reconnaissance—the essential prelude to *manned* exploration—can be carried out from Earth orbit. It is probably no exaggeration to say that a good orbiting telescope could give us a view of Mars at least as clear as did Mariner 4. And it would be a view infinitely more valuable —a continuous coverage of the whole visible face, not a signal snapshot of a small percentage of the surface.

Nevertheless, there are many tasks that can best be carried out by unmanned spacecraft. Among these is one that, though of great scientific value, is of even more profound psychological importance. I refer to the production of low-altitude oblique photographs. It is no disparagement of the wonderful Ranger, Luna and Surveyor coverage to remind you that what suddenly made the Moon a real place, and not merely an astronomical body up there in the sky, was the famous photograph of the Crater of Copernicus from Lunar Orbiter 2. When the newspapers called it the picture of the century, they were expressing a universally felt truth. This was the photograph that first proved to our emotions what our minds already knew but had never really believed—that Earth is not the only world. The first high-definition, oblique photos of Mars, Mercury and the satellites of the giant planets will have a similar impact, bringing our mental images of these places into sharp focus for the first time.

The old astronomical writers had a phrase that has gone out of fashion but that may well be revived: the plurality of worlds. Yet, of course, every world is itself a plurality. To realize this, one has only to ask: How long will it be before we have learned everything that can be known about the planet Earth? It will be quite a few centuries before terrestrial geology, oceanography, and geophysics are closed, surprise-free subjects.

Consider the multitude of environments that exists here on Earth, from the summit of Everest to the depths of the Marianas Trench— from high noon in Death Valley to midnight at the South Pole. We may have equal variety on the other planets, with all that this implies for the existence of life. It is amazing how often this elementary fact

is overlooked and how often a single observation or even a single ex-
trapolation from a preliminary observation based on a provisional
theory has been promptly applied to a whole world.

It is possible, of course, that the Earth has a greater variety of
more complex environments than any other planet. Like a jet-age
tourist "doing Europe" in a week, we may be able to wrap up Mars
or Venus with a relatively small number of "landers." But I doubt it,
if only for the reason that the whole history of astronomy teaches us
to be cautious of any theory purporting to show that there is something special about the Earth. In their various ways, the other planets
may have orders of complexity as great as ours. Even the moon—
which seemed a promising candidate for geophysical simplicity less
than a decade ago—has already begun to unleash an avalanche of
surprises.

The late Professor J. B. S. Haldane once remarked—and this
should be called Haldane's Law—"The universe is not only stranger
than we imagine, it is stranger than we *can* imagine." We will encounter the operation of this law more and more frequently as we
move away from home. And as we prepare for this move, it is high
time that we face up to one of the more shattering realities of the
astronomical situation. For all practical purposes, we are still as geo-
centrically minded as if Copernicus had never been born; to all of us,
the Earth is the center, if not of the Universe, at least of the Solar
System.

Well, I have news for you. There is really only one planet that
matters; and that planet is not Earth but Jupiter. My esteemed col-
league Isaac Asimov summed it up very well when he remarked: "The
Solar System consists of Jupiter plus debris." Even spectacular Saturn
doesn't count; it has less than a third of Jupiter's enormous mass—
and Earth is a hundred times smaller than Saturn! Our planet is an
unconsidered trifle, left over after the main building operations were
completed. This is quite a blow to our pride, but there may be much
worse to come, and it is wise to get ready for it. Jupiter may also be
the *biological,* as well as the *physical,* center of gravity of the Solar
System.

This, of course, represents a complete reversal of views within a
couple of decades. Not long ago, it was customary to laugh at the
naïve ideas of the early astronomers—Sir John Herschel, for example—
who took it for granted that all the planets were teeming with life.
This attitude is certainly overoptimistic; but it no longer seems as
simple-minded as the opinion, to be found in the popular writings of
the 1930s, that ours might be the only solar system and, hence, the
only abode of life in the entire Galaxy.

The pendulum has, indeed, swung—perhaps for the last time; for in another few decades, we should know the truth. The discovery that Jupiter is quite warm and has precisely the type of atmosphere in which life is believed to have arisen on Earth may be the prelude to the most significant biological findings of this century. Carl Sagan and Jack Leonard put it well in their book *Planets:* "Recent work on the origin of life and the environment of Jupiter suggests that it may be more favorable to life than any other planet, not excepting the earth."

The extraordinary color changes in the Jovian atmosphere—in particular, the behavior of that Earth-sized, drifting apparition, the Great Red Spot—hint at the production of organic materials in enormous quantities. Where this happens, life may follow inevitably, given a sufficient lapse of time. To quote Isaac Asimov again: "If there are seas on Jupiter . . . think of the fishing." So that may explain the mysterious disappearances and reappearances of the Great Red Spot. It is, as Polonius agreed in a slightly different context, "very like a whale."

Contrary to popular thinking, gravity on Jupiter would not pose insurmountable difficulties. The Jovian gravity is only two and a half times Earth's—a condition to which even terrestrial animals (rats in centrifuges) have managed to adapt. The Jovian equivalent of fish, of course, couldn't care less about gravity, because it has virtually no effect in a marine environment.

Dr. James Edson, late of NASA, once remarked, "Jupiter is a problem for my grandchildren." I suspect that he may have been wildly optimistic. The zoology of a world outweighing 300 Earths could be the full-time occupation of mankind of the next 1000 years.

It also appears that Venus, with its extremely dense, furnace-hot atmosphere, may be an almost equally severe yet equally promising challenge. There now seems little doubt that the planet's average temperature is around 700 degrees Fahrenheit; but this does not, as many have prematurely assumed, rule out all possibility of life—even life of the kind that exists on Earth.

There may be little mixing of the atmosphere and, hence, little exchange of heat between the poles and the equator on a planet that revolves as slowly as Venus. At high latitudes or great altitudes—and Venusian mountains have now been detected by radar—it may be cool enough for liquid water to exist. (Even on Earth, remember, the temperature difference between the hottest and the coldest points is almost 300 degrees.) What makes this more than idle speculation is the exciting discovery, by the Russian space probe Venera IV, of oxygen in the planet's atmosphere. This extremely reactive gas combines with so many materials that it cannot occur in the free state—unless it is continuously renewed by vegetation. Free oxygen is an almost infallible indicator of life: If I may be allowed the modest cough of the minor prophet, I developed precisely this argument some years ago in a story of Venusian exploration, *Before Eden.*

On the other hand, it is also possible that we shall discover no trace of extraterrestrial life, past or present, on any of the planets. This would be a great disappointment; but even such a negative finding would give us a much sounder understanding of the conditions in which living creatures are likely to evolve; and this, in turn, would clarify our views on the distribution of life in the Universe as a whole. However, it seems much more probable that long before we can certify the Solar System as sterile, the communications engineers will have settled this ancient question—in the affirmative.

For that is what the exploration of space is really all about; and this is why many people are afraid of it, though they may give other reasons, even to themselves. It may be just as well that there are no contemporary higher civilizations in our immediate vicinity; the cultural shock of direct contact might be too great for us to survive. But by the time we have cut our teeth on the Solar System, we should be ready for such encounters. The challenge, in the Toynbeean sense of the word, should then bring forth the appropriate response.

Do not for a moment doubt that we shall one day head out for the stars—if, of course, the stars do not reach us first. I think I have read most of the arguments proving that interstellar travel is impossible. They are latter-day echoes of Professor Newcomb's paper on heavier-than-air flight. The logic and the mathematics are impeccable; the premises, wholly invalid. The more sophisticated are roughly equivalent to proving that dirigibles cannot break the sound barrier.

In the opening years of this century, the pioneers of astronautics were demonstrating that flight to the Moon and nearer planets was possible, though with great difficulty and expense, by means of chemical propellants. But even then, they were aware of the promise of nuclear energy and hoped that it would be the ultimate solution. They were right.

Today, it can likewise be shown that various conceivable, though currently quite impracticable, applications of nuclear and medical techniques could bring at least the closer stars within the range of exploration. And I would warn any skeptics who may point out the marginal nature of these techniques that, at this very moment, there are appearing simultaneously on the twin horizons of the infinitely large and the infinitely small, unmistakable signs of a breakthrough into a new order of creation. To quote some remarks made recently in my adopted country, Ceylon, by a Nobel laureate in physics, Professor C. F. Powell: "It seems to me that the evidence from astronomy and particle physics that I have described makes it possible that we are on the threshold of great and far-reaching discoveries. I have spoken of processes that, mass for mass, would be at least a thousand times more productive of energy than nuclear energy. . . . It seems that there are prodigious sources of energy in the interior regions of some galaxies, and possibly in the 'quasars,' far greater than those produced by the carbon cycle occurring in the stars . . . and we may one day learn how to employ them." And, if Professor Powell's surmise is correct, others may already have learned, on worlds older than ours. So it would be foolish, indeed, to assert that the stars must be forever beyond our reach.

More than half a century ago, the great Russian pioneer Tsiolkovsky wrote these moving and prophetic words: "The Earth is the cradle of the mind—but you cannot live in the cradle forever." Now, as we enter the second decade of the age of space, we can look still further into the future.

The Earth is, indeed, our cradle, which we are about to leave. And the Solar System will be our kindergarten.

COMMENTARY: ANALOGY AND PREMISES

No popular writer on science or author of science-fiction enjoys a higher reputation for his knowledge and imagination than does Arthur C. Clarke. This brilliant article reveals also his optimism concerning the long-range results of present scientific research. His *stance* thus is directly contrary to that of Frederic Nelson, who admits he fears that Man will become enslaved or even destroyed by the machines he is continuing to produce. Mr. Clarke shares none of this pessimism or skepticism. Although admitting the great shocks awaiting mankind, he sees the best is yet to come.

To lead up to this reassuring conclusion, he had to establish, or *verify,* the three *premises* which appear in the opening paragraph as evidence, he says, of "a widespread misunderstanding of the possible scale, importance and ultimate implications of travel to the planets." If he can clear up this "misunderstanding" on these three points, he will be able to show his readers that travel to the planets is not only within man's easy reach but also essential for man's ultimate discovery of his real place in the universe.

As we see them being taken up one after the other, his premises can easily be formulated as *evaluative statements:*

> Before long we will have technology to make interplanetary travel inexpensive.

Exploration of the planets is important for the new knowledge it will provide.
It will open the universe to man.

If we accept these premises, we can hardly refuse to go along with him and adopt his conclusion.

To convince us of the "truth" of his first premise, he resorts to comparison in the form of *analogy*. He describes the problems and progress of aeronautics with that of astronautics and maintains that just as inventions and new knowledge made air travel possible, so also "near space" exploration now going on will produce the necessary breakthroughs in technology necessary to make planetary exploration easily possible. He *assumes* that such improvements in machines and propellants are inevitable. He argues from the belief that just as great thinkers and inventors in past centuries led step by step to the wonders of today, so will equally gifted scientists and engineers solve space problems.

He even uses the *appeal* of interplanetary travel becoming a bargain. Imagine only ten dollars for propellant fuel say to the moon or 300 dollars for a jaunt to Jupiter and all way points! How inexpensive rocket fuel must be if it takes only 50 cents worth to escape from the surface of the moon!

His second premise is bolstered with some impressive statements of "fact." Among these is one saying that all the years of astronomical observations have produced only "a few hours" of really reliable information regarding planets and stars. It follows, then, that in space stations free from the distortions of the earth's atmosphere, astronomers will be able to gather accurate information about the solar system and the galaxies. He *assumes* also that as yet we do not have "any *reliable* knowledge about planetary conditions." In support of this contention he cites numerous old misconceptions that space flights have already exploded. As part of his argument he warns against continuing to hold the assumption "that there is something special about the Earth." On the basis of present information he projects the *hypothesis* that geographical conditions on the planets may be just as varied and complex as are those on Earth.

When contemplating the "implications" of the new knowledge that will result from planetary exploration, he adopts the language of prophets. His expression becomes highly *connotative* as he seeks to share his vision with his readers:

The Earth is, indeed, our cradle, which we are about to leave. And the Solar System will be our kindergarten.
There are appearing simultaneously on the twin horizons of the infinitely large and the infinitely small, unmistakable signs of a breakthrough into a new order of creation.

With such connotative language appealing to our hopes and desires for great adventure and discovery, he ends his presentation of his third premise, and at the same time he states his conclusion regarding the wonders awaiting man in the stars.

Is his evidence and the logic in support of his optimistic thesis more convincing than Frederic Nelson's when he made his far less hopeful evaluation of Man's future? Both have asked the same question: "Will Man eventually master his machines?"—and both have answered it. Which answer is true? Can either be verified, or is this a question that semanticists term "meaningless"—that is, not answerable, since there is no evidence at hand to verify any answer?

WHAT DOES IT SAY?

1. Besides providing the reader with a bit of humor what other persuasive effect does this advice have: "If you are ever stranded on Jupiter, you'll have to buy almost $300 worth of energy to get home. Make sure you take enough traveler's checks!"?

2. Does knowing that astronauts have found "good honest dirt" and rocks on the moon affect your feelings about exploration there?

3. Why does Mr. Clarke use the term "culture shock" to identify the effects to be expected on man's first learning accurate knowledge about the planets?

4. How does saying "All the planets lie far out on the gentle slope of the solar field . . ." make trips to the planets sound more feasible?

5. Have you any idea as to what is contained in "all the little black boxes that are sold by the carat"?

6. What is the name for the kind of argument wherein present "no-margin-for-error technology" in space trips is compared to having a car designed solely to complete "a mission" to a parking meter?

7. How do you interpret Einstein's statement: "The good Lord is subtle, but He is not malicious"?

8. In saying "Jupiter may also be the *biological* as well as the *physical* center of gravity of the Solar System," what is Mr. Clarke trying to tell us?

WHAT DO YOU THINK?

1. Arthur C. Clarke offers many more or less controversial statements deserving of an essay-length discussion. Select one of your own

from the essay or one of the following that you agree or disagree with:

(a) "Einstein once said: 'The good Lord is subtle, but He is not malicious.' "

(b) "Every world is itself a plurality."

(c) "So it would be foolish, indeed, to assert that the stars must be forever beyond our reach."

(d) "Perhaps I had better deal here with those strange characters who think that space is the exclusive province of automatic, robot probes and that we should stay at home and watch TV, as God intended us to."

(e) "Unless the record of the past is wholly misleading, we are going to see much the same sequence of events in space."

(f) "And with these, the Solar System will become an extension of the Earth—if we wish it to be."

2. Here are some statements often heard when the topic of space travel and exploration is discussed. For an essay, state the case one of its proponents would make, and then analyze it for its logic:

(a) "Instead of spending all that money on space, we should spend it to make life on Earth here more livable."

(b) "We may have to fight the Russians for possession of the mineral rights on the moon."

(c) "Space exploration will end up only with the United States and Russia, despite all treaties, using space stations for missile launching pads."

(d) "Man in his pride should pay heed to the Biblical account of the building of the Tower of Babel."

(e) "Very likely in planetary exploration man would encounter whole new strains of viruses and bacteria that could wipe out the whole human race."

(f) "There are intelligent beings in far space who are already trying to get in touch with us."

(g) "Space travel from other planets? Why we already have it. What do you suppose all these Flying Saucers are?"

(h) "If God wanted us to go traipsing about the planets, He would have made it possible for us in the first place."

(i) "Why spend all this money when we won't get any good out of it in our own lifetime?"

3. Discuss in writing some of the basic assumptions you have found common to most of the science-fiction you have read.

4. Write a logical analysis of a science-fiction film you have seen.

Should Scientists Play God?
by EDMUND R. LEACH

Human scientists now have it in their power to redesign the face of the earth, and to decide what kind of species shall survive to inherit it. How they actually use this terrible potentiality must depend on moral judgments, not on reason. But who shall decide, and how shall we judge? The answer to these questions seems to me repugnant but quite plain: There can be no source for these moral judgments except the scientist himself. In traditional religion, morality was held to derive from God, but God was only credited with the authority to establish and enforce moral rules because He was also credited with supernatural powers of creation and destruction. Those powers have now been usurped by man, and he must take on the moral responsibility that goes with them.

Our idea of God is a product of history. What I now believe about the supernatural is derived from what I was taught by my parents, and what they taught me was derived from what they were taught, and so on. But such beliefs are justified by faith alone, never by reason, and the true believer is expected to go on reaffirming his faith in the same verbal formula, even if the passage of history and the growth of scientific knowledge should have turned the words into

Reprinted from *The Saturday Evening Post,* November 16, 1968. Copyright E. R. Lêach. Reprinted by permission of author.

plain nonsense. Everyone now knows that the cosmology that is presupposed by the language of Christian utterance is quite unrelated to any empirical reality. This explains why so many religious-minded people exhibit an extreme reluctance to inquire at all closely into the meaning of basic religious concepts.

But just what *do* we mean by the word God? In Christian mythology, as represented by the Bible, God is credited with a variety of functions. He is the creator who first set the cosmological clock in motion; He is the lawgiver who establishes the principles of the moral code; He is the judge who punishes sinners even when human law fails to do so; He is also a kind of trickster who intervenes in human affairs in a quite arbitrary way so as to test the faith of the righteous; and, finally, He is a mediator between sinful man and his destiny. He is not only the judge of sinners but their salvation. These attributes of God are by definition "superhuman," but they are nevertheless qualities of an essentially human kind. The God of Judeo-Christianity is, in all His aspects, whether creator, judge, trickster or mediator, quite explicitly anthropomorphic. And the converse is equally true: There is necessarily something godlike about every human being.

Anthropologists, who make it their business to discover just how human beings perceive themselves as differing from one another and from other natural species, will tell you that every community conceives of itself as being uniquely "human." This humanity is always felt to be a quality of civilization and orderliness that "we" alone share; "other" creatures, whether they be foreigners or animals, are members of inferior species and are described by labels such as "savage," "wild," "lawless," "heathen," "dangerous," "mysterious."

There is a paradox here: When we affirm that *we* are civilized and that the *others* are savage, we are claiming superiority over the others, but the mythology always explains the origin of this superiority by a story of the Adam and Eve type. "In the beginning God created our first ancestors and gave them the moral rules that are the basis of our present civilization." But this "God" himself belongs to the category of "others": He is nonhuman, He is above the law, He is dangerous and mysterious, He existed even before the beginning, He is Nature itself. So we find that, in religious terms, culture—that is, civilization —stands in a curiously ambivalent relationship to nonculture—that is, nature. At one level we, the men of culture, are dominant over nature, but at another level God and nature merge together and become dominant over us.

All this is more relevant to my title than might at first appear, for scientists, like God, have now become mediators between culture and nature. Modern science grew out of medieval alchemy, and the alchemists were quite explicitly men who sought to do what only gods might properly do—to transform one element into another and to discover the elixir of immortal life. They pursued these revolutionary objectives in the atmosphere of a very conservative society. Official doctrine held that the order of nature had been established once and for all in the first six days of the Creation, and that the proper station and destiny of every individual had been preordained by God. The alchemists, therefore, were very properly regarded as blasphemous heretics, for they were attempting to tamper with God's handiwork, they were claiming that "laws of nature" could be altered by human intervention, they were playing at being God. Moreover, they lived in a world of fantasy: The heretical miracles that they claimed to perform were imaginary.

But at the present time the ordinary everyday achievements of science, which we take quite for granted, are of precisely the kind that our medieval forebears considered to be supernatural. We can fly through the air, we can look in on events that are taking place on the other side of the earth, we can transplant organs from corpses to living bodies, we can change one element into another, we can even produce a chemical mimicry of living tissue itself.

In the traditional mythology, the performance of miracles is only a part (and on the whole a minor part) of God's function. God's major role is moral—He is the source of the rules, He punishes (or redeems) the wicked. The scientist can now play God in his role as wonder-worker, but can he—and should he—also play God as moral arbiter? If you put this question to any group of actual scientists, the great majority will answer it with an unhesitating "No," for it is one of the most passionately held formal dogmas of modern science that research procedure should be objective and not tendentious. The scientist must seek to establish the truth for truth's sake, and not as an advocate of any particular creed. And on the face of it, this principle is self-evident: If we are to attain scientific objectivity, moral detachment is absolutely essential.

Yet this viewpoint, too, is a product of history. Modern science can be said to have begun when Copernicus and Galileo established the fundamental bases of modern astronomy. In order to do this, they had to achieve moral detachment and deny the truth of the Ptolemaic cosmology, which at that time had the official sanction of the Church. As both these men were good Catholics, and several of the cardinals, including Galileo's Pope, were excellent scientists, the conflict of values led to the utmost tribulation on all sides. And so it has continued even down to the present. Again and again leaders of the Church have felt themselves compelled to declare that some finding of science—such as evolution by natural selection, or the chemical origin of life, or the capacity of the human race to reproduce itself beyond the limits of its food supply—is contrary to religious doctrine, and they have demanded that the scientists recant. Against this coercion the scientists have erected their own counterdogma: The pursuit of scientific truth must be free of all moral or religious restraints.

But the claim to moral detachment is not absolute. In actual practice all scientists draw the line somewhere, and they usually draw it between culture and nature. Freedom from moral restraint applies only to the study of nature, not to the study of culture. Even the Nazi scientists who experimented with human beings as if they were monkeys, rats or guinea pigs, would not have challenged this distinction. They merely drew their line in a different place: From their point of view the Jews were not really human, but just a part of nature.

But discriminations of this sort are very ungodlike. God is the creator and protector of *all* things: He does not destroy one part of His creation in order to give benefit to another; creation is a totality, one and indivisible. In contrast, we human beings habitually act as if all other living species, whether animals or plants, exist only for our own convenience; we feel free to exploit or destroy them as we think fit. It is true that some sentimental laymen have moral qualms about vivisection, but no orthodox scientist could ever have any hesitation about experiments involving "mere animals." All the same, there are always some kinds of experiments that any particular research worker would *not* be prepared to carry out. Each individual does, in practice, "draw the line somewhere," so the question arises whether he might not with advantage draw it somewhere else.

The moral doubts of those who helped to design the first atomic bombs have become notorious, and today there must be thousands of highly qualified scientists engaged on hundreds of different chemical and biological research projects who face similar difficulties. It is not simply a matter of trying to measure the positive value of a gain in human knowledge against the negative value of powers of military destruction; the merits and demerits of our whole biological history are at stake. It is no good for the scientist to suppose that there is some outside authority who can decide whether his experiments are legitimate or illegitimate. It has become useless to appeal to God against the Devil; the scientist must be the source of his own morality.

Because God traditionally had unlimited power to intervene and alter the natural course of events, it made sense to treat Him as the ultimate moral authority as well. But today when the molecular biologists are rapidly unraveling the genetic chemistry of all living things— while the radio astronomers are deciphering the program of an evolving cosmos—all the marvels of creation are seen to be mechanisms rather than mysteries. Since even the human brain is nothing more than an immensely complicated computer, it is no longer necessary to invoke metaphysics to explain how it works. In the resulting mechanistic universe all that remains of the divine will is the moral consciousness of man himself.

So we must now learn to play God in a moral as well as in a creative or destructive sense. To do this effectively, we shall have to educate our children in quite a different way. In the past, education has always been designed to inculcate a respect for the wisdom and experience of the older generation, whose members have been credited with an intuitive understanding of the wishes of an omniscient God. From this point of view, the dogmas of religion represent the sum of our historical experience. So long as it appeared that "natural law" was eternal and unalterable—except by God—it was quite sensible to use history in this way as a guide to virtue. But in our changed circumstances, when we ourselves can alter all the ground rules of the game, excessive deference to established authority could well be an invitation to disaster. For example, as long as medical science was virtually impotent—as it was until the beginning of this century—it made perfect sense to accept the traditional theological principle that it is always virtuous to save a life. But today the doctors, provided they are given sufficient resources, can preserve alive all manner of deformed infants and senile invalids who would, in the natural course of events, have been dead long ago. But the cost of preserving these defective lives is ultimately borne by those who are normal and healthy, and at some point the burden will become intolerable, and saving life will become morally evil. When we are faced with moral paradoxes of this kind—and science presents us with new ones every day—it is useless to console ourselves with the conventional religious formulas. We ourselves have to decide what is sin and what is virtue, and we must do so on the basis of our modern knowledge and not on the basis of traditional categories. This implies that we must all share in a kind of immediate collective responsibility for any action that any one individual performs. Perhaps this all sounds like a pie-in-the-sky doctrine. But unless we teach those of the next generation that they can afford to be atheists only if they assume the moral responsibilities of God, the prospects for the human race are decidedly bleak.

COMMENTARY: SEMANTICS AND ARGUMENT

Dr. Edmund R. Leach, the distinguished British scientist, has constructed a formidable argument in favor of his thesis, or *proposition*, that since science has gone as far as it has, "There can be no source for these moral judgments except the scientist himself." His reasoning takes on the form of a carefully woven chain of arguments, each link of which he skillfully forges before moving on to the next. Naturally, since the term *God* must play an essential part in this reasoning, the author will need to do much defining and explaining of that term.

The opening paragraph contains in essence the whole argument. It consists of a series of evaluative statements along with other statements that many readers will probably accept as historical facts. But it is the final sentence of the paragraph that will set some teeth on edge: "Those powers have now been usurped by man, and he must take on the moral responsibility that goes with them."

As the study of *semantics* has long since established, words can make or ruin our lives. Among the most powerful of these words has been the three-letter word *God* when spelled with a capital letter. Its connotations have been built up through the centuries of our Judaic-Christian culture. Most likely for that reason Dr. Leach begins by attempting to show that "our idea of God is a product of history" and that faith may be perpetuated as merely "a verbal formula" having little to do with reason. Any number of modern theologians would accept his statements as being factual.

He next moves to the analysis of what "we mean by the word *God*," and he lists the "variety of functions" historically credited to this "God." He infers from these six complex, and even contradictory, "functions" that our idea of the Deity is "quite explicitly anthropomorphic," and has resulted in man's giving himself certain godlike attributes. Such statements he also assumes to be accepted facts.

Having now explained the historic origins and meanings of the term "God" to his satisfaction, he turns to anthropology to show that every society thinks of itself as "favored" and that the "Adam and Eve myth" has supported this self regard. The anthropomorphic concept of God, he says, becomes a paradox, however, when "God" is also identified with "Nature," which is nonhuman.

Until now, he points out, scientists were content to remain in their historic role as objective thinkers, working only with the things of "nature" and not interfering with the concerns of "culture." These were to be left to the religions. The history of science attests to this enforced separation. But now that scientists can perform feats that once would have been considered "miracles," they are also compelled to face up to the responsibilities of making moral decisions in matters of "culture." So he argues that the concept of "scientist" has taken on new meaning, while the old concept of "God" has lost its meanings. And since there no longer is a God or a Devil to appeal to, "the scientist must be the source of his own morality." Dr. Leach repeatedly drives this point home.

In his closing paragraphs, Dr. Leach draws some further conclusions from the evidence he had earlier presented. He infers that, like the universe, human beings are mechanisms and that "all that remains of the divine will is the moral consciousness of man himself." And as he assumes he has adequately shown, it has always been the scientists who have shown the rest of mankind the facts of existence; it remains then for scientists to take the next logical step: "So we must now learn to play God in a moral as well as a creative or destructive sense." His details of what science is doing, for example, in medicine to prolong and alter life support his contention that no longer can scientists bow to other authorities such as those formerly fortified by "natural law." He repeats his thesis in various terms, even some traditional ones: "We ourselves have to decide what is sin and what is virtue. . . ."

A careful study of this essay will reveal how logically Dr. Leach supports his thesis, even though that thesis may be distasteful to many readers. Certainly it can arouse debate, for the issues herein intrude upon the areas of both fact and faith, the most controversial of all boundary lines!

WHAT DOES IT SAY?

1. In the second paragraph the author speaks of "the cosmology that is presupposed by the language of Christian utterance." What is this "cosmology," this "language"?

2. How possibly can the Bible ever be said to make "God" appear as "a kind of trickster"?

3. From what language is the word anthropomorphic derived?

4. What is a paradox?

5. In what way may the alchemists be regarded as being akin to modern scientists?

6. What is meant by the statement that in the past it was thought that "research procedure should be objective and not tendentious"?

7. Describe some of the features of the "Ptolemaic cosmology" that Copernicus and Galileo attacked in opposing Church doctrine.

8. What, to you, are the implications of this statement: "Since even the human brain is nothing more than an immensely complicated computer, it is no longer necessary to invoke metaphysics to explain how it works"?

WHAT DO YOU THINK?

1. Taking care to be logical, defend or attack one of the many evaluative statements found in Dr. Leach's essay. You might try your hand on one of these:

   (a) "Every community conceives of itself as being uniquely 'human.'"

   (b) "God is the creator and protector of *all* things: He does not destroy one part of His creation in order to give benefit to another; creation is a totality, one and indivisible."

   (c) "But in our changed circumstances, when we ourselves can alter all the ground rules of the game, excessive deference to established authority could well be an invitation to disaster."

   (d) "It is no good for the scientist to suppose that there is some outside authority who can decide whether his experiments are legitimate or illegitimate."

   (e) "But unless we teach those of the next generation that they can afford to be atheists only if they assume the moral responsibilities of God, the prospects for the human race are decidedly bleak."

2. Do you have strong feelings regarding the relationships between science and humanitarian ethics? If so, express your views on one of these complex subjects:

   (a) Physicians who, although trained to save lives, aid in the study of viruses and bacteria to be spread among civil populations as weapons of war.

   (b) Communities that welcome missile bases because "it's good for business."

   (c) Physicians and counselors who treat drug addicts and youthful runaways but refuse to cooperate with local police agencies.

   (d) Clergymen who support moral teachings that they themselves fear are not true.

3. In the light of Dr. Leach's essay, define and explain your idea of one of the following:

A moral person	Progress
An atheist	Immorality
A believer in God	Freedom
A hypocrite	Responsibility

1969 to 2019
by PAUL BRODEUR

The proliferation of problems in this increasingly complex society of
ours has led to a proliferation of conferences on how to deal with the
problems, which, in turn, has given rise to seemingly endless discussion
about what sort of projections to make, plans to draw up, and policies
to implement in order to solve the problems that, in Mother Goose
progression, led to the conferences that gave rise to the discussion—or
so it seemed to us by the time we had finished looking in on the
American Institute of Planners' Conference that was held for two
days recently in the Sert Room of the Waldorf-Astoria. The conference
was entitled "Building the Future Environment—An Atlantic Region
Perspective to the Year 2020," and was attended by more than four
hundred businessmen, government officials, architects, planners, and
educators. When we arrived for the first seminar, we found Boris
Pushkarev, planning director of the Regional Plan Association, in the
midst of delivering a paper that presented a detailed forecast for living
and working conditions in the urbanized northeastern-seaboard cor-
ridor. Mr. Pushkarev was speaking from a lectern that stood in front
of an electronic digital-display unit, which, to dramatize the problems
facing the now and future inhabitants of Megalopolis, had been set to

advance at the rate of one year for every half hour of the conference, and as he launched into a description of a phenomenon he called "spread city," the machine clicked, new numbers fell into place, and the year changed from 1969 to 1970.

According to Mr. Pushkarev, "spread city" is an amorphous development pattern, neither urban nor suburban nor rural, that occurs when living, working, and shopping facilities are scattered in random fashion over the landscape. "The motor-vehicle traffic generated by such a pattern necessitates the building of freeways that wiggle around and between pieces of developed land, and through the 'spread-city' centers," he said. "The result is a highway map that looks like a bowl of spaghetti." Mr. Pushkarev finished his talk with a discussion of the pros and cons of high-speed ground-transportation schemes, such as automated highways, tracked air-cushion vehicles, and gravity-vacuum transit, and he was followed to the lectern by Jerome P. Pickard, director of the Department of Housing and Urban Development's Program Analysis and Evaluation Staff, who started out by quoting H. G. Wells—"Human history becomes more and more a race between education and catastrophe"—and ended by saying that if present trends continue, today's population of forty-eight million in the Atlantic Metropolitan Region will have increased to eighty-two million by the year 2020.

At this point, a short recess was called to enable those attending the conference to fill out an electronic punch-card opinion survey consisting of questions and multiple-choice answers. The first question was "Present trends will raise the forty-eight million population of the Atlantic Region to eighty-two million in 2020. What is your reaction to this forecast?" The possible answers were "Trend O.K.—We can swing it. No problem for twenty years. Too many too fast—need time to get ready." When the cards had been collected, Professor Benjamin Chinitz, chairman of the Department of Economics of Brown University, delivered a critique of the papers given by the two speakers. "What I find distressing is the business-as-usual spirit with which the authors go about their task," Professor Chinitz said. "We've got to put aside the old concepts of city planning. Our dialogue about urban development must now be directed to the overriding problems of poverty and racial equality." A second critique was then offered, by Lawrence K. Edwards, president of the Tube Transit Corporation of Palo Alto, California, who suggested that automobiles be kept out of overcrowded city centers, and gave way to Elmo Roper, founder and senior consultant of Roper Research Associates, Inc., who proceeded to give the results of the opinion survey. According to Mr. Roper, forty per cent of the audience found the population trend O.K. and manageable; eight per cent felt that there would be no problem for twenty years; forty-four per cent believed that the growth rate was too fast to be accommodated; and eight per cent were unable to answer the question.

When we dropped by on the second day of the conference, it was ten o'clock in the morning (our time) in the digital-clock-year 2007, and Marion Clawson, director of the Land Use and Management Program of Resources for the Future, was delivering a paper entitled "New Responsibilities for Government"—responsibilities that he said rested upon the basic assumptions that men, as rational beings, can choose the kinds of lives they want, that long-range planning is practical, and that such planning should include the maximum permissible range of choice for the individual. A critique of Mr. Clawson's paper was given by Emilio Q. Daddario, representative from Connecticut and chairman of the House Subcommittee on Science, Research, and Development, who started out by questioning Mr. Clawson's basic assumptions. "What philosophical or empirical basis can be used to support these assumptions?" Representative Daddario asked. "There's much evidence, after all, to suggest that man is emotional rather than rational. Furthermore, long-range planning has been tried extensively throughout history, from ancient China down to the Soviet Union, with little conclusive proof that the rational plans of bureaucrats produce results superior to those of the marketplace."

The year had advanced to 2015 when Herman Kahn, director of the Hudson Institute, got up to deliver a paper entitled "New Roles for Private Enterprise," for the afternoon seminar. According to Mr. Kahn, the Western world has suffered since the Second World War a failure of nerve similar to that which occurred in Hellenistic Greece and Imperial Rome. "We're full of guilt and pessimism, which are bad for morale," Mr. Kahn said. "Perhaps we can take comfort from the fact that during the reign of the pessimists, which lasted six hundred years, Athens was better governed than ever before. It was not, of course, as creative, but in my opinion we're in for a similar era—an era of big public works that raise morale and turn people on. It doesn't take great art to make a Lincoln Center, you know. It just takes money and good consultants." Mr. Kahn went on to say that he had devised a plan for turning New York into a "water city," and a scheme for increasing the size of Central Park. "The first idea consists of building a commercial center on the scale of Rockefeller Center on the lower tip of Welfare Island and on filled land extending south to Belmont Island, at Forty-second Street," he said. "The island could then be connected to Manhattan by a broad, low bridge wide enough to have restaurants and stores on both sides. This would provide a huge marina in what is now the west channel of the East

River, which would encourage New Yorkers to take to the water by the boatload. As for Central Park, I'd like to double its size by selling small pieces at the southern end and extending it right up through Harlem to the Harlem River."

Mr. Kahn concluded his paper by stating that a city's future depends upon emphasizing the positive as well as the negative, and he was followed to the lectern by Max Ways, a member of the board of editors of *Fortune,* who said that the general attitude toward the city had changed in his lifetime from complacent boosterism to masochistic despair. "To keep saying that the city is ungovernable, unlivable, and impossible is giving in to social hypochondria," Mr. Ways declared. "Cities are attracting people in a mass migration unparalleled in history because people at all economic, social, and educational levels are moved by a profound desire to be where the action is."

Mr. Ways sat down, to considerable applause, and was replaced at the lectern by Anthony Downs, who is executive vice-president of the Real Estate Research Corporation, of Chicago, and one of the authors of the Kerner Report. Mr. Downs began his critique by accusing Mr. Kahn of not addressing himself to the problem of how to get his new schemes accepted. "We've had some ideas paraded before us in magnificent clothes that the emperor does not possess," Mr. Downs declared. "Herman Kahn depends too much on what I call proof by assertion. Let's not forget to differentiate between words and reality, between rhetoric and events. Where, for example, do you put all the people who will be displaced by doubling the size of Central Park? Why, this seminar reminds me of some kind of intellectual Kiwanis Club meeting! Personally, I disagree with all the emphasis on positive thinking. I think a period of dark perception is a healthy thing. We need to take a hard look at what we're really like."

At this point, with the year at 2019, we decided to call it a day.

COMMENTARY: INFERENCES AND DEDUCTIONS

Over the years "The Talk of the Town" section of *The New Yorker* Magazine has become famous for the fact that although the essays may be written by different authors, their style remains consistent in tone and manner. This piece by Paul Brodeur (his name does not appear in the magazine as author) is a fine example of that style. It also affords us a chance to examine some aspects of logic.

The typical "Talk of the Town" item bases its thesis upon inferences, or deductions, drawn from a reporter's observations while attending some unusual event such as this conference on "Building the Future Environment—An Atlantic Region Perspective to the year 2020." As in other "Talk" pieces, the thesis is implied rather than bluntly stated. By *thesis,* in this instance, we mean what the author really thought of this two-day meeting at which various experts presented a wide variety of conflicting views and solutions to the basic problem facing the conference.

What is Mr. Brodeur's conclusion? Judging by his opening and concluding remarks, he seems to be implying that this gathering of hundreds of experts achieved little or nothing more than an exchange of conflicting opinions. Thus he plays the typical *New Yorker* role of being the impressed, but somewhat skeptical, reporter who has just witnessed another of the unusual and puzzling social phenomenon that life in this great metropolis affords.

His opening *statements* are ones of *evaluation* or *judgment* and become the *assumptions* upon which his account will rest. They make the points that the "proliferation of problems" leads to "a proliferation of conferences on how to deal with the problems." These conferences, in turn, give rise "to seemingly endless discussions" that result in additional, inconclusive conferences. To support these assumptions, he relies upon the persuasive devices of *example* by telling us of his experiences with this particular conference. His method of reporting what he saw and heard is also of importance in influencing the reader to accept these assumptions.

He makes dramatic use of the conference's "electronic digital-display unit, which . . . had been set to advance at the rate of one year for every half hour of the conference." Against this symbolic time-lapsing machine, he presents first a planning director's "spread city" statements, which seem to be a combination of fact, evaluative judgment, and perhaps even of emotion. Next he summarizes an urban planning specialist's evaluative statements, given to us only as unsupported assumptions to be taken for granted since the author has condensed the speech.

His summary of the "punch-card opinion survey" taken by opinion-poll expert Elmo Roper indicates by its results that the specialists remain divided despite the two reports they have just heard. He continues then with more brief quotations and summaries of talks by other such experts as an economist, another land management planner, a state politician, an area institute director, a *Fortune* magazine editor, and a Chicago real estate researcher.

In making these summaries, Mr. Brodeur suggests the weak base of assumptions on which these discussions seem to rest. He quotes Representative Daddario: "What philosophical or empirical basis can be used to support these assumptions?" But does this political spokesman then get down to hard facts of evidence himself? On reading his following remarks, one can only conclude that this politician also relies upon evaluative statements and judgments that have no ready facts to support them. How else can one regard this passage?

> There's much evidence, after all, to suggest that man is emotional rather than rational. Furthermore, long-range planning has been tried extensively throughout history, from ancient China down to the Soviet Union, with little conclusive proof that the national plans of bureaucrats produce results superior to those of the marketplace.

From these words we infer that the speaker holds the consideration of long-range plans and the anticipation of problems to be a waste of time and effort. Other inferences are that by letting business firms and corporations go their own way and then by having political agencies deal with resulting problems as they arise, everything will eventually turn out well.

Mr. Brodeur concludes his essay with a Chicago real estate researcher's attacks on the proposals made by the Hudson Institute director for the improvement of Manhattan. Again, according to the quotations afforded us, we find the attacker using the language of good logic: "Herman Kahn depends too much on what I call proof by assertion. Let's not forget to differentiate between words and reality, between rhetoric and events." But, again, these statements fail to be any other than merely emotional, evaluative ones.

No wonder, according to this quoted evidence, the author, in typical *New Yorker* fashion, ironically decides "to call it a day." Are you convinced by the evidence presented in this essay that the inferences found in the opening are justified? Or has the author "stacked the deck" by his selection of quotations?

WHAT DOES IT SAY?

1. How can "the proliferation of problems" be said to lead to "a proliferation of conferences"?

2. Of what was the "electronic digital-display unit" a symbol?

3. Give the literal meanings of the words making up the term *megalopolis*.

4. As you know them, what are the connotations of "spread-city centers"?

5. Identify, as to type, the following statements:

> Forty-four per cent believed that the growth rate was too fast to be accommodated.

We're full of guilt and pessimism, which are bad for morale.
Why, this seminar reminds me of some kind of intellectual Kiwanis Club meeting!

6. Explain the *allusion* in this statement: "We've had some ideas paraded before us in magnificent clothes that the emperor does not possess."

7. Has any essay in this book been said to rely upon "proof by assertion"?

8. What is the important difference between "words and reality"?

WHAT DO YOU THINK?

1. On the basis of your observations of the behavior and speech of the participant, write an essay having inferences and conclusions drawn from a typical meeting or discussion—"bull session"—of one of the following:

Your dormitory or house residents

A particular cafeteria or student center group

A church social club

A politically affiliated body: student Republicans, Democrats, S.D.S., and so on

A special social committee

A joint faculty-student committee

A student government session

2. Having care for supporting evidence, write an essay agreeing or disagreeing either in whole or in part with one of the following statements appearing in "1969 to 2019":
   (a) "There's much evidence, after all, to suggest that man is emotional rather than rational."
   (b) "It doesn't take great art to make a Lincoln Center, you know. It just takes money and good consultants."
   (c) "Cities are attracting people in a mass migration unparalleled in history."
   (d) "I think a period of dark perception is a healthy thing. We need to take a hard look at what we're really like."

(e) "Human history becomes more and more a race between education and catastrophe."

3. Supporting your evaluative statements with good evidence and sound inferences, try to convince your classmates to accept your views on one of the following problems:

(a) Mass transportation for your city

(b) Proper zoning for suburban areas

(c) Good new housing units

(d) Proper recreational areas

(e) Hunting laws and preservation of wild game

(f) Vacation vehicle control: speedboats, trail motorcycles, snow-mobiles, surfboarding, and so on.

(g) Small plane flight regulations

4. Systematically describe some features of your own neighborhood that appall you, and then point out what should be done to remedy the situation.

Breathes There a Man
by GOODMAN ACE

Twenty-two years ago, on July 1, 1946, the United States moved the inhabitants of Bikini Atoll to another atoll in the Marshall Islands so that our government could conduct some underwater atomic bomb tests.

Now President Johnson has announced that the Bikini Atoll is safe again, and that the natives could return to their homes. So a committee of nine Bikini islanders came back to Bikini to investigate and to report to their countrymen on the state of the tiny island which has been kept clear of human inhabitants since 1946.

"The island is changed," *The New York Times* reported the high commissioner to have said. "Most of the trees have gone."

This remark must not have set too well with our government man in charge of making this move back to Bikini.

"Look," he said, "you people have been hollering you want to come back home. Remember, home is where you hang your hat."

"I know," replied the dissident Bikini islander. "But all the hall trees have been blown away, too. The island is not the same."

"That's what you said when we moved you away from here twenty-two years ago to Rongerik Atoll. So we moved you to the Kili

Reprinted from *Saturday Review*, October 26, 1968. Copyright 1968 by Saturday Review, Inc. Reprinted with permission of author and publication.

Atoll. Now when you say you want to come back to Bikini, you're complaining about this atoll. If you keep raising issues like that, how can you have a life of law and order on this atoll? Seems to me you people don't like any atoll at all."

"Well," said the Bikinian, "when you moved us to Rongerik Atoll, we found poisonous fish in the lagoon."

"So we moved you to Kili Island. Besides, all our scientists have stated quite clearly that radiation levels have dropped to a point where Bikini is safe again for habitation."

"Yes, I know they said that. But I don't see any of them habitating up here. There must still be some radiation."

"Oh, I suppose there will always be a little bit of radiation. But it's safe for you to live with."

"Well, maybe for me, yes. But some of our women are a little bit pregnant. They want to be sure that their newborn . . ."

"There you go raising issues again. Let's take it from the top. You will agree that our country had to make these underwater atomic tests, right?"

"Well, we don't understand why they . . ."

"Why? Because our country is trying to get a nonproliferation treaty signed. We want all nations to sign it. How could the United States sign a nonproliferation treaty if we didn't test enough atomic bombs so we could get some proliferation to nonproliferate with?"

"How's that again?"

"You people refuse to understand."

"What we don't understand is why you picked our homeland to shoot off so many atomic bombs?"

"Why? To contain Communism. Don't you know if one small country falls, the next one topples and then they all topple. That's the domino theory."

"Yes, but we think of it as the chess theory. It seems to us we're the pawns, and we've been rooked by the kings and queens."

"Nobody's doing anything to you. Our government is going to rehabilitate this whole island. That concrete blockhouse over there is coming down; also that giant communication tower in the jungle back there. On this beach here is going to rise the new, magnificent Hilton Bikini. Do you think we'd build a big hotel if it weren't safe? Didn't you hear General Curtis LeMay say that since those atomic tests were exploded here even the rats on Bikini have grown bigger and fatter? Now don't quote me saying the Hilton Bikini is going to have fat rats. I didn't say that."

"But we don't need a hotel. We need hospitals and. . ."

"OK, we'll build you a hospital."

"Then there are all our little children."

"OK, we'll build them a schoolhouse."

"Our culture is a mixture of Polynesian and Melanesian blood."

"Oh, I get you. So we'll build two schools. We'll even give you the buses to bus the kids. What do you say, you going to move back here?"

"Well, we're just a committee of nine. We must report to our people in Kili."

"OK, you do that. Tell 'em we're going to make this an island of paradise. We'll build playgrounds, a Disneyland. We'll give you houses, Coca-Cola, churches, roads. In no time at all you'll be getting social security, welfare, unemployment insurance. Tell 'em an atom bomb that gives you all this can't be all that bad."

COMMENTARY: FALLACIES AND FALLACIES

Goodman Ace, one of our country's sharpest social critics, is obviously attacking government policy on the proposed return of former Bikini Atoll islanders to that island now officially declared "safe" for resettlement. To make his criticism amusing, he has chosen the device of a dialogue between the government agent and the spokesman for the islanders. But, as analysis reveals, Ace has made the government agent a kind of "salesman" who employs all of the fallacious reasoning a very shrewd (or very simple-minded) talker might use. Needless to say, Ace makes these fallacies also ridiculous.

Let us begin with a look at the language and reasoning of this "government man." His highly idiomatic vocabulary and sharp tone suggest a rough, undiplomatic character—someone like the proverbial used-car dealer: "Look, . . . you people have been hollering you want to come back home." This remark is followed by the illogical statement: "Remember, home is where you hang your hat." This is a *non sequitur*, since the islanders do not wear hats, and besides, this boorish remark implies that any place is good enough for these people.

The *allusion* to "law and order" is a facetious echoing of a familiar expression which lacks any relevance in this context and is meant to distract the islanders from the real issue of the argument: Is the island *now* suitable for the proposed return? The allusion is immediately followed by the *pun,* or *paronomasis,* "atoll at all," indicating the speaker takes the whole matter most lightly.

In the next bit of exchange, the government man "begs the question" by pretending that the question as to the presence of dangerous radiation has already been settled. He dismisses it, saying, "Oh, I suppose there will always be a little bit of radiation. But it's safe for you to live with."

The reply of the islander reveals again his clear thinking, and all-observing character, as well as his ironic wit: "Well, maybe for me, yes. But some of our women are a little bit pregnant. . . ." Instead of admitting the dangerous effects of radiation upon unborn children, the government man returns with a ridiculous counter-attack: "There you go raising issues again. . . . You people refuse to understand. . . ." (This device of retorting to the charge of an adversary by counter-charge is called *antanagoge*.) He continues with a plea in justification of the use of the atoll as an atomic bomb test site in the first place: "Why? Because our country is trying to get a nonproliferation treaty signed. . . . Why? To contain Communism." (This is the abuse of another rhetorical device called *antistasis,* which is a plea in justification of an action because it obviated something worse.)

In replying to the "domino theory," the islander adopted the very sophisticated figure of speech called *antitrophon* (an argument retorted on or turned against an opponent): "Yes, but we think of it as the chess theory. It seems to us we're the pawns, and we've been rooked by the kings and queens." The word *rooked* here is also a pun for the vernacular meaning of "cheated."

In his persuasive attempts, the agent also asks *rhetorical questions* that are ridiculous in the eyes of the islanders: "Do you think we'd build a big hotel if it weren't safe? Didn't you hear General Curtis LeMay . . .?" In trying to bribe them, the government man resorts to *epitrope* (concession to an opponent, sometimes ironic): "Oh, I get you. So we'll build two schools. We'll even give you the buses to bus the kids." And he ends up with a final, extravagant, and totally irrelevant speech of *aparithmesis* (enumerating of particulars to produce a cumulative, or even anticlimactic, effect): "OK, you do that. Tell 'em we're going to make this an island of paradise. We'll build playgrounds, a Disneyland . . . give you houses, Coca-Cola. . . ." In the final sentence the word *all* being used in two different senses is an example of *antanaclasis* (repetition of a word in a different sense).

Goodman Ace may not be familiar with all of these jawbreaker terms of argument, but he certainly knows how to employ the patterns of language they stand for. By the time we have reached the ironic end of this dialogue, we can see that he has extended his attack on the Bikini policy to include criticism of many features of United States cultural stereotypes and criticism also of the scientists and military leaders who created and used the atom bomb. He also demonstrates how these language devices can be twisted and perverted by glib speakers who lack conscience.

In this light, the title itself, "Breathes There a Man," sets the ironic tone of the piece. It is taken from "The Lay of the Last Minstrel" by Sir Walter Scott, wherein the exile thinks of his former homeland and says:

Breathes there a man with soul so dead
Who ne'er to himself hath said,
"This is my own, my native land!"

WHAT DOES IT SAY?

1. The opening complaint of the Bikini commissioner—"Most of the trees have gone"—suggests what basic fact that none of the government agent's arguments can explain away?

2. In argumentation what is the meaning of *issues*? Why is the agent being ridiculous in his accusation that the commissioner is "raising issues"?

3. What is an *atoll*? What contradictions does the combination of the words "Bikini atoll" and "atomic bomb" hold for you?

4. Notice that the commissioner says, "There must still be some radiation" and the agent replies, "Oh, I suppose there will always be a little bit of radiation." What in their contexts is the difference here between *some* and *little*?

5. Why would the commissioner be puzzled by the agent's remark that the United States needed to test atomic bombs "to get some proliferation to nonproliferate with"?

6. Is there any irony in the agent's referring to "that giant communication tower in the jungle back there"? How could that particular tower be at all correctly called a "communication tower"?

7. What connotations would the expression "the Hilton Bikini" hold for you?

8. Is the commissioner implying that he has racial troubles when he speaks of "a mixture of Polynesian and Melanesian blood"? Or is this remark only another of the author's means of pointing a finger at conditions in the United States?

WHAT DO YOU THINK?

1. In the age when ever more powerful missiles with atomic warheads remain aimed at potential targets everywhere, including the cities of our own country, it is not easy to forget the horrible realities they symbolize. Consider one of the following subjects as a possible starting point for summing up your own feelings regarding these threats.

(a) Can we never have enough missiles for the defense of our country?

(b) Are there any dangers in underground testing of nuclear devices?

(c) What has happened to the nuclear arms test-ban treaty?

(d) Does anyone still say, "I'd rather be red than dead"?

(e) Are missile-launching sites in space becoming realities?

(f) Is it true that the stronger the military power of the United States, the better the chance for peace in the world?

(g) Can nuclear energy used for peaceful purposes be easily turned into weapons of war?

2. Examine copies of weekly news magazines for the past several weeks, and report your findings on their agreement or disagreement on questions concerning nuclear weapons or power.

3. If you have some knowledge of the subject, select one of the following general topics and "come down the abstraction ladder" to give it a specific, concrete treatment:

(a) The industrial-military complex that President Eisenhower warned against as a great danger to the United States.

(b) The lasting effect of the Hiroshima and Nagasaki atomic blasts.

(c) The effectiveness of organized religions in preserving international peace.

(d) Scientific research on campus and projects having possible military application.

(e) Should engineers ever question the uses to which the products they design or build will be put?

(f) Can scientists "afford" to have a conscience?

(g) How far can a person go in excusing himself for performing some ugly duty by pleading: "I was only carrying out the orders given me by my superiors"?

Should the United States Install an ABM System?
pro: HON. JOHN O. PASTORE, UNITED STATES SENATOR, RHODE ISLAND

Today we are living in a mad world, and indeed it is a mad world. There are enough nuclear and thermonuclear bombs to burn this world to ashes.

One thing has saved mankind. Through some miracle, after Hiroshima and Nagasaki, no atomic bomb has been dropped on human beings. Today, figuratively speaking, we have atomic bombs coming out of our ears, not only in the arsenals of America, not only in the arsenals of Russia, not only in the arsenals of other countries, like Great Britain, but now we also see that the Red Chinese have detonated seven devices having a sophistication that has surprised the members of our committee and the scientists of this country. The Red Chinese have achieved a hydrogen bomb.

But now the big question arises. One day, when Red China builds up its arsenal and becomes a world threat with nuclear weapons, we can kiss Formosa goodbye; we can kiss South Korea goodbye. If that day should ever come, I would not know why we should ever have struggled in Southeast Asia. There is turmoil in Korea. There is turmoil in Vietnam. There is turmoil in the Middle East. There is turmoil in Cyprus. There is turmoil all over the world. Yet man has it within his power to destroy himself completely.

Reprinted from *Congressional Digest*, Vol. 47, No. 11 (November, 1968). "The Controversy Over a U.S. Anti-Ballistic Missile System, Pro & Con." Reprinted by permission.

Should the United States Install an ABM System?
con: HON. EUGENE J. McCARTHY, UNITED STATES SENATOR, MINNESOTA

There is every reason to question the decision to proceed with a light antiballistic missile system.

The case for it has been based on four premises:

First. That Chinese progress in developing strategic nuclear capabilities had proceeded so far that considerations of the U.S. leadtime could no longer allow deferral of a decision to deploy a defense.

Second. That a light ABM defense would be highly effective for a number of years against any emerging Chinese threat.

Third. That such a deployment would not have a significant impact on the strategic arms race between the United States and the Soviet Union, or on our efforts to achieve a nuclear nonproliferation treaty.

Fourth. That a light ABM deployment might provide protection against an accident.

All four of these premises are open to question.

First, since the September decision to go ahead with the anti-ballistic missile system, administration spokesmen have said that missile developments in China have not proceeded as rapidly as they anticipated they would proceed. Despite this reevaluation, there

Reprinted from *Congressional Digest*, Vol. 47, No. 11 (November, 1968). "The Controversy Over a U.S. Anti-Ballistic Missile System, Pro & Con." Reprinted by permission.

(pro—continued from p. 272)

We have heard that the ABM system will cost a large sum of money, and that the dollar is faltering. I regret that. No Member of this body favors frugality more. No Member of the Senate wants peace more. We have been struggling for peace since 1946.

There was the Baruch plan, and it was rejected by the Soviet Union even when we had a monopoly of the atomic bomb.

I remember three crises. The first arose over the question, Shall we have nuclear submarine propulsion? Many people asked, "Why waste the money?" But there was one quiet voice—Captain Rickover's. That one quiet voice became louder and louder and louder until the President heard it. President Truman reversed some of the skeptics and gave the go-ahead sign in December 1947, when he authorized the building of the submarine *Nautilus*. Today we call Polaris nuclear propelled submarines our first line of defense.

A secret hearing within the Joint Committee on Atomic Energy heard that the Russians are catching up with us in nuclear submarines and will be ahead of us within 4 to 7 years if we don't take some action. Where will our first line of defense be then? I know we cannot build a defense system that will protect every American life. But where is the justification for this idea that if you cannot save 50 million Americans, let them all die? This is the logic here today: If you cannot save 50 million, let them all die.

America knows that it will not be the aggressor. We will not shoot the first atomic bomb. And these bombs should not be used; only as a last resort. I have kept my fingers crossed; and the last prayer I say every night when I go to bed is that some irresponsible person will not say, "Shoot one in Southeast Asia," as they were saying, "Shoot it in Korea." I heard those voices, even on the floor of the Senate. I dread the day when that ever happens. If that day ever comes, God help us.

So what are we trying to do here? We are not trying to build a bigger bomb, as the Russians did when they broke the moratorium and detonated a 60-megaton bomb. We are not trying to do that. We are not trying to destroy others.

They talk about offensive weapons as being the answer. Why should we be an offensive nation? We can spend $5 billion every 2 months in South Vietnam—every 2 months—to give freedom to the South Vietnamese, and we cannot spend $5 billion over 4 or 5 years to protect American lives? Oh, where is our reason?

We are not building an offensive weapon. We are building a defensive weapon. Yet we are shedding crocodile tears that, if we try to protect American lives, that is going to accelerate the arms race in Moscow.

(con—continued from p. 273)

apparently has been no reconsideration of the administration time table.

It seems to me that since we are postponing other vital expenditures in this country, this is one expenditure we might postpone in view of what is supposed to be accurate information from administration spokesmen.

Second, eminent scientists such as George Kistiakowsky and Jerome Wiesner, who have for a long time been involved in the technology of missiles and also concerned about the nuclear and political and moral implications of these weapons, and upon whom we depended for advice for many years, have questioned whether the Sentinel deployment or even a better system to that—and also one which would be more costly—would provide real protection against the Chinese threat, if we assume there is a Chinese threat. Scientists concede there is great uncertainty about the potential effectiveness of the Sentinel deployment. In view of this uncertainty, and also considering the potential damage to the United States and the waste of money if the system is ineffective, it seems to me most unwise to proceed on the assumption that this system would be effective, or to base any national policies on that assumption.

The massive offensive capability of the United States must certainly continue to be counted as the effective deterrent against any rational decision by the Chinese to employ any nuclear weapon against us. Of course, if the decision is to be irrational, it must be doubted whether any defense could be effective.

In my opinion, as we proceed to deal with nuclear weapons, the one assumption we have to continue to make is that everyone is somewhat rational. If we go beyond that, there is no basis on which we can make a policy. I think the record shows that as people have nuclear weapons their rationality grows stronger. We hope this will be the case with any nation that has the kind of power incorporated in nuclear weapons.

It would be most unwise for the United States to frame its policies on a system which in the judgment of many would not in itself be effective, or which if effective would not be so excepting under the most rational and restrained conditions.

This reminds me of the great concern we had over fallout shelters 5 or 6 years ago. Today, I do not know of anyone who is selling fallout shelters. I understand they are beginning to collapse in the backyards of those who did construct them.

Third, our going forward with the Sentinel system could have a profound effect on the Soviet-American arms race, which I think is the most significant arms race in the world today.

(pro—continued from p. 274)

How naive can we get? Here are the Russians, building a system to save Russians. Are Russians better than Americans? Is it better to live as a Russian and die as an American? If they can save their lives, why cannot we save ours?

Oh, woe be to us.

I wish we could take the $80 billion we spend on military matters every year and save it. If I could be sure this afternoon that no one will ever use an atomic weapon, I would sit right down now and keep my peace.

But who will give that guarantee? Who can give me that guarantee? How do we know they will not use them? They have them. How do we know that some mad triggerman, some day, will not lose his sense of balance and say, 'Let them have it'? And when they come over here with those 25-megaton bombs, what will we do?

If we could take a 25-megaton bomb, make it into the equivalent amount of dynamite, and load it onto a freight car, that freight car would extend from the Atlantic Ocean to the Pacific Ocean diagonally from Maine to Lower California.

A few years ago, we had the Cuban missile crisis. Nobody wants to become aggressive. Nobody wants to become offensive. But what we are talking about is survival. We are talking about the second strike.

America has a military posture that if they bang us, maybe we will hit them back. The big question is, what are we going to hit them back with? They have this fractional orbiting thing now, where they can shoot a missile up in orbit, and let it come down, and not in violation of the United Nations Treaty, because they can shoot it up and bring it down without a full orbit.

We have made some small steps; the Nuclear Test Ban Treaty, and I hope they will sign the Nonproliferation Treaty. But that is not enough. As long as we have one nuclear bomb in this world, we have to do something about protecting ourselves against it. The idea is that if they bang us good, we will bang them better. It all depends on how tough that first bang is.

Today, with the technology that has been developed, with fractional orbiting, they have cut down the warning time from 15 minutes to 3 minutes. Mind you that. And we have nothing to challenge this; nothing to challenge it at all.

So I say to my friends, "Go ahead and save your dollars. Keep pouring them into Vietnam and not regretting it. But do not spend a quarter to protect American lives."

If that is the philosophy of America, I am ashamed. But I do not believe it is. I am not the conscience of this body, and I will do

(con—continued from p. 275)

The U.S. ABM decision has to date been couched largely in terms of American security without sufficient attention to the fact that it has an immediate impact on other nations, particularly Russia, and thus could set in motion within other countries, such as the Soviet Union, a series of political pressures quickly translated into decisions on military budgets and resources allocated. In short, the American decision must be looked at in a total world context where there is, of course, a kind of unending change going on today.

It is quite reasonable to assume that the Soviet Union would respond in some way to our Sentinel deployment, although perhaps to a lesser degree than would be the case if we were to begin the building of a massive antiballistic missile system which may follow.

Antiballistic missile defenses introduce such large uncertainties into the whole calculation of the power bloc in the world that efforts to secure any agreement on strategic armaments limitations would be seriously prejudiced.

National security for the United States still seems to be perceived by many as having a quantitative base, and it is assumed that by a simple kind of arithmetical addition, security can be increased. In my judgment, this is no longer valid once nations have reached technological parity. We have to begin to make efforts of another order. Once nations have reached the point of military strength sufficient to destroy each other, the question of parity on a kind of physical or mathematical basis, in my judgment, becomes almost irrelevant. This is the relationship we have reached with Russia and we may well reach it with other nations in the not too distant future.

Since many nations of the world feel that a clear indication of Soviet-American willingness to end their nuclear race is a necessary condition to their acceding to the Nuclear Nonproliferation Treaty, our ABM deployment would have a negative effect on our efforts to get acceptance of that treaty around the world. In some ways, the bringing to an end of the Soviet-American nuclear race may have more important bearing upon reducing the possibility of nuclear warfare than bringing to an end the proliferation of limited nuclear power among the other nations of the world.

Fourth, the last premise upon which the ABM is being advanced is that it would protect the U. S. population against accidental nuclear launches by other nuclear powers, seems highly questionable. The likelihood of an accidental launch or detonation of a missile warhead of any kind is, in the first place, very small. However, it would seem at least as likely that there would be a nuclear explosion resulting from an accident in the ABM system as one resulting from an accidental launch of a foreign ballistic missile, or one of our own ballistic

(*pro—continued from p. 276*)

as I feel I should do, and I know other Senators will also, even though they disagree with me. I know that money is short; and I know that frugality is the theme song of the day.

I know all that. It is going to be hard to dramatize this, because Pastore can never come in here and say, "I told you so," because he would be dead by that time. And that is the pity of it. One of the hardest things to do in the world is to sell life insurance to a healthy man. A healthy man thinks that he will never die.

It is our responsibility to look down that long road. Senators who want to save perhaps a half billion dollars in the budget had better get started now. Red China will have an ICBM capability by the mid-seventies. Make it 1974. Make it 1973. Make it 1972. Make it 1971. Make it any year one wants to. However, I am talking about history. I am talking about all of the tomorrows, every single one of them. And if we get going late, we will end up late.

Yes; I know the answer is complete disarmament. And I live and yearn and pray for that day when we have complete disarmament. But until that day, Red China and Red Russia will do all they can to gain superiority in this field. We had better beware.

Everyone says, "But this is not meant against Russia. This is against Red China." I know that, but in everything there must be a beginning. And I say the time to start is now.

(con—continued from p. 277)

missiles. This follows from the fact that large numbers of such defensive missiles must be kept in a very high state of readiness at all times if they are to be effective against the accidental launch of offensive weapons, by other nations, or accidental launching of our own.

Thus, the light Sentinel ABM deployment would be another escalatory move in a senseless strategic arms race between the two super powers; a move which could only lead to an exacerbation of tensions with a net reduction in the security of both, and to a diversion of resources on both sides from what I think are more pressing needs.

The decision is a good example, unfortunately not an isolated one, of an attempt to buy security through a kind of misplaced, simplistic reliance on technology rather than by facing up more realistically and constructively to problems that are in fact primarily political in nature: in this case, the problem of the relationships between the United States and the Soviet Union, the United States and China, and the other nations of Asia and of the world.

The decision seems to have been reached without adequate consideration being given to its effects on other nations throughout the world, its impact on the quality of life in the United States, to the alternative uses to which the resources might be put, and to the overall risks to our security of a continuing arms race which actually may be far greater than the risks involved in arms control measures.

Even though it is presented to us here in the name of defense, as have been most of the expansions of our military power over the past 15 years, in my judgment, no adequate case has been made for the Sentinel thin antiballistic missile.

I believe that the judgment of the Senate should be one against its approval.

COMMENTARY: APPEALS, ASSUMPTIONS, AND PREMISES

These two speeches made by eminent United States senators are highlights of the debate of June 24, 1968, on the floor of the Senate regarding a bill to authorize construction of antiballistic missile installations. They provide us with excellent examples of basic contrasts in persuasive styles and logical argument. Both the *pro* and the *con* speeches reflect the difference in temperament, background, and political philosophy of their spokesmen.

The opening statements set the tone and approach to the problem taken by the speakers. Senator Pastore begins: "Today we are living in a mad world, and indeed it is a mad world. There are enough nuclear and thermonuclear bombs to burn this world to ashes." On the contrary here is Senator McCarthy's unadorned opening: "There is every reason to question the decision to proceed with a light anti-ballistic missile system. The case for it has been based on four premises. . . ."

Obviously Senator Pastore wants his fears to be shared by his audience, whereas Senator McCarthy intends to attack the logic that has led defenders of the missile system to reach the conclusion forming the basis for the bill being debated. By listing the "four premises" and then attempting systematically to prove them fallacious, Senator McCarthy appears as the restrained, rational speaker. On the contrary, Senator Pastore's emotional utterances voice fears and concerns, often in the form of appeals:

> . . . We can kiss Formosa goodbye; we can kiss South Korea goodbye. No Member of this body favors frugality more. No Member of the Senate wants peace more.
> This is the logic here today: If you cannot save 50 million, let them all die.
> If that day ever comes, God help us.
> Oh, where is our reason?
> Yet we are shedding crocodile tears that if we try to protect American lives, that is going to accelerate the arms race in Moscow.
> Oh, woe be to us.
> But do not spend a quarter to protect American lives.
> If that is the philosophy of America, I am ashamed. But I do not believe it is. I am not the conscience of this body, and I will do as I feel I should do . . .
> One of the hardest things to do in the world is to sell life insurance to a healthy man.
> And I live and yearn and pray for that day when we have complete disarmament. . . . We had better beware.

In cold print the emotion-charged voice and delivery that would give these emotive statements their dramatic urgency may be missing, but the emotional overtones are unmistakable.

Restraint and refusal to take alarm characterize Senator McCarthy's highly rational approach. He cites testimony by experts, draws parallels with "the great concern we had over fallout shelters five or six years ago," sees opportunities for better relationships with Russia and China, and also doubts the efficiency of the proposed missile system.

In a controversy such as this one, where experts with many sources of information available to them disagree, it is difficult for the ordinary citizen to determine which side is absolutely right and which completely wrong. What further clouds the argument and its issues are the personal and political conflicts the dispute gives rise to. There seems to be a profusion of evidence, but how is the evidence to be evaluated?

David J. Barrios

If Senator Pastore seems given to emotive statements, Senator McCarthy is seen relying upon some assumptions requiring far more evidence than is provided them; for example, his assurance of the rationality of powers having nuclear weapons at their disposal, and their willingness to reach mutual agreements.

WHAT DOES IT SAY?

1. If a *euphemism* is a substitute term for one too plain or shocking *(restroom, mortician)*, what is the effect of Senator Pastore's euphemism: "The idea is that if they bang us good, we will bang them better. It all depends on how tough that first bang is"?

2. What exactly was he referring to when he said, "It is going to be hard to dramatize this, because Pastore can never come in here and say, 'I told you so,' because he would be dead by that time. And that is the pity of it"?

3. What effect was he seeking when he described "a 25-megaton bomb" in terms of TNT?

4. In context, how appropriate do you consider his statement that "the last prayer I say every night when I go to bed is that some irresponsible person will not say, 'Shoot one in Southeast Asia,' as they were saying, 'Shoot it in Korea' "?

5. Restate in your own words the point you think Senator McCarthy is making in this argument: "The massive offensive capability of the United States must certainly continue to be counted as the effective deterrent against any rational decision by the Chinese to employ any nuclear weapon against us. Of course, if the decision is to be irrational, it must be doubted whether any defense could be effective."

6. Which of the two senators uses longer sentences and more abstract terms?

WHAT DO YOU THINK?

1. By now everyone knows how the ABM controversy has been dealt with. Are you in agreement with the present policy? How does it square up with the following statement made by an "experienced negotiator": "To deny the President the ABM system would be like throwing away his hole card in a stud game. . . . What we spend on it, if it is later abandoned, will be money well wasted. It is the best chance we have."[1]

2. Consult current or back issues of *Congressional Digest* and select for analysis a pro-con argument on another controversial question that interests you.

3. What are your feelings and thoughts about terms such as the following that have kept popping up in discussions regarding numbers and potency of missile systems: "security gap," "survival gap," "sufficiency," "superiority," "parity," and "overkill"?

4. Being as logical as you can, write your response to the following questions asked by Dr. Lee A. DiBridge: "If it is a contest in which we have 1000 hydrogen warheads and the Russians have 900, is that good or bad? Or should we have 1500 to their 900? Or are they going to get 1500 and only have 1000?"[2]

5. Select one of the following as an essay topic:

A letter I should write to my Congressman

[1] *Newsweek*, April 7, 1969.
[2] *The New York Times*, December 17, 1968.

Campaign promises and post-election realities

Atom bomb movies are not so funny

Do I have Strontium 90 in my bones?

Will Howard Hughes prevent further underground nuclear tests in Nevada? Is Alaska a safer area for such tests?

It's something out of *Mad* magazine

Life of an officer assigned to a missile site "silo"

part VII
LITERATURE AND ART

WHAT IS STYLE?:
SENTENCES, PARAGRAPHS, AND DICTION

So far, without always calling direct attention to them, we have tried to explain and apply many of the insights and skills provided by both the traditional and the "new" rhetorics. But since the complex subject of "style" especially demands it, we need now to take a look at some specific, recent discoveries illuminating the writing process.

One of these fresh insights into the nature of composition comes from the linguistic approach to sentences and paragraphs known as *tagmemics*. It properly stresses the fact that style is greatly concerned with the *choices* any writer must make *before* he begins writing as well as *during* the actual writing of his composition. Here is a tagmemic definition of style:

> A writer's style, we believe, is the characteristic route he takes through all the choices presented in both the writing and *prewriting* stages. It is the manifestation of his conception of the topic, modified by his audience, situation, and intention—we might call his "universe of discourse."[1]

[1] Richard E. Young and Alton L. Becker, "Toward a Modern Theory of Rhetoric: A Tagmemic Contribution," *Harvard Educational Review,* XXXV (Fall, 1965), p. 466. Editor's italics.

A writer's style, as this definition states, comes from the choices he makes: of the facts about himself, about his subject, and about the audience he is addressing—facts that every essay and commentary in this book emphasize. Style reflects a writer's passion, or lack of it, for his subject, his planning and arrangement in presenting it, and his care for its logic as well as for its appeal. And above all, as this treatment of *style* hopes to show, the writer's choice of language, sentence structure, and paragraph pattern of sentences will determine the effectiveness of his composition.

Closely related to this tagmemic approach to the sentence and the sentence-in-the-paragraph are the discoveries of Francis Christensen. He has noted that many excellent authors make their sentences "cumulative," in effect, by adding details which can be said to "generate" from the feelings and knowledge of the writer as these have been aroused by close observation. The more a writer sees, the more specific his observation becomes and the richer the texture of his sentences. It is by the *addition* of these details, appearing either before or after the main clause, that the writer makes his statements specific and concrete.[2]

The main clause of a sentence, as Francis Christensen observed, contains a general or abstract idea which the author will add to in order to make his meaning, or impression, definite and clear. Consider this main clause statement: *He was the first one*; obviously, it requires details. Here is how William Faulkner treats it in the opening of his *Intruder in the Dust*:

> He was the first one, standing lounging trying to look occupied or at least innocent, under the shed in front of the closed blacksmith's shop across the street from the jail where his uncle would be less likely to see him if or rather when he crossed the square toward the postoffice for the eleven o'clock mail.[3]

Note that as the sentence progresses, the picture grows more and more vivid, more specific and concrete with particulars.

Without distinguishing between free and imbedded modifiers, here is how the Christensen method and grammatical terminology can be applied to that sentence to point up its dramatic cumulative effect:

[2] Francis Christensen, "A Generative Rhetoric of the Sentence," *Notes Toward a New Rhetoric* (New York: Harper & Row, Publishers, 1967), pp. 1–22.

[3] William Faulkner, *Intruder in the Dust* (New York, 1948), p. 3.

1 He was the first one (main clause)
  2 standing (verb cluster)
  2 lounging (verb cluster)
  2 trying to look occupied or at least innocent (verb cluster)
    3 under the shed (prepositional phrase)
      4 in front of the closed blacksmith's shop (prepositional phrase)
        5 across the street from the jail (prepositional phrase)
          6 where his uncle would be less likely to see him (subordinate clause)
            7 if or rather when he crossed the square (subordinate clause)
              8 toward the postoffice (prepositional phrase)
                9 for the eleven o'clock mail. (prepositional phrase)

Seen in this skeletal form, the sentence reveals the basic fact that as ideas or impressions generate additional details, the sentence becomes more meaningful. The closer the observation, the more penetrating the thought and the richer the texture. We speak these sentences, even though we may not be able to give names to their grammatical structures. Regrettably, we cannot here enter into any further presentation of the exciting but intricate forms and concepts of transformational, or generative grammars.

The Christensen approach to sentences within the paragraph is similar and can also be most helpful to any student writer. We will apply this method of analysis to one of the paragraphs in "Writers I Have Met" by John Updike in an attempt to show some of the features of his writing style. But here is the way the method can be applied to an ordinary paragraph.

1 Mac's grandfather was a very rich and shrewd man.
  2 As a pioneer he was able to buy vast sections of land.
    3 At one time he owned almost half of the county.
  2 He naturally acquired interests in banks and profited from the great investment opportunities they offered him.
    3 His holdings included among many others the Sun Empire enterprises, the Legal Insurance Company, and the P&S transportation system.
  2 At his death he left an estate of eight million or more, carefully set up to take advantage of the inheritance tax loopholes of his day.

By means of this method we can see at a glance how, like the sentence, a paragraph is also "cumulative" in structure, and how with its added information, it makes specific and concrete the more or less abstract idea in the topic sentence.

STYLE AND DICTION

Like all writer styles, the student writer's style is shaped by the choices he makes not only in building his sentences and paragraphs, but also by his choice of words. In fact, Jonathan Swift's famous definition of *style* still applies: "Proper words in proper places." *Proper* here, however, does not mean that every word has just one meaning; on the contrary, it means choosing a word having a denotation or connotation that will make definite the point you wish to make in any group of words. Language, for the most part, is not neutral in its power of suggestion. Indeed, it is often difficult to select words that do not reflect the attitude of the writer, with its consequent influencing of the reader. Deliberate slanting of words in an attempt to make the reader share the bias of the author is common practice. To call someone "stout" is not the same as calling him "obese." Obviously, if you want to reach your reader and persuade him to accept your point of view, you are going to use whatever device comes to mind in order to do so—language which is weighted in favor of your predilections is always one of your most effective methods.

For example, a review of Philip Roth's best-selling novel, *Portnoy's Complaint,* contained this sentence: "On one level, since few writers are as hip as Roth to the nuances of middle-class neuroses or as tuned in with such a show-biz sense of mimicry to the diction of the American Jewish milieu, Portnoy's past comes off as a kind of universal pop boyhood of the forties, with a Jewish accent and comic twist."[4] The word choice here reveals a mixture of language levels that evidently satisfies the reviewer's sense of a style suitable for his purposes in this article; he wanted a "hip" tone.

"Proper words" means, then, choices that will adequately convey what the author wants his readers to understand or imagine. In an article in the *Saturday Review* some years back, John Ciardi remarked that the writer begins with a conceptual "buzz" that starts him writing. His readers, however, do not have that "buzz," and it is the writer's job to create it in them by means of words in certain patterns or rhythms.

What are the words that best convey what you feel, what you see, what you want your readers to understand or visualize, and what will make those readers *identify* with you?

---

[4] Josh Greenfeld, " 'Doctor, This Is my only Life . . . ,' " *The New York Times Book Review* (February 23, 1969), p. 1.

Since we live in a sense world, and since our perceptions come to us primarily through our senses, it should be obvious that we must rely heavily upon sense words in those details which clarify our general statements. And also, since specific observation requires specific diction to convey it to our readers, it stands to reason that the more specific the words we use, the sharper the image.

Faulkner, in the previously quoted sentence, speaks of someone *lounging* (a particular visual term); and note where: "under the shed in front of the closed blacksmith's shop, across the street from the jail." He could hardly be more specific! And note further, Faulkner does not say, simply, that the lounger would be noticed when his uncle "came for the mail" but when he would "cross the square" for the "eleven o'clock mail." Again, the general idea of wealth in the paragraph about Mac's grandfather is converted into the specific details of Sun Empire enterprises, Legal Insurance Company, and the P&S transportation system.

In addition to leaning heavily on specific and sense words, good writers take advantage of comparisons to make their readers "buzz" with them. The most common comparisons are metaphors, in which the relation of one thing to another is made strikingly evident on the instant and does what long explanations would fail to do as well. To say that man *bulled his way* through all opposition, to indicate that the ditchdigging machine *clawed* at the earth, to state that one's mind became a *vacuum* is to reach your readers more effectively than to *lumber along* with a succession of explanatory statements.

Other figures of speech such as *irony* ("That's the most intelligent solution to campus unrest I've ever heard!"—meaning to the informed listener that it is the least intelligent) or *litotes* or understatement ("Being caught in an outright lie like that was a trifle embarrassing") have their advantages upon occasion. And there are other effective choices such as words whose sound helps to convey the sense: words like *crack* or *hiss,* which are imitative of the sound (*onomatapoeia*) and words like *jump* or *soothing* that suggest an idea. Then there are words in combination, whose repeated initial or stressed sound (*alliteration*) helps to enforce an idea: *a particularly appropriate passage,* for example.

Negatively, there are expressions to avoid because they either tell your readers little or nothing, or because they positively annoy your readers with their flatness or staleness. One should avoid using *jargon,* which is a kind of substitute for communication: vague, abstract, sometimes technical terminology that obscures rather than clarifies a thought.

One should also avoid *trite expressions,* that is, shopworn figures that have long since lost any vividness, and *clichés* such as "flat as a pancake" or "what a nice time we had last evening."

In previous chapters we have discussed these and other aspects of diction, all elements of an effective style. And in the essays which follow, they will repeatedly be called to your attention. Remember that good style is expression that brings your readers into close communion with you.

Writers I Have Met
by JOHN UPDIKE

The lust to meet authors ranks low, I think, on the roll of holy appetites; but it is an authentic pang. The county where I and my literary ambitions were conceived held only one writer, whose pen name, Mildred Jordan, masked her true identity as an unmeetably rich industrialist's wife. At Harvard I stood with crowds of other students to hear, and to glimpse in the mysterious flesh, anthology presences like Eliot, Sandburg, Frost, and Wilder. After his lecture in Sanders Theater, Eliot, a gem of composure within a crater of applause, inserted his feet into his rubbers, first the right, then the left, as we poured down upon him a grateful tumult that had less to do with his rather sleepy-making discourse on poetic drama than with the fabulous descent of his vast name into an actual, visible, and mortal body. Whereas Sandburg, playing ballads in New Lecture Hall, rambled

Reprinted from *The New York Times Book Review,* August 11, 1968. © 1968 by The New York Times Company. Reprinted by permission of publication and author.

Introduction
The thesis idea appears in the opening sentence, supported by a list of the first literary figures seen in person.

on into our dinner hour; as the audience noisily diminished he told us, his white bangs glowing in the gloom, that it was all right, that often in his life he had sat in hotel rooms with only his guitar for company.

Body
Joyce Cary, his first social acquaintance with a famous novelist and the effect the meeting had on Updike's sensibilities.

The first author I met socially was Joyce Cary. It was in England's Oxford. Someone kindly had us to tea, and into the stiff little party bounced a well-knit sandy man with light, quick eyes and an intensely handsome chin; unhesitatingly he assumed his right to dominate the conversation. He was full of a tender excitement, the excitement of those certain they are loved, and anxious to share, before it spills over and is wasted, the bubbling treasure of themselves. He described to us his sitting in Paris writing at an outdoor table while around him in the Tuilleries little boys were going pee-pee; he read us, with an excessive Irish accent, the opening and then the closing words of "Finnegans Wake," to show that they interlocked.

His youthful indiscretion at that meeting.

Now I had never read Cary, but had myself recently tasted the black emboldening blood of print. When he stated that Joyce's influence was enormous, I churlishly grunted disagreement; he cited e. e. cummings, and I absurdly shook my head No. His eyebrows lifted, and for a second I lived within the curiosity of those very quick eyes. They flicked away, and somewhat later I began to read him, and found him to be—above all in his two African novels—a splendid writer, peculiarly alive to nuances of power and competition such as my jealous rudeness that afternoon. For years the incident embarrassed me in memory, and in 1957 Cary heroically suffered his prolonged death, and I lost forever my chance to apologize.

His long anticipated meeting with James Thurber, the famous wit, and his disappointment with the experience.

Quite different was my preparation for meeting James Thurber, in London later that year. As a boy I had hoarded pennies to buy Thurber's books, and owned them all; he was for me the brightest star in that galaxy of New York wits I yearned to emulate, however dimly. A college acquaintance who knew of my adoration arranged the meeting: into her flat Thurber was led by his wife, Helen. He was taller than I had expected, not Walter Mitty but a big-boned blind giant, and his upstanding hair was snowier than photographs had led me to expect, and there could have been no anticipating the alarming way his eyes caromed around under the refracting magnification of his glasses.

He sat, talking and drinking tea until I wondered why his bladder didn't burst. We listened, I raptly at first and finally becoming, to my own amazement, bored. Though Thurber cocked his head alertly at my poor fawning attempts to make conversation, these attempts did not appreciably distract him from the anecdotes of Columbus, Ohio, he had told a thousand times before, and that I had read 10 years before, in their definitive, printed versions. Pages of "The Thurber Album" and "My Life and Hard Times" issued from his lips virtually intact.

His performance, though remarkable, was, alas, a performance; I had been privileged to join an auditory audience slightly less anonymous than readership, and there was no question of living for even a second in his curiosity. Fifteen years later, with another adored writer, Jorge Luis Borges, I was to re-experience the disappointing revelation that blindness and fame and years do island a man, do isolate him within a monologue that, if he is a literary man, he has delivered to you already, in finer and grander form—"grander" because literary obsessions appear to have been selected from an infinite field, whereas personal obsessions seem to betray a mere narrowness. Sad to say, my love of Thurber's works was slightly stunted ever after his generous teatime monologue.

All the writers I have met—and they have not been many; I must be one of the few Americans with a bachelor-of-arts degree who has never met either Robert Lowell or Norman Mailer—carry around with them a field force that compels objects in the vicinity to conform

The visit as a performance by the famous author.

A similar disappointment in discovering how disillusioning a conversation with a famous poet can turn out to be.

The powerful "field force" that seems to surround writers who have strong personalities.

to their literary style. Standing next to E. B. White, one is imbued with something of the man's fierce modesty, and one's sentences haltingly seek to approximate the wonderful way his own never say more than he means. Whereas Thurber's humor bore a trace of the tyrannical, a wish to impose confusion from above, White's seems to stem from an extreme of attentiveness that would grant to things the graceful completion they lack in reality. Once I barged through a door in The New Yorker offices, and powerfully struck an obstacle on the other side; White had been hurrying down the hall, and stood there dazed. Reading in my face my horror, my fear that I had injured this sacred and fragile person, this living embodiment of the magazine's legend, he obligingly fell down as if dead.

E. B. White an example of this power to influence those whom he meets.

A room containing Philip Roth, I have noticed, begins hilariously to whirl and pulse with a mix of rebelliousness and constriction that I take to be Oedipal. And I have seen John Cheever, for 10 days we shared in Russia, turn the dour world of Soviet literary officials into a bright scuttle of somehow suburban characters, invented with marvelous speed and arranged in sudden tableaux expressive, amid wistful neo-Czarist trappings, of the lyric desperation associated with affluence. As if transported to the moon, people in Cheever's neighborhood lose half their bodily weight. My most traumatic experience of gravitational attraction came with John O'Hara. I had consented to read at a White House entertainment for the National Honor Students; crossing the lobby of the Hay-Adams, I spied brooding on a chair a broad-shouldered presence strongly reminiscent of the back of a book jacket. Deferentially I moved closer. "Mr. O'Hara?" said I.

Some other well-known authors who exert this "field force" capable of affecting a social environment surrounding them.

The "traumatic" experience of meeting John O'Hara in unusual circumstances.

O'Hara held out his hand. "Pull," he said. I hesitated. "My back," O'Hara explained. I pulled. He grunted in pain but did not budge. "Again," said O'Hara.

This time he made it, wincing, to his feet.

Our laconic but characteristic dialogue continued. He, too, was attending the White House function. I offered him a ride in the limousine that had been sent for me, since I was one of the entertainers. I explained to the suspicious driver that this gentleman was John O'Hara, a very great writer and a guest of the President. The driver with maximum grudgingness made space for him in the front seat, while my wife and I settled regally in the back.

Within the few seconds of this encounter I had been plunged into a cruel complex of stoic pain and social irony—a Negro chauffeur and a stammering light-verse writer had transformed a millionaire author into a front-seat hitchhiker. Mortified by the situation, feeling all its edges grating on O'Hara's acute nerves, I fled conversationally to the state of Pennsylvania, which we had in common. O'Hara moved us to a plane both higher and more concrete—the number of Updikes in Princeton, New Jersey. At the White House he showed a distinct preference for the company of Marianne Moore, bending his big ear to her tiny precise voice like a schoolboy listening to a transistor radio he has smuggled into class.

These not entirely fanciful reminiscences (which have omitted how I met Bernard Malamud in a museum lavatory, or how James Dickey entertained me one hungover 6 A.M. with a concert of country guitar music that fetched tears to my hillbilly eyes) mean to suggest that writers, like everyone else, see a world their personalities to some extent create. Denis de Rougemont states that Chateaubriand could never have written Stendahl's essays on seduction because seduction was simply no problem for Chateaubriand. The cosmos of delay and obfuscation rendered in "The Castle" surely in part reflects the special environment Kafka's neurotic mannerisms spun around him. And we all recall how Hemingway scouted the world for those marginal places where violence might feed his style.

Some other unusual circumstances in the meeting of Bernard Malamud and James Dickey, prompting the view that "writers, like everyone else, see a world their personalities to some extent create."

Conclusion

Analysis of the tempera-
ments who turn to writing
fiction and the psycho-
logical reasons why a personal meeting between
writer and reader must result in a "performance" by
the writer.

Also, as one who in a small way is himself
now and then "met," I suggest that forces
within the writer-reader personal encounter
foment unreality. The reader comes equipped
with a vivid, fresh, outside impression of works
the writer remembers wearily from the inside,
as a blur of intention, a stretch of doubting
drudgery, a tangle of memories and fabrica-
tions, a batch of nonsensical reviews, and a
disappointed sigh from the publisher. The
reader knows the writer better than he knows
himself; but the writer's physical presence is
light from a star that has moved on.

Evasive temperaments are drawn to the
practice of fiction. Their work is done far behind the heat-shield of face and voice that
advances against a room of strangers. The performance can be a shambling and ingratiating
one as much as a cocksure and intimidating
one, but performance it is: a pity, for these
anonymous devoted readers who press affec-
tionately toward a blind man are his lovers, who
have accepted into themselves his most intimate
and earnest thrusts. I would like to meet, I
suppose, Vladimir Nabokov and Henry Green,
but recognize the urge as superstitious, a seeking of a physical ritual to formalize the fact that
we already are (I write as a reader) so well met.

OUTLINE

Thesis: Admiring readers desire to meet their authors but find the
meeting to be a "performance."

  I. At Harvard, John Updike enjoyed the excitement generated by the
appearances of famous poets.
    A. Although somewhat prosaic in his talk, T. S. Eliot's appearance
was awe-inspiring.
    B. Carl Sandburg was a relaxed visitor.
 II. Famous authors create an atmosphere of "gravitational attraction."
    A. Joyce Cary at once dominated the conversation.
      1. He told of Paris and read from "Finnegan's Wake."
      2. Much to his later regret, Updike disagreed with him.

    B. James Thurber gave a "performance."
      1. He repeated already published anecdotes.
      2. Jorge Luis Borges did the same.
    C. E. B. White's presence dominated conversational styles.
      1. His humor differed from Thurber's.
      2. He liked to complete what is lacking in reality.
    D. Other writers also create their own atmosphere.
      1. Philip Roth's is Oedipal.
      2. John Cheever's is lyrically suburban.
      3. John O'Hara's manner is laconic.
        a. The meeting in Washington was traumatic.
        b. O'Hara was surprisingly attentive to Marianne Moore.
    E. Writers create a world their personalities seem to need.
      1. Bernard Malamud and James Dickey do so.
      2. Stendhal, Kafka, and Hemingway did also.
III. Meetings with authors must always have an air of unreality.
    A. The reader knows the author through his works.
    B. The author sees his published work in a different light.
    C. These circumstances make the author give a "performance."

COMMENTARY: SENTENCE AND STYLE

John Updike owes much of his reputation as an author of distinctive short stories to his choice of language in his descriptions of place and character. A quick glance at the opening paragraphs of this personal essay shows Updike's taste for concrete and specific words that make images and convey sensuous impressions. Here are some of those colorful words and expressions: *lust, holy appetites, pang, anthology, presences, the mysterious flesh, a crater of applause, sleepy-making discourse, the fabulous descent, rambled on, his white bangs glowing in the gloom, the heat-shield of face and voice, shambling and ingratiating, cocksure and intimidating, lovers, intimate and earnest thrusts, the urge, a seeking of a physical ritual.* Highly connotative language such as this serves to communicate the intensity and freshness of the feelings the author experienced in meeting these famous personages.

    His skill in making vivid his memories of these meetings appears also in his sentence structures and their arrangements in the paragraph. As the following schema applying the Christensen principles shows, he took great care to support the abstract with the specific and concrete. The sentence patterns in the second paragraph afford us our example:

1 The first author I met socially was Joyce Cary.
2 It was in England's Oxford.
  3 Someone kindly had us to tea, and
  3 into the stiff little party bounced a well-knit sandy man. . . .
  3 He was full of a tender excitement. . . .
  3 He described to us his sitting in Paris . . . ;
  3 he read us with an excessive Irish accent, the opening. . . .

Notice, too, how Updike keeps his readers clued in by using the device of *parallelism* through repetitions of the pronoun *he* as subject of subsequent clauses in order to keep the reader's attention focused on the "well-knit sandy man."

Every sentence adds additional concrete details to the image of Joyce Cary as Updike remembers him that day; each statement contributes a vivid impression of the man and makes specific the promises implied in the topic sentence. Take, for instance, the fourth sentence as an example of this development by addition of details:

1 He was full of a tender excitement,
2 the excitement of those
  3 certain they are loved,
  3 and anxious to share,
    4 before it spills over and is wasted,
2 the bubbling treasure of themselves.

Seen in this fashion, the sentence reveals the fascinating architecture of the "cumulative" sentence which, by its adding of details, helps the reader identify with the experience John Updike is recalling to share with him.

Diction, sentence architecture, and paragraph pattern, then, are some of the elements that go into the making of a style. And as this Updike piece should suggest, every style is unique, having at least some idiosyncrasies distinguishing it from that of other writers, as we shall also see in the essays following this one.

WHAT DOES IT SAY?

1. Why is it appropriate to call "Eliot, Sandburg, Frost, and Wilder" *anthology presences?*

2. What does Sandburg's admission "that often in his life he had sat in hotel rooms with only his guitar for company" suggest about the lives of famous authors?

3. How is Updike's statement that "I had . . . myself recently tasted the black emboldening blood of print" appropriate to the theme and language of this essay?

4. Who is "Walter Mitty," and why was James Thurber unlike him?

5. Can you identify the figure of speech to be found in this sentence: "All the writers I have met . . . carry around with them a field force that compels objects in the vicinity to conform to their literary style"?

6. Why could E. B. White be considered the "living embodiment" of *The New Yorker Magazine's* "legend"?

7. What generally is meant by "a traumatic experience"?

8. Identify the figure of speech in this expression: "bending his big ear like a schoolboy listening to a transistor he has smuggled into class."

WHAT DO YOU THINK

1. Somewhat in John Updike fashion, attempt to sum up your impressions of meetings or conversations with representatives of one of the following occupations:

Bus drivers	School principals
Policemen	Dog owners
Disc jockeys	Golfers
Waitresses	Track athletes
Television stars	Models
Campus dignitaries	Poets
Visiting lecturers	Boy Scout leaders
Campus rebels	Insurance salesmen

2. Write a personal essay expressing as vividly as possible your pleasure or displeasure concerning one of these:

Experimenting with ice cream flavors

Cutting classes

Going to drive-in movies

Eating church dinners

Camping out

Delivering newspapers

Visiting with relatives

Taking part in campaigns

Preparing for certain occasions

Borrowing or lending money, clothes, cars, and so on

3. In his closing sentence John Updike says that as readers "we already are . . . so well met" with the authors we admire. If you have read any of his novels—*Run, Rabbit, Run, The Centaur, Couples*—write your description of what you think meeting him socially would be like.

The Big Lies About Mind-Affecting Drugs

by JEREMY LARNER

As one who has written about drug effects and the philosophical issues raised by drug taking, I have a confession to make. Drugs can be very boring. And talk about drugs is even more boring.

When it comes to drugs and writers, editors can usually find a hip pedant who will trace the history of which poets took which drugs to write which poems back to the Stone Age. Then he will put on his social-science seriousness and speculate that some of the poets would have written the same poems anyway, or better, or worse, or different, or more, or not at all.

But really . . . does any semi-educated reader doubt that from time to time certain poets and writers have used mind-affecting drugs? And no one needs to remind us, I hope, that when the drug gets more important than the writing—as drugs have a tendency to do—the writing isn't worth the bag.

Yet people will talk, and especially they will talk about what they are afraid they may be missing. I suppose it is inevitable that culture gobblers will feast upon symposia convened to decide how drugs might be employed in pursuit of what people who don't have it call "creativity." But I think they miss the point and end up discussing the wrong question. For the fact that writers can use drugs to jazz their minds, or—as Faulkner used alcohol—to keep them going, is not what lends a titillatory quality to the subject.

The titillation comes from forces beyond our control: Specifically, the social and historical forces that have created for the first time in American life an official drug culture. The existence of such a culture (or cult) and the price which American writing is already beginning to pay for it are to my mind far more critical than whether and how a given artist may stimulate himself.

The drug culture is populated by two overlapping types of people. First, the people who organize their psyches around the taking of drugs, and who claim that it is a more beautiful thing they do. Second, the publicists—the writers, editors, teachers, and media men—who may or may not use drugs themselves or know much about them but who identify themselves with drug taking and who promote it as a tremendously significant act.

Currently these people are extending an invitation which is implicit in everything that labels itself *hip*, whether in movies, advertising, magazines, pop music, or television commercials (all of which are increasingly interchangeable). We are cordially invited, before it's too late, to dissolve ourselves into the drug culture, to share the magic secret of turning on, and to base our daily life, our art, and indeed our whole personalities, such as they are, on the recognition of a stupendous in-joke. Because the in-joke is the centre of the drug existence. The joke is that all of *them*, out there, are sick, dull, and square. They are responsible for the impenetrable mess they call a world, but the joke is that the world is unreal. Only we inside people and the insides of our heads are real. Though we may look as lost and ugly as anyone else, we make the scene together, baby, we tune to the basic primitive vibrations, *and we swing*.

The invitation is tempting. Life is sweeter when a man can join something—even if it's a slick-cover, cellophane underground. In these hysterical times of bombing and blabbing, there's not much going above-ground that commands our allegiance. And when it comes to writing, how much do we have that's worth holding on to? Let's admit it: This is not one of the great moments for novel writing or for poetry (though they are not being replaced, as nitwits would have it, by nitwit impressionistic essays). The modern writer faces enormously difficult problems in a world where the assumptions that once bound individuals together and made relations significant seem increasingly inappropriate and absurd. It's not my purpose here to define these problems at any length; the occasional successes in modern literature have done that far better than I could hope to. Every writer who's worth a damn struggles with them in his own way and comes up with his own sort of solutions, most of them tentative, anguished, twisted, and incomplete.

But much of our writing, I'm sorry to say, lacks even these pitiful virtues. Much of it is simply empty, blank, sterile, and lacking in emotion, in wonder, or in any sense of human possibility. In its capacity to stir us, change us, or give a shape to our confusion, this writing is already drugged. It is drugged because its perpetrators, whether high or straight, are under the spell of a deadly cultural demimonde.

We see in some of the most fashionable writing at least six symptoms of an ordinary marijuana high: 1. An ecstatic melting, in which all things are seen as equally groovy. In this state one is relieved of troublesome moral problems. Whatever looks good, is good. 2. A depersonalization, in which the emotions of others are cause for mere amusement, or objects for aesthetic arrangement. An increasing number of craftsmen absorb themselves in creating intricate game-novels, in which the reader pulls back strand after strand of symbolic wrapping paper only to find the author crouched at the centre like a grinning toad. 3. Paranoia, in which every item in the social and political landscape is registered as a portentous menace to the lorn and lonely self. 4. Superprojection, in which the environment takes on the face of one's own desires. One melting novelist emits novel after novel in which he discovers that all of America from politics to sex is none other than himself and his own magnificent wish for pathic humiliation. Which leads me to 5. Narcissism, in which all the complexity and diversity of the world is whittled down and funnelled into one's own interest with one's own dear poor wonderful person. Which makes one a pigeon for self-pity and also 6. False illumination. Anyone who has ever smoked grass knows the grand swelling feeling of unprecedented Insight. Often you think the person grinning back at you is thinking the same thing—but you'd better not check, and you can't anyway while you're high. Of course, writers can test their illuminations by writing them down. Some people throw them away in the dawn's early light. Others publish them.

America's crying need for Instant Vision has led to a new form of hero worship which I might call guru worship. Anyone who has something simple to say that will raise up the chosen and put down the others can build himself into a guru, especially if he has some claim to being young, soft to touch, or from a primitive society, preferably dark in colour. No doubt, like rising drug sales, guru worship stems from the desperation we all feel. But there are alternative outlooks—harder but maybe more worthwhile—for those who aspire to write something that will be more than a symptom.

Meanwhile it is not only tempting but financially rewarding to pander to the mass appetite for the Mystic Word To End All Words. Recently New York subways have been plastered with portraits of Che Guevara decked out as Christ, and no doubt the appropriate publications will carry words and music to match. Soon there will be a Guevara men's cologne. Perhaps Che would indeed make a better messiah than Lyndon or Dylan, Westmoreland, Stokely, or Allen Ginsberg. (Perhaps not.) But when writers dissolve themselves in prose which deifies one or the other, paints him in drug-radiations of holy simplicity, they must destroy some part of themselves that they need to write with.

I refer to the part that thinks, that makes distinctions, that sees in detail, that seeks to understand, that worships vastness and variety, that wants to know—and to show—how big things and little things work together and how they look, down to their private parts, and in their public parts, too.

The greatest thing writers have going for them—every one of them, even the most debased hack, flack, or parasite—is the possibility that an individual might stand back for a moment and truly see something, all by himself, and tell us what he sees without falling back on the staleness of any in-group vision or the magic of any medicine.

Luckily there will always be a few scribblers too rough-edged and ornery to accept the invitation. You can't make a slick fop from a sow's ear, no matter how many prescriptions, subscriptions, or media mixtures you expose him to. But the drug cult has been joined by many, is getting its message to many more, and in fact has already succeeded, through its truly remarkable advertising contacts, in connecting itself with art. (Of course as distinctions blur in a haze of pot smoke, the turned-on huckster becomes a self-appointed artist, with a page from McLuhan as an I.D. card.) In an age when for many God and Country have receded into the wallpaper, art is believed in more urgently than ever. This is good in a way—it will put more bread on the table for good writers as well as for the rest. But the kind of art in which one man sits down all alone and lays his soul on the line to get something right is likely to be too hard and too bulky for slick packaging. Art is increasingly a product to be merchandised like any other product—and so is the artistic identity. According to all the popular buying guides, one consumes the artistic identity in the form of drugs. To quote William Burroughs, "Wouldn't you?"

What happens to most faithful consumers is not very pleasant. I don't know how well-known this is to people who have an ideological admiration for drug taking as the mark of a brave new generation which will save the world and make it pure. But I have had too many friends who started out as artists—talented, promising people, not just "sensitive" —who ended up as mental cases, suicides or, more often, just plain vegetables—owing to drugs. Now I know, to anticipate a sophisticated objection, that without drugs most of these people would have found some other potentially destructive experience, as artists always have. But for me the point is that nearly any other dangerous experience is more conducive to growth, more useful as literary material.

The number of wasted souls is particularly evident among would-have-been writers under twenty-five years old. I suspect there's a compulsion for a young ambitious person to take whatever's going as a challenge, as Fitzgerald and many others did with liquor. With drugs, the results can be even more disastrous. Even if we forget about the more dramatic cases, we still are faced with the man who manages to grow older without ever having been alone with himself straight. There's nothing more pathetic than a forty-year-old hipster, coming home from his creative day at the agency or studio to put a teen-age record on the stereo, get high, and giggle. When he's really high, he'll go out and go shopping: I'm afraid that buying the truly freaky is the ultimate act of existential rebellion in the drug culture.

I want to mention, finally, a less metaphysical effect that drugs have on writers and artists. As D. H. Lawrence once wrote, "When men want to be supernatural, be sure that something has gone wrong in their natural stuff."

A few years ago I remember arguing about drugs with a friend of mine who had been on the Greenwich Village scene since the early fifties, a lady who has had intimate knowledge of more poets and painters than anyone I could conceive of. The lady has since changed her mind about everyday drug takers, for the most basic of reasons. "I don't know anyone," she said, "who's been on speed, junk, dex, or alcohol to any large extent who's been able to enjoy sex or really to stick with it." And she adds a piece of sociology that is probably more acute than anything I've said here: "The young artist comes to the city and everything gets up tight—the air, the pressures, the competition, the confusions over sex, the different scenes. And he figures drugs are a door. The door opens real crazy. But it slams shut right on his sex life."

COMMENTARY: DICTION AND SENTENCES

In this article Jeremy Larner once again speaks out on the subject that he knows, from first-hand experience, fascinates our times: drugs and their mind-hallucinating effects. Like John Updike's, his style is personal and conversational but more direct in addressing the reader, as is apparent in the three sentences making up the 34 words of the opening paragraph. Evidently with hopes of being hardhitting, he makes three separate sentences out of closely related ideas that most writers would probably have phrased in no more than two or possibly even in one such as this: "As one who has written about drug effects and the philosophical issues raised by drug taking, I have a confession to make: drugs can be very boring, and talk about them even more boring." But for good or bad, Jeremy Larner made the *choice* to say it in three brief sentences. After that opening, however, he drops this somewhat telegraphic manner, and without at all ceasing to address the reader chooses more conventional sentence forms and lengths.

His "speaking" tone comes partly from his choice of words, which are drawn from the vocabulary he presumes is current among his readers: "the writing isn't worth the bag," "culture gobblers," "jazz their minds," "hip," "in-joke," "sick, dull, and square," "baby, we tune to the basic primitive vibrations, *and we swing*," "a pigeon for self-pity," "bombing and blabbing," and "groovy."

Yet careful examination reveals he soon stops relying upon such expressions, and for the major part of his essay settles down to a use of comparatively standard diction. Without sacrificing any of his hold on his readers, he remains direct and idiomatic even when analyzing the "six symptoms of an ordinary marijuana high."

Note, for example, the effectiveness of: "Life is sweeter when a man can join something—even if it's a slick-cover cellophane underground," which conveys in a vivid, concrete metaphor what would take several sentences to say, less well, in flat explanatory phrases. Note the effectiveness of the alliteration in "bombing and blabbing," with "blabbing" a deliberate choice for the alliterative "b" over, say, an equally suggestive word such as "chattering." Note the effective irony of speaking about oneself as "one's own dear poor wonderful person" in talking about Narcissism, and the effective echo-allusion in remarking about disillusioned writers discarding the next morning effusions that looked good the night before: "Some people throw them away in the dawn's early light." And finally, note the concrete, figurative way of characterizing intricate game-novels . . ." in which the reader pulls back strand after strand of symbolic wrapping paper only to find the author crouched at the centre like a grinning toad."

If "style is the man," then we should be able to detect at least some of this author's traits and background as revealed in this essay on the very controversial topic of writing and the use of drugs. It is clear that he agrees with the D. H. Lawrence quotation: "When men want to be supernatural, be sure that something has gone wrong in their natural stuff" and applies this judgment to any writer, poet, or artist who turns to drug-taking as a source of inspiration. Likewise, as his language also makes emphatic, he considers the writer's task to be one of facing up to "enormously difficult problems," and he says: "Every writer who's worth a damn struggles with them in his own way and comes up with his own sort of solutions, most of them tentative, anguished, twisted, and incomplete."

Do you admire such convictions? Can you identify with them? Whether you do or not, everyone must admit that these statements reveal Larner to be speaking with an earnest sincerity often edging on pitying anger, as he does in the concluding sentences: "And he figures drugs are a door. The door opens real crazy. But it slams shut right on his sex life."

His ability to make a phrase adds special force to his statements. Take this one, for example: "America's crying need for Instant Vision has led to a new form of hero worship which I might call guru worship." In these days of synthetics, when everything from tea and coffee to some art works boasts the term "instant," Larner's expression "Instant Vision" is dramatically apt as is his "guru worship" and his "a page from McLuhan as an I.D. card." His variation of an old axiom also spices up his views: "You can't make a slick fop from a sow's ear." This comes, of course, from "You can't make a silk purse out of a sow's ear." These and other phrase coinages act as persuasive appeals to heed the author's basic warning which may thus be summed up: "Art and drugs don't mix."

WHAT DOES IT SAY?

1. In his introduction, Jeremy Larner stresses the fact that regarding the subject of drugs, "The titillation comes from forces beyond our control." In this context what is the meaning of *titillation?*

2. Define *hip* as a label for a certain air of sophistication.

3. What does his statement that some people "organize their psyches around the taking of drugs," suggest to your imagination?

4. List some connotations you associate with the expression "and we swing."

5. What is *Narcissism,* and why is it said to be a symptom of "an ordinary marijuana high"?

6. Who was Che Guevara? Also identify those included in this quotation: "Lyndon or Dylan, Westmoreland, Stokely, or Allen Ginsberg."

7. What drugs are known by these names: *speed, junk, dex?*

8. How do you define a "hipster"?

WHAT DO YOU THINK?

1. By means of specific examples explained in detail, discuss your agreement or disagreement with *one* of these statements appearing in Jeremy Larner's article:

   (a) "When the drug gets more important than the writing . . . the writing isn't worth the bag."
   (b) ". . . Social and historical forces . . . have created for the first time in American life an official drug culture."
   (c) "Only we inside people and the insides of our heads are real."
   (d) "In these hysterical times of bombing and blabbing, there's not much going above ground that commands our allegiance."
   (e) "In an age when for many God and Country have receded into the wallpaper, art is believed in more urgently than ever."
   (f) "Art is increasingly a product to be merchandised like any other product—and so is artistic identity."
   (g) " 'And he figures drugs are a door.' "

2. Show in a brief essay how one or the other of the following may contribute to "the drug culture" said to exist in the United States.

Television advertising	Modern art
Magazine advertising	Parental attitudes
Current movies	"God is dead" thinking
Rock and roll music	"Miracle" medicines
Underground press	Vietnam war
Organized crime	City slums
Racism	Alcoholism

You Will Not Be Lonely

by WALTER KERR

With The Living Theater, you will never be lonely. You will be quiet, for very long periods of time, if you care for quiet. Each of the three productions that I saw at the Yale University Theater last week and that are now being offered, together with a fourth, at the Brooklyn Academy of Music opens in prolonged silence. The "Antigone" begins with members of the company, in twos and threes, appearing against the naked backstage wall to hesitate, stare at the audience, shield their eyes, move again ever so slightly, hesitate again. The staring continues for 10 minutes. Four members of the company then drop to their knees, scratch at the floor, and utter low moans. The moans continue for 15 minutes, after which the first word of the play is spoken.

The "Frankenstein," a company improvisation rather than an adaptation of Mrs. Shelley's novel, has already found its silence before we enter the theater. The company is seated—has been seated for how long?—cross-legged on the stage, staring at us once more. It is meditating, and we are told, briefly, that the purpose of the meditation is to enforce the levitation of a girl, long blond hair bathing her expectant body, at stage center. If the girl levitates, the event will have been consummated and nothing further need be done; we will presumably get

Reprinted from *The New York Times,* October 6, 1968. © 1968 by The New York Times Company. Reprinted by permission.

up and go home. After 15 minutes of wordless concentration, the meditation gives way to three minutes of yoga exercises; we are assured, in a sentence, that following these three minutes the girl *will* levitate. On the evening I attended she did not levitate, which meant that the play had to be performed, as indeed it was for some hours afterward. (I was forced to leave at 11; the third act had not yet begun.)

The opening of "Paradise Now," an improvisation meant to take the theater into the streets when the police are willing, opens less quietly, though at a whisper. Members of the company rustle through the auditorium, leaning solicitously over those in aisle seats, murmuring "I'm not allowed to travel without a passport," "I don't know how to stop the war," "You can't live if you don't have the money," "I'm not allowed to smoke marijuana," "I'm not allowed to take my clothes off." Each of these statements is developed separately, in ascending repetition, ending at last in a roar; each roar subsides suddenly, however, to a new whisper, so that hush tends to predominate over clamor. The practice continues for one hour after the announced curtain time, at which point the members of the company take off their clothes.

You will, at certain moments, be interested. You will not be interested in the players stripped to G-strings, for their bodies are in the main ugly, the males scrawny, the girls undeveloped. (An exception must be made for Rufus Collins, whose physique would please a sculptor; he also possesses the company's only distinguished speaking voice, which he is going to destroy if he continues to scream as required.) You will be interested, at least during the "Frankenstein," in gimmickry. Once the 18 minute silence is over, murders erupt everywhere on a three-story jungle gym: a man swings into space by the neck, others are garroted, gassed, guillotined; a girl is hurled alive into a coffin and carried through the house. You will not have heard a girl screaming inside a coffin before. There is a slight prickle to it.

Tubes are now attached, tangled as on a telephone switchboard, to a male corpse in an effort to restore destroyed Man to life. While a blinding, spinning, pure white light rattles at our eyeballs, the corpse turns green, red, green, red, with a lantern representing the human heart flickering and fading as hope soars, fades. The corpse is given a foot, a brain; a red eye is placed in its navel. The tubing begins to pulse, pale yellow, then to run a new course away from the experiment, climbing the high scaffolding until it leads us to eight or nine silhouetted bodies, suspended in midair, forming the outlines of a moving man. The massive image is unexpected. There are visual busynesses to attend to.

But, quiet or mildly bemused, you will not be lonely. The players are always with you. They are in the aisles with their feet arched high, ready to kick you in the face. They are behind you, massaging your head. They are beside you, having crawled to the center of the row, to touch you—touch your hair, touch your cheek, touch whatever happens to be in your pockets as they explore them. "Holy pencil," they say as they find your pencil, "Holy glasses" as they find your bifocals. When the words happen to call for sibilants, it is sometimes necessary to wipe the player's spittle from your face. In this theater, this "free" theater, we are all one. There are no actors, no spectators, no critics—thanks be to God, no critics—only "human beings." Human beings being together.

It is right here that light-mindedness vanishes and, if you *are* a human being with human sympathies, your heart begins to break. For there is no togetherness, no secret sharing, no impulsive return of the performer's intimate gesture, no yes. Though you are not alone, these players are. It is true that a few students at Yale, seated onstage to begin with, did partially strip and join hands with the company to go into the streets on the opening night of "Paradise Now"; one or two were arrested along with directors Judith Malina and Julian Beck. But these were *efforts* at joining, attempts at participation to see what participation might be like. I doubt very much that any of them will be returning to Europe with the Becks when their American journey is done, transformed, absorbed, committed to the cult. I doubt that the experience was.

Plainly it was not for the hundreds of spectators who sat patient, tolerant, willing, detached on three nights. The audience was calmly, responsibly, even respectfully neutral. It did not laugh openly very often. It did not shout out many ripostes. It did not become irritated; those who slipped away generally did so unobtrusively. If there was no hostility in the house, there was no commitment, either, no fusion with the event. But it was not the spectators who were isolated. They had each other. They exchanged glances with one another, little jokes with one another, friendly reassurances with one another. They knew who they were; *they* constituted a body. It was the Becks, and their companions on the stage, who were isolated—alien, earnest, believing, begging, trying, trying, trying so hard, sharing with one another something they could not project beyond themselves, hopeful, self-hypnotized, phantoms on an empty playground.

The almost unbearable truth is that life and the theater have passed The Living Theater by. Their group gropings, hands sliding over loin-clothed bodies piled high as a funeral pyre or clutching at their genitals in masturbatory dance, no longer seem adventurous; they seem a mild, if not senile, form of O'Horganism. Who would arrest these vacant-eyed children? Their gimmickry, even when it still catches the eye, is ancient, incredibly innocent charade. The business of arranging seven

bodies to look like one, or of putting curled and twisted bodies together so as to spell out the word "Anarchy," is Aquacade stuff, Busby
Berkeley come late; it is done better every Saturday afternoon on football fields.

The application of this technique to regular dramatic passages, as
in the "Antigone," is achingly literal: To show that Creon is trampling
on men Creon walks on the back of a man, to show that Creon is
catered to by sycophants five or six performers crawl on their knees
after him, licking his thighs and rubbing their heads against his stomach.
It is small wonder that Creon (Mr. Beck) cannot speak well in the
circumstances, or that the thought of the play is reduced to kindergarten level; but speech is no better when the principals are freed of
their barnacles. The mystique has swallowed speech, made it cheap;
the confrontation between Mr. Beck's insanely grinning Creon and Miss
Malina's petulant and bewildered Antigone seems, in the reading, a confrontation between a Halloween pumpkin and Poor Pitiful Pearl. Nor
is the sacrifice of speech compensated for by acrobatic skill. A girl spun
off a revolving line of bodies comes away clumsily; a flutter of fingers
seems almost arthritic; a man solemnly stepping backward should not
really step on the hair of the nearest kneeling girl, not if he has been
rehearsed.

At one time, before The Living Theater lost its quarters here and
was exiled to Europe, Miss Malina, as a director, was often able to impose a clear discipline on a production. Whether one cared for the
materials being produced or not, a firm, skilled, passionate hand could
be felt at work: "The Brig" was a drill, expertly organized. Now, in the
new freedom, all disciplines have gone soft. In her infrequent appearances onstage, Miss Malina herself seems lost, somehow hurt. Mr. Beck
continues to seem pontifical, and untalented. The majority of the performers do not seem to be actors at all. They are converts.
The intellectual life of the group has been reduced to this. On
the second night at Yale, there were some 200 students who had not
been able to buy tickets; the house was sold out, and more—perhaps
150 additional spectators had been permitted to sit on the stage. A
chant went up outside: "The theater belongs to the people!" (Were
there no people inside, filling every inch of available space?) The Living
Theater performers became very agitated about the exclusion of those
others who had wanted admission. They proposed, heatedly, that the
door be thrown open to all who wished to enter. (The aisles, bear in
mind, were already filled with members of the company.) Word came
back that the theater was over-crowded and that the fire department
would admit no more. Fury now raged from the stage. How could the

theater be *free,* how could the country be *free,* so long as there were fire departments?

This theater of freedom means to be a theater of joy. It is more nearly a matter for tears.

COMMENTARY: VIVIDNESS AND TONE

Walter Kerr, dramatic critic for *The New York Times,* in this commentary on The Living Theater, demonstrates the skill that has made him one of the most powerful and respected theater critics of our day. Note his vivid reconstruction of what goes on in this recent experiment in the theater; note the careful control of tones, the gross understatements that convey his pitying disapproval, leading to his conclusion that the "joy" which the new theater intends to convey is "more nearly a matter for tears."

His initial remarks discuss the opening portions of three of the productions that he witnessed, all of which, he says, opened "in prolonged silence." "You will," he says, "be quiet for very long periods of time," adding, offhand, "if you care for quiet." Then he proceeds to elaborate, as he does throughout his critique, in such vivid detail that we readers can share his experience as a spectator.

In "Antigone," we look on with him as the "members of the company"—he carefully refrains from calling them actors—stare out at us for ten minutes, then drop to their knees to scratch and moan for some 15 minutes more. Notice, incidentally, the impotence and futility suggested in the word "scratch." In "Frankenstein," we watch "the company" stare at us quietly for 15 minutes, followed by three minutes of "yoga" exercises in an attempt to "levitate" a girl with long, blond hair who is sitting in the center of the stage. Note, again, the implication in referring to these actions as "yoga" exercises, the suggestion of something extraneous to the circumstances. In "Paradise Now" we listen with him to the whispered comments of the "members of the company" as they "rustle" for an hour through the auditorium, leaning over those seated on the aisle.

When he goes on to depict the action, or "gimmickry," as he calls it, in "Frankenstein" he is specific and concrete in his details. We look on with him as he pictures in vivid terms the various murders that erupt on a "three-story jungle gym." With him, too, we get a "slight prickle" as we hear the screams of a girl who has been "hurled alive" into a coffin, as that coffin is carried through the house. We watch, with him, the detailed efforts to bring a corpse back to life: the appearance of foot, brain, navel, with the red eye glowing in it; the pulsing yellow tubing, the silhouetted bodies suspended in the air.

All of our senses are accosted, as they clearly are in the theater: our head is massaged, our cheek touched. We feel the hand in our pocket, the wet spittle that we wipe from our face after the strolling players have sprayed us in their close-up enunciation of "sibilants."

Again, when Kerr accuses The Living Theater of being dated, old hat, he is once more specific and concrete in his illustrations: the twisted bodies spelling out "Anarchy"; Creon walking on the back of a man or being followed by crawling sycophants who lick his thighs and rub their heads against his stomach; naked bodies piled up like a funeral pyre, or dancing, clutching their genitals. All this outmoded technique he calls "achingly literal," and compares it with the formations of the swimmers in the Aquacades of former time or with the band formations between halves in a football game.

Along with this detailed representation of what goes on at a production of The Living Theater is the careful enunciated criticism of it. A key phrase is the one he states at the outset: "You will never be lonely." This, in itself, is somewhat ambiguous, suggestive, even, of a compliment. Loneliness is not, ordinarily, desirable. But gradually the full force of that statement becomes apparent. You will never be lonely because "the players are always with you." They massage your head, touch your hair, your cheek, explore your possessions, spray you in the face as they whisper "unwarranted" restrictions of society in intimate close-ups. And yet, Kerr indicates, all these frantic attempts to involve the spectators fail. They generate no "impulsive return." It is, Kerr indicates, heart-breaking for anyone with "human sympathies," heart-breaking that The Living Theater should so fail in its attempt to be intimate and significant. Spectators remain "patient," and "tolerant," but "respectfully neutral," while the players, "self-hypnotized," keep "begging, trying, trying, trying so hard" to project themselves.

The tone through all this is one of pitying regret. The fact that "life and the theater have passed The Living Theater by" is called an "almost unbearable" truth. Oh, Kerr concedes that "at certain moments" you will be "interested." Not in the nudity of the players, he hastens to add. Their bodies, with the one exception of Rufus Collins, are ugly. But some of the "gimmickry" is of interest (the word itself suggests "gadgets," not true art), and you may be "mildly bemused." Faint praise, indeed.

For the most part, however, Kerr proceeds to damn the whole concept of The Living Theater with an air of quiet authority that strips it of any real value. As he moves ahead with his critical comments he becomes more outspokenly condemnatory, although his tone remains consistently urbane. The "gimmickry," the one thing he had faintly praised, he calls "incredibly innocent." Its technique is not only outmoded but practiced "better every Saturday afternoon on football fields." Applied to drama, this technique results in the "thought of the play" being childish, "reduced to kindergarten level." As actors, the two principal exponents of The Living Theater, Mr. Beck and Miss Malina, have little to recommend them. Mr. Beck is referred to as "pontifical" and "untalented," his expressions as Creon "insanely grinning." Miss Malina, as Antigone, is "petulant and bewildered." Her confrontation with Creon is compared to a "confrontation between a Halloween pumpkin and Poor Pitiful Pearl." Once a disciplined director, she now appears to have "gone soft," so that in the "new freedom" the performers "do not seem to be actors at all," even their acrobatics being "clumsy," their gestures "arthritic."

Certainly, language in the hands of a skilled writer like Walter Kerr becomes a formidable tool. Unlike the invective that appeared at times in Thomas Edwards' remarks about Marshall McLuhan or the often informal and colloquial tone of Jeremy Larner's strictures about those writers who rely upon mind-expanding drugs for their inspiration, Kerr keeps his diction formal and controlled, even when he is being most pitiless in his condemnation. He gains his effects, not by any cleverness of phrase, but by the accuracy and vividness of his words and, at times, his apt comparisons and occasional metaphor; for instance, "when the principals are free of their barnacles," a reference to those hindrances he has mentioned that hamper the actors.

WHAT DOES IT SAY?

1. Who wrote the original "Antigone"? What, in general, is the subject of the drama that would account for the opening of The Living Theater's production?

2. Calling the production of "Frankenstein" a "company improvisation rather than an adaptation" of Mary Shelley's novel would suggest what about the performance?

3. What do all of the "whispers" spoken by the players in "Paradise Now" have in common? What are they intended to suggest?

4. A "jungle gym" is an apparatus found on children's playgrounds. Why is Kerr's description of the setting in these terms effective?

5. *Bemused* has as one meaning the idea of being absorbed. What other meaning does it have? Do you see anything effective in this double suggestion?

6. What is a riposte, and what would the failure to "shout out" ripostes indicate about the reaction of the audience?

7. Who is the Halloween pumpkin referred to in the reference to the confrontation by Miss Malina as Antigone? In context, do you find this comparison effective?

8. The concluding anecdote is intended to convey what about the "intellectual life" of the performers in The Living Theater?

WHAT DO YOU THINK?

1. "Paradise Now," the title of one of The Living Theater productions which Kerr witnessed, would suggest a presentation of a better world than the one we now live in. Write an essay in which you elaborate on a few aspects of what you would consider essential to such a paradise.

2. In some productions of The Living Theater the players removed their clothes and invited members of the audience to come on stage and do likewise. How do you regard such demonstrations?

3. Tom Prideau, dramatic critic of *Life* magazine, made the following comment about nudity on the stage: "Because some players have already grown fairly accustomed to stage nudity, they are beginning to take it for granted—providing it is a valid force in the play and is not paraded for pornographic kicks."[1] What is your reaction to this comment, and how would one determine when nudity was a "valid force" in a play?

4. The Living Theater is only one of a number of recent experiments in drama. Discuss some other experiment with which you are familiar—the theater of the absurd, for example. Follow Kerr's method of giving an accurate, vivid description of a performance before you turn to critical comment about it.

5. Select any other form of modern art—painting, sculpture, music, prose, fiction, poetry—and write a critical commentary about it. Be sure to choose something you are familiar with, and be sure to write in specific, vivid terms.

6. Society puts a number of restrictions upon the actions of the individual, presumably for the common good. Some of these restrictions are suggested by the players' whispers in "Paradise Now." Discuss any restrictions imposed by law that you feel are undesirable—any unnecessary, unwarranted intrusions upon a person's freedom of action.

[1] Tom Prideau, "The Man Who Dared to Enter Paradise," *Life* Magazine (November 22, 1968), p. 123.

New York
by JOHN A. WILLIAMS
(from THE MAN WHO CRIED I AM)

One press day afternoon, in the fall, Max lay on his couch reading. Beside him rested a clipboard; sometimes while reading, a passage triggered ideas. The desk light was on and there was paper in the typewriter. His hemorrhoids had been bothering him; it was best to take it easy. But, whenever he glanced at the empty clipboard, the desk, and the typewriter with its surly white paper waiting to be filled, he felt uneasy and guilty about lying down.

He forced himself to read. A little later he felt chills and then was suddenly nervous. He shifted his position. Then he got up and turned off the desk light and returned to the couch. Once more he rose and went to the desk and ripped the paper out of the typewriter. But now his hands were shaking. He was overwhelmed by the idea that he was not a writer, but a pretender, like so many others he had met in Harlem or down on 8th Street. No real writer would be lying on his can when there was work to be done. He had stumbled into a dead-end street, that was all. A writer had to stand the silences that came with being alone, and he hated being lonely and yet it comforted him. You could think when you were alone, and writers needed to think.

He picked up the clipboard and tossed it across the room, where it clattered against a wall and fell to the floor. Dilemma. How in the hell did it happen? What had started it? He could get out; he wasn't going to spend the rest of his life like Harry—never knowing what the next phone call or mail delivery would or wouldn't bring; never knowing what life would hold for you at forty-nine or fifty-nine. No. He was going to apply himself; he was going to scheme and jive, dance in the sandbox, Tom, kiss behinds, and wind up managing editor of the *Democrat.* He had a little prestige now. No one else at the office had written a novel and they weren't planning to, either!

His chills and shakes persisted. He thought he would feel better outside. He pulled on a sweater and walked rapidly to the corner and then across the street into the park. There he sat in the sun, but even as he did, his mind floated up words to describe what he was seeing and feeling. A young sharpie in draped coat and pegged pants strolled by, arms held stiffly behind his back. A barge, belly-deep in water, steamed slowly up the Hudson, froth leaping from its bows. Max looked at the Palisades and descriptions came for that sheer mass of stone rising from the west bank of the river. And words came for the color of the sun, for the sounds of the children playing near him, for the arching spiral of a battered football and the taut freckled face that watched its flight. The words kept coming, even when he closed his eyes, words and ways of using them that he knew no newspaper could ever use.

He was twenty-four and he knew he hadn't lived much. He hadn't been anywhere, really, not even to Niagara Falls, the Canadian side. Going to college had only taught him that he would never be able to read all the things he wanted to or should. And if he hadn't read so much or traveled so much, how in hell could he feel so much?

Why me? He asked himself bitterly. He looked at the bouncing back of the sharpie. Why couldn't I have been like him? Anybody who walked like that and dressed like that, well, he seemed to be able to live life as he found it. Why can't *I* wear zoot suits, dance the Lindy better, until my nuts fall, laugh like hell instead of just smiling? Why can't *I* be loud and loose and drunker than I ever let myself get? Why am I the way I am? Mutant, freak, caprice, fluke. Maxwell Reddick.

He thought about his childhood, his parents, and dismissed them. No, it went beyond that, beyond them. He remembered a childhood photo. He still had it, somewhere. It was a photo which, when his parents had passed it around, drew the comment: "Three? He looks so old and wise." Was there something in that silly photo that could give him answers? So old, so wise, God, about *what?* He would study it once more when he returned to his apartment. What in the world had made him look so old and wise at only three? His family had never starved. His parents had been good to him and perhaps even loved him, coming late in their lives as he had. He didn't know, had never assumed that they had not loved or at least liked him. That had to count for something, although the old man was hell on wheels right up until they laid him out, four years to the exact day and hour after his mother had died. What did that mean? That look he had at three. . . . Which spermatozoid, which ovum, preserved for generations in the secret places of bodies, had sensed the presence of each other, finally, and, fiercely subcopulating, created him? Had they come out of the past at all, the future? But why, *why?*

The next time he saw Harry, Max asked, "Do you ever question the way you are, why you're a writer?"

"Every day."

Max waited for him to go on. It was a Saturday afternoon and the uptown bar had not yet filled with dapper Negroes starting the second leg of the weekend; Friday night was the first; Saturday into Sunday was the second, which was brought to an end only by habit of going to church Sunday morning or sleeping into Sunday afternoon.

Harry laughed. "Well, you're colored and you wonder how come you're a writer because there is no tradition of colored writers. Are we related to some ancient Yoruba folklorist, to Phillis Wheatley? I think about that. Then, somehow, it doesn't matter about the tradition; what matters is now. You wrote a book, Max, and published it. As I see it, that makes you, like me, a very special person among all the people who've ever lived. That's cause for some pride, I think; that's cause to produce more books. That also makes you dangerous because they don't burn people anymore, they burn books, and they don't always have bonfires. I love it like this; let there be a little danger to life, otherwise life is a lie.

"I'm the way I am, the kind of writer I am, and you may be too, because I'm a black man; therefore, we're in rebellion; we've got to be. We have no other function as valid as that one." Harry grinned. "I've been in rebellion, and a writer, I guess, ever since I discovered that even colored folks wanted to keep me away from books so I could never learn just how bad it all was. Maybe, too, to keep me from laughing at them. For taking it. My folks had a deathly fear of books."

Harry took a deep drink of his beer and gazed moodily around the bar, then he said, "There's something wrong with this ritual these people have here. Oh, hell, I like kicking it around all weekend, too, but that doesn't mean I can't see what's going on. A writer worth his salt is not going to write about how damned lovely it is; it isn't, that's why so many people tell themselves it is. But they don't want to hear what you've got to say if it isn't the same thing they can see or believe, and that's going to make you a target. Talk about sitting ducks! You against them, and all you've got is a beat-up typewriter and some cheap rag bond. And your head.

"If your first book is any indication, you're a rebel, too, just as you should be. Don't be guilty if you make it and Negroes themselves start shooting you down; your subject will always be America or Americans. You didn't make the bed; you just have to lie in it. Even so, when my name is mentioned, I want people to jerk up and look for trouble; I want trouble to be my middle name when I write about America. I wouldn't like it if a single person slept well. We—you, me, Warren and the others—have that function. I'll tell you why.

"In our society which is white—we're intruders they say—there has got to be something inherently horrible about having the sicknesses and weaknesses of that society described by a person who is a victim of them; for if he, the victim, is capable of describing what they have believed nonexistent, then they, the members of the majority, must choose between living the truth, which can be pretty grim, and the lie, which isn't much better. But at least they will then have the choice.

"It must be pretty awful for a white man to learn that one of the things wrong with this society is that it is not based on dollars directly or alone, but dollars denied men who are black so dollars can go into the pockets of men who are white. It must make white men ponder a kind of weakness that will make them deny work to black men so that work can be done by men who are white. How it must anger them to know finally that we know they deny women who are white to black men, while they have taken black women at will for generations.

"And don't they know or want to know that the absence of black voices in the state legislatures and in Congress, unheard since the Reconstruction, wounds them to the death? How painful would it be for them to admit that millions of acres of black men's lands were ripped from them by night riders and county clerks, and are still being held by the descendants of the thieves? Very painful. They'd have to give back those lands, those dollars, that work.

"Ah yeah, there's quite enough to be in rebellion about," Harry said, morosely. "I quit the Party because I became damned sick and tired of white men telling me when I should suffer, where and how and what for. And, Max, I was suffering all the time! And I got tired of writing what I knew was wrong for me, our people, our time, our country. I got tired of seeing young Negroes, *young*, man! beat when they drifted into the Party looking for hope and found nothing but another version of white man's hell. Karl Marx was not thinking about niggers when he engineered *The Communist Manifesto*; if he was, why didn't he *say* so? None of the 'great documents' of the West ever acknowledged a racial problem tied to an economic problem, tied to a social problem, tied to a religious problem, tied to a whole nation's survival. And that's why, man, none of them, unamended, are worth the paper they were written on." Harry jabbed himself in the chest. "Somewhere you know this and you're thinking twice about starting to work. Your job is to tell those people to stop lying, not only to us, but to themselves. You've written and in the process, somewhere in that African body of yours, something said, 'I am—a writer, a man, something, but here for today. Here for right now.' "

Harry waved to the waiter for more beer.

"That could make a man start thinking he's pretty important stuff, couldn't it, Harry?"

"Damn, Max. Don't you understand? If you don't have the perspective of yourself, can you expect other people to have it?"

But during the next weeks no amount of talking seemed to help. Max had a thousand abortive starts on the new novel, but none of them went past page three or four. In despair, he turned to his essays, but finally came to distrust them; he could not begin one with a question and answer it logically. "Does American democracy work?" Logically the essay could be completed by adding two letters: "No."

When he wrote, Max wanted to soar, to sing golden arias. But Zutkin's editor friends wanted emotion: anger, unreasonable black fury; screeching, humiliation, pain, subjects which evaded the essay; articles, yes; the essay, no. Do not sing, Max, the editors seemed to be saying. Instead, tell us, in your own words, in ten thousand words or less, just how much we've hurt you! We will pay handsomely for that revelation.

Until the Moses Boatwright case, few of the Harlem doings had touched Max. There were murders, yes, and reefer raids, the burglaries. There were the big bands at the Savoy and the Apollo; the Garvey diehards, the Ras Tafarian street fights, the dances. After Moses Boatwright Max didn't want to sing at all, ever. Or, he knew it would take him a long time to learn how to sing again and even if he did, he would never sing the way he imagined he could. Maybe he would sing a rumbling, threatening basso like Harry Ames.

COMMENTARY: STYLE AS THE MAN

In portraying Maxwell Reddick and Harry Ames as black writers and rebels, John A. Williams evidently gives voice to his own deepest feelings as another black author. Like Langston Hughes, Richard Wright, James Baldwin, Ralph Ellison, and LeRoi Jones, Williams himself identifies with this role as protester who, as the cliché has it, "tells it like it is." The "message" of this portion of his novel is clearly stated and indicates the author's deep involvement with a common cause.

We see this fervent conviction embodied in the language of Harry Ames' long speech, which begins: "In our society which is white— we're intruders they say—there has got to be something inherently horrible about having the sicknesses and weaknesses of that society described by a person who is a victim of them. . . ." In the rest of this speech we are told the dilemma confronting all white people, and this dilemma, as Williams describes it, has "horns" that are cruelly sharp. Can they be avoided? Do white people have choices other than those two presented them by Williams?

He thinks not, and he seems as unhappy about the unavoidability of those horns as are his readers. He is also harshly aware of the only role left for the black writer to play in this most painful situation: a duty expressed in most realistic terms: "You've written and in the process, somewhere in that African body of yours, something said, 'I am—a writer, a man, something, but here for today. Here for right now.' "

Since the rest of the novel hinges upon the choices the talented black writer must make between going along with the Establishment or opposing its racial injustices, this speech is most important for Max Reddick, the man who must make such a choice. Any reader of *The Man Who Cried I Am* will have no doubts as to which choice Williams thinks is the only right one.

Despite his concern for his "message," however, Williams never forgets that his primary purpose is to tell a story and to keep that narrative moving. As his manner in the following paragraph shows, he takes pains to keep his readers aware of "what happens next" and to carefully build the suspense. Underline for yourself the words that show the sequence of time marking the acts leading to one climactic state of frustration:

> He forced himself to read. A little later he felt chills and then was suddenly nervous. He shifted his position. Then he got up and turned off the desk light and returned to the couch. Once more he rose and went to the desk and ripped the paper out of the typewriter. But now his hands were shaking. He was overwhelmed by the idea that he was not a writer, but a pretender, like so many others he had met in Harlem or down on 8th Street. No real writer would be lying on his can when there was work to be done. He had stumbled into a dead-end street, that was all. A writer had to stand the silences that came with being alone, and he hated being lonely and yet it comforted him. You could think when you were alone, and writers needed to think.

The third person pronoun *he*—referring to Max—serves as the "key word" giving a coherent point of view to almost all of the sentences, including by implication the *you* of the final sentence. The time-signal words indicating a succession of acts are these: *a little later, then, once more,* and *but now.* These terms are aided, of course, by the shift in verb tenses in the last four sentences, wherein *would* and *could* intensify Max's frustration by presenting ideal notions of "a writer."

All that has been previously said in this book regarding elements and aspects of effective writing from the "new rhetoric" point of view can be applied to the discussion of "style" in this and any other selection. Every writer's style is shaped by many things, including his choice of subject, his stance, his order of arrangement, his logic, his kind of appeals, his choice of diction, and certainly his pattern of grammatical forms.

By now, too, you know from your own writing experiences how applicable these concerns are to you in your efforts to attain a suitable style. Let us hope that your ever improving style of writing will testify to your willingness to apply what you have learned.

WHAT DOES IT SAY?

1. Why is the following expression a most apt one for almost any writer: "the typewriter with its surly white paper waiting to be filled"?

2. If in order to become an editor Max was tempted "to scheme and jive, dance in the sandbox, and Tom,"—what would he have been doing?

3. Max thinks of himself as a "mutant, freak, caprice, fluke." Are all of these terms applicable to human beings?

4. Define *spermatozoid, ovum.*

5. Identify the following: "Yoruba folklorist," "Phillis Wheatley," "the Reconstruction."

6. Why can some people have "a deathly fear of books"?

7. The word *intruders* has a special meaning as Harry Ames applies it to black people. How do you feel about it?

8. In what respects, as Harry Ames describes it, is the Communist Party "nothing but another version of white man's hell"?

WHAT DO YOU THINK?

1. Write a dialogue between two persons who have opposing ideas on one of the following questions:

    (a) Should 18-year-olds have the right to vote?
    (b) Is marijuana less harmful than alcohol?
    (c) Should there be only two grades in college—pass and no-pass?
    (d) Are people in our local community "racists"?

(e) Should campus administrators in any way assume responsibility for the moral or social life of their students?
(f) Should white students be required to take any courses in a Black Studies curriculum?
(g) Is it necessary for black people to be complete rebels?
(h) Is it right that the present generation of white people should bear the brunt of trying to right the racial wrongs of all of the past?
(i) Was Che Guevara a hero in real life?

2. Write an analysis of the views and arguments to be found in one of the following books:

   The Autobiography of Malcolm X

   Malcolm X Speaks

   Soul on Ice, Eldridge Cleaver

   Fire Next Time, James Baldwin

   Black Boy, Richard Wright

   The Affair At The Algiers Motel, John Hershey

   The Dutchman, LeRoi Jones

   Invisible Man, Ralph Ellison

3. Write as vivid a narrative as you can of an experience in which you came to realize the potentials of fear and hostility present in racial confrontations.